MW00795590

'*Root Narrative Theory and Conflict Resol*
retical umbrella highlighting fundament
modern, often seemingly intractable,
impressive array of scholarship in the servi   ...veloping a useful conceptual tool
for understanding reciprocal relationships between power, conflict, and values.
Readers from a variety of backgrounds will find points of agreement while engaging disparate, too often isolated, literatures.'

—*Steve Hitlin, The University of Iowa, USA*

'Solon Simmons promises a "big picture book," and he delivers one. Root Narrative Theory is a major advance in our understanding of radical disagreement and
protracted social conflict. It offers a new way to conceptualize power in the etiology and dynamics of conflict: conflict is about the perception and experience of
social power abusively and unjustly deployed. Narrative is the way individuals "story,"
remedy, and resist the abuse. Four iconic thinkers, Hobbes, Locke, Marx, and Fanon,
illustrate forms of abuse as threats to security, liberty, equality, and dignity, and provide
frameworks for a "moral politics" raised in response. Simmons builds on the moral
psychology of Haidt and the family metaphor theory of Lakoff, to remind us that root
narratives, however motivated by emotions or framed by cognition and metaphor,
have a sociological dimension, anchored in the social ecology of institutions, social
relations and structures. Empirically grounded and richly illustrated with examples
drawn from an impressive array of thinkers (Arendt, Polanyi, Hayek, and Habermas,
among them), and practitioners (Robespierre, Reagan, and Martin Luther King...),
Simmons argues for the productive analysis of deep conflict as the unpacking of root
narratives in mutual contention, and of peace, if it is to come, as the refashioning of
narratives and the overcoming of legacies of abusive power.'

—*Kevin Avruch, George Mason University, USA*

'Solon Simmons' new book *Root Narrative Theory and Conflict Resolution* presents an
incredibly thoughtful and important tool for analyzing conflict stories, particularly
in the field of moral politics. However, his Root Narrative Theory is not just a
diagnostic – it has practical uses for building understanding, dialogue and peace.
Simmons' arguments are drawn from political and social theory. While often dis-
cussing dense concepts, Simmons keeps the content accessible and the tone con-
versational. He presents a broad range of sources, ranging from the deeply
philosophical to popular media, to establish the foundations of his theory. His
theory introduces twelve root narratives, which he suggests form the basis of conflict discourse in modern politics. He provides numerous illustrations of each,
drawing from historical texts to recent political campaigns. Simmons' work
demonstrates the inherent relationship between power, moral values, and storytelling. It is essential reading for anyone involved in politics, media, conflict resolution and peacebuilding.'

—*Samantha Hardy, CCI Academy, Australia*

'Solon Simmons' lively, insightful exploration of the four "root narratives" (stories that stimulate and organize our feelings about security, liberty, equality, and dignity) makes a major contribution to our understanding of what drives and shapes modern social conflicts. By linking recent discoveries about the role of narrative in conflict to key theories of social and political structure, his work opens the door to new forms of conflict resolution practice. A must read for people interested in resolving current sociopolitical and cultural conflicts.'

—*Richard Rubenstein, George Mason University, USA*

'With Root Narrative Theory, Solon Simons offers an original perspective for understanding protracted conflicts. This book exhibits a stunning breadth of scope and depth of detail, drawing upon thinkers of the past for developing a moral vision of conflict resolution practice. Students, professors, and scholar-practitioners of conflict will benefit greatly from the books' boldly creative themes that are crafted carefully through rigorous discursive analysis.'

—*Daniel Rothbart, George Mason University, USA*

'As a practitioner who is committed to engaging with narratives for peace, I especially appreciate this important work on Root Narratives. I believe that as peacebuilders, we have to hold ourselves to a higher standard of engaging with narratives in a way that is restorative in the public sphere and not just force upon others our own ways of making meaning in the world. Thank you Professor Simmons for this framework that is helpful in exploring our own root narratives and those of others, so we can better work for social and political change that is both healing and more effective.'

—*Julia Roig, PartnersGlobal, USA*

ROOT NARRATIVE THEORY AND CONFLICT RESOLUTION

This book introduces Root Narrative Theory, a new approach for narrative analysis, decoding moral politics, and for building respect and understanding in conditions of radical disagreement.

This theory of moral politics bridges emotion and reason, and, rather than relying on what people say, it helps both the analyst and the practitioner to focus on what people mean in a language that parties to the conflict understand. Based on a simple idea—the legacy effects of abuses of power—the book argues that conflicts only endure and escalate where there is a clash of interpretations about the history of institutional power. Providing theoretically complex but easy-to-use tools, this book offers a completely new way to think about storytelling, the effects of abusive power on interpretation, the relationship between power and conceptions of justice, and the origins and substance of ultimate values. By locating the source of radical disagreement in story structures and political history rather than in biological or cognitive systems, Root Narrative Theory bridges the divides between reason and emotion, realism and idealism, without losing sight of the inescapable human element at work in the world's most devastating conflicts.

This book will be of much interest to students of conflict resolution, peace studies and International Relations, as well as to practitioners of conflict resolution.

Solon Simmons is Associate Professor of Conflict Analysis and Resolution at George Mason University, USA.

ROUTLEDGE STUDIES IN PEACE AND CONFLICT RESOLUTION

Series Editors: Tom Woodhouse and Oliver Ramsbotham *University of Bradford*

The field of peace and conflict research has grown enormously as an academic pursuit in recent years, gaining credibility and relevance amongst policy makers and in the international humanitarian and NGO sector. The Routledge Studies in Peace and Conflict Resolution series aims to provide an outlet for some of the most significant new work emerging from this academic community, and to establish itself as a leading platform for innovative work at the point where peace and conflict research impacts on International Relations theory and processes.

For more information about this series, please visit: https://www.routledge.com/ Routledge-Studies-in-Peace-and-Conflict-Resolution/book-series/RSPCR

ROOT NARRATIVE THEORY AND CONFLICT RESOLUTION

Power, Justice and Values

Solon Simmons

Routledge
Taylor & Francis Group

LONDON AND NEW YORK

First published 2020
by Routledge
2 Park Square, Milton Park, Abingdon, Oxon OX14 4RN

and by Routledge
52 Vanderbilt Avenue, New York, NY 10017

Routledge is an imprint of the Taylor & Francis Group, an informa business

British Library Cataloguing-in-Publication Data
A catalogue record for this book is available from the British Library

Library of Congress Cataloging-in-Publication Data
Names: Simmons, Solon, author.
Title: Root narrative theory and conflict resolution : power, justice and values /
Solon Simmons.
Description: Abingdon, Oxon ; New York, NY : Routledge, 2020. |
Series: Routledge studies in peace and conflict resolution | Includes
bibliographical references and index.
Identifiers: LCCN 2019045060 (print) | LCCN 2019045061 (ebook) |
ISBN 9780367422073 (hbk) | ISBN 9780367422066 (pbk) | ISBN
9780367822712 (ebk)
Subjects: LCSH: Conflict management. | Narration (Rhetoric)
Classification: LCC HD42 .S56 2020 (print) | LCC HD42 (ebook) |
 DDC 303.6/9–dc23
LC record available at https://lccn.loc.gov/2019045060
LC ebook record available at https://lccn.loc.gov/2019045061

ISBN: 978-0-367-42207-3 (hbk)
ISBN: 978-0-367-42206-6 (pbk)
ISBN: 978-0-367-82271-2 (ebk)

Typeset in Bembo
by Taylor & Francis Books

For Andrea, Alessandra, and Gabriela

CONTENTS

ACKNOWLEDGEMENTS

This is a big-picture book, the kind that has developed over such a long period of time that it is hard to remember all of the people who played important roles in helping me to develop the ideas represented in it. I have been trying to wrap my head around a narrative approach to politics from the early days of the Ross Perot campaign in 1992 when, as I was traveling in Europe after college, I looked back on my country and wondered what was going on. Clearly Perot was onto something, and it struck me that that something was political storytelling. When I began my graduate studies soon after at the University of Wisconsin–Madison, I had countless encounters with students and faculty in both formal and informal settings that helped me to develop what would become Root Narrative Theory.

If I am honest, the most important impetus for developing this meta-philosophical model was my decision to join the faculty of the Institute for Conflict Analysis and Resolution (ICAR) at George Mason University in 2006. This little institute that later became a school, was exactly the sort of open setting that made it possible for me to explore the big ideas of political history with the kind breadth and courage it would take to risk taking on a project like this one.

Everyone knows that those of us who work in the human realm—in the humanities and social sciences—retreat to disciplinary corners when we do our serious work. I was trained to read and cite sociologists, while critiquing and ignoring political scientists (very hard to do). Others do the same across whatever disciplinary boundary they consider to be important for their careers. This was not how things worked at ICAR. In order to flourish in that kind of interdisciplinary setting, I had to read things that seemed just a little off—somehow related to my projects but with all the wrong assumptions built in. It was a little bit like a high school reunion, cast back into relationships with people who had taken very different roads in their lives, and who just didn't get what my life and work were really about. Now I think that it is this very sort of intellectual context that is likely to be the most productive and satisfying. In a place like that, you just can't hide behind your disciplinary bromides, which most intellectuals tend to do.

A onetime adviser of mine, Byron Shafer, put it well when he said something to me like 'most people are theorizing politics on a postage stamp when we need to be thinking about the big picture.' Root Narrative Theory is certainly an example of the latter. If the theory turns out to be as useful as I expect it could, it will owe its success to the perpetual high school reunion of the mind that is my daily life at George Mason University, where I face weird questions from anthropologists, communications scholars, historians, lawyers, peacebuilders, philosophers, political scientists, psychologists, theologians, and others who all wonder why I have made choices that just seem natural to me. After all of these multidisciplinary body blows, my work has moved into a state of a 'new natural.' Root Narrative Theory is not just an example of sociology, but something different, and I owe this to the students and faculty at the School for Conflict Analysis and Resolution (SCAR) who know who they are.

I do want to give a special call-out to the SCAR students who have been subjected to various versions of this theory over the years. One of the best things about a multidisciplinary setting, especially one focused on practice and the application of ideas, is that one is encouraged to feed living or cutting-edge research into the classroom discussion. This helps keep things current. I certainly abused this opportunity and have introduced my own take on how narrative, conflict, and peacebuilding interrelate at every chance I have had. Because of this, Root Narrative Theory builds in ideas, insights, and qualifications from literally dozens of students over the past eleven years, when the critical insight of the theory—that protracted conflict is all about perceptions about the abuse of power—first came to me in a class discussion. Since then, some version of this theory has appeared in every one of my classes, and the ways that students have reacted to my impositions has made the theory whatever it has become. I do want to call out two special classes that were helpful through the course of my writing, the Spring 2019 class on "Conflict and Discourse Analysis" and the 2019 Summer session class focused on "Narrative Interventions in Conflict Resolution." These students know what Root Narrative Theory is and what it is not because they have all used it in either research or conflict engagement projects. I was truly lucky to have the opportunity to work with these gifted students, and I learned a lot from them.

I also want to thank those colleagues who read some version of the manuscript or gave me an opportunity to present the material, providing me with the chance to receive critical feedback. Although I am sure I am forgetting many important people, these were Kevin Avruch, Joe Bock, Elena Cirmizi, Mohammed Cherkaoui, Sara Cobb, Gbenga Dasylva, John DeRosa, Cheryl Duckworth, Michael English, Steve Hitlin, Fakhira Halloun, Landon Hancock, Doug Irving-Erikson, Lauren Kinney, Karina Korostelina, Soyoung Kwon, Sungju Lee, Angelina Mendes, Jay Moon, Qing Gao, Arthur Romano, Dan Rothbart, Rich Rubenstein, Mara Schoeny, Sergei Samoilenko, Julie Shedd, Peter Stearns, and Roland Wilson.

Along with these colleagues, I should mention my long-standing friends who have had to endure my pontifications on these matters over the years, Aaron Stalnaker, Brad (Roald) Severtson, Keenan Yoho, and Eric Zimmerman. They appear in this book whether they know it or not.

And finally, I need to thank my family. I know most people appreciate their families deeply, but I am fully convinced that I was surprisingly lucky in this life to find myself with the little tribe I have. Thanks to my parents, Jim and Joan Simmons, and those that raised them, for their undying support (my father is a political scientist and all these ideas were hatched long ago as I stole through his ample library). Thanks to everyone in my wife's family, especially her indefatigable mother Lili Sanchez Ruiz for everything she has done for us over the years. But most all thank you to the nucleus, my brilliant, kind, and courageous wife, Andrea Robles, and my two daughters Alessandra Simmons-Robles and Gabriela Simmons-Robles. I am so proud of everything they do. They are what this is all for.

1

RADICAL DISAGREEMENT AND ROOT NARRATIVES

How do you identify the emotional core of a rational argument? If you can do that, you have lit the spark for conflict transformation, because the emotional core of the rational argument is a force that can be used to change the world. Indeed, it is all that ever has.

The emotional core of a rational argument becomes so powerful in peace and politics precisely because it harnesses our primitive emotional instincts to our near infinite capacity for rational problem solving, making us what Giovanni Pico della Mirandola called "a creature neither of heaven nor of earth." Both research and world events are converging on the idea that that space in which emotional forces are yoked to reason is narrative—the structures that make storytelling possible. Accordingly, this will be a book about narratives, not just about any old story someone wants to tell, but the kind of narratives that define the emotional core of our rational arguments: what I call the root narratives. Therefore, it will be a book about philosophy and core values, about power and politics, but also about how our deepest convictions fall into identifiable patterns that can be recognized in practice and turned to more positive ends. This is a book about the sources of moral authority and the hope for peace.

Because hope is not a strategy, this also has to be a book about the current state of peace thought. I use the somewhat cumbersome word "thought" in the way it would have once been used in the phrases "political thought" or "social thought," a broad term meant to capture contrasts between quite different justifications for systems of social, political, and economic forms of organization, as was typical in the milieu that produced Hannah Arendt, Reinhold Niebuhr, Max Horkheimer, Friedrich Hayek, Leo Strauss, and Karl Polanyi, among others.[1] We need a broad term like this to capture the spirit of the conversation of peace and conflict studies, because events have conspired to drive the field into the open again in ways that it might not have been for some time. If you wonder why everyone seems so intent on controlling the narrative, it is because big ideological shifts are underway, big enough, perhaps, to represent a shift in world history on the scale that only our grandparents would recognize.

One way to mark this transition is through the dramatic changes in the political scene in the United States in which Barack Obama, the first African American president, was succeeded by the first truly reactionary president, Donald Trump. The importance of the transition is critical, even when considered in relation to previous shifts like those that brought Richard Nixon and Ronald Reagan to power. The transition from Obama to Trump not only signals major changes in the domestic affairs of the United States, but also a major change in the structure of international politics, one not seen for almost a century. In the new system, older or more thoroughgoing forms of authority as represented by Xi Jinping in China, Vladimir Putin in Russia, Recep Tayip Erdoğan in Turkey, Rodrigo Duterte in the Philippines, Andrzej Duda in Poland, and Narendra Modi in India appear to be in vogue. The standard assumptions of the liberal international order[2] are no longer as immediately relevant as they once were. We no longer live in Eleanor Roosevelt's world. Ours is increasingly less defined by the West and its categories, and more by what Oliver Ramsbotham has called radical disagreement[3]—disagreement at the level of basic political values and moral intuitions—which is alive in conflicts around the world in ways that it has not been in a long time.

As Lou Kriesberg has argued, conflict resolution developed as a field of basic research in the context of the Cold War when some questions were too hot to address, which was nevertheless a world of relative stability enforced by the antagonism of two ideologically opposed super powers.[4] We no longer operate in a stable world in which things like democracy, socialism or the international community can be taken for granted. Peace thinkers again have to think big as they did in the run up to the First World War, because the equilibrating trends that have displaced the West have also brought the global diversity of ideological perspectives into conversation in quite radical ways. We have yet to catch up with the implications.

Ideology, the most intensified form of political narrative, is both logical and passionate, demonstrating what Hannah Arendt described as a "curious logicality."[5] In his famous book on the subject, *The End of Ideology*, written just prior to the Kennedy era and the 1960s,[6] the sociologist Daniel Bell wrote, "what gives ideology its force is its passion... one might say, in fact, that the most important, latent, function of ideology is to tap emotion" (p. 400). Bell's book—or maybe just its title—became famous because, among other things, it predicted a major shift in political narrative in the mid-twentieth century; class divisions and their attendant ideologies, having roiled global politics since the last decades of the nineteenth century, were fading. The old ideologies were no longer effective, closing the book "on an era of easy 'left' formulae."

Although some of my readers may remember this era directly, most of us have grown up after the "end of ideology," and therefore never knew what "easy left formulae" felt like. In our time, class analysis was really hard to do. Questioning capitalism in any mainstream setting required great critical effort and was always confronted by powerful pushback, if not outright derision. Sometime after 1978,[7] the era of class struggle had given way to Fukuyama's neoliberal "End of History."[8] And if class warfare was outmoded, so too was the strongman; few still considered that authoritarian modes of legitimation had much of a serious future, even if a few outliers held on here and there for reasons of the expediency of great power politics.

But today, everything is up for grabs in global affairs, not just in the seminar room but also the stateroom. In this way, our time resembles 1968 less, tumultuous as it was, and 1945 or 1914 more. We seem poised either to adapt a new moral politics to the demands of peace as was done after the Second World War, or to shuffle the deck with faith in a gamble on apocalypse as was true of 1914. We can hope that the rise of both the destructive power of nuclear weapons and the spread of the humanizing technologies of modern media will render war on the scale of the last century unthinkable, but the conflicts we face together are no less foundational than were those faced by our grandparent's grandparents.

This unsettled nature of our times helps to explain the rise of an analytic concept that seemed outré when I began to use it in the early 1990s, that is narrative. It is hard to turn on the television, let alone read a conflict analysis without someone speaking about the importance of controlling, crafting, managing, or directing "the narrative."[9] I have taken to referring to this trend in reference to the vogue that developed around the concept of "attitude" in the social sciences in the 1920s and 1930s: "narrative is the new attitude."[10] And my explanation for our attraction to the concept, having something to do with generational replacement and the maturation of philosophical trends, has even more to do with our need to address the unsettled nature of the times. Where once Bell could refer to ideology as a concept that applied almost exclusively to economic affairs and the future of capitalism, ideology, his "will fused with ideas," is precisely what most people are grasping for in their frustration today. Uncertainty displaces expertise and emboldens the layperson's intuitive and emotional relationship to ideas. Accordingly, many new schools of thought have arisen to help us think better about the intuitive nature of political thought.[11]

Although our unsettled times will demand technical analysis of careful plans and policy agendas for social and political change, in crises, technical rationality is buried under the public's emotional reactions to arguments. If we plan to work for peace, we had better develop a better understanding of how ideas become fused with will, and if we can ever hope to faithfully describe the illusive concept of ideology, we had better come to terms with this slippery concept of narrative, the only concept that works both at the level of reason and emotional intuition, values and interests, concurrently.

We are ready for a mature theory of ideology, one that simultaneously recognizes our animal nature and our angelic rationality. We can work with concepts that walk and chew gum at the same time, that give emotional primacy its due, without losing sight of the fact that politics is about power and who wields it for what ends. In this sense, every conversation in the study and practice of peace and conflict resolution is already about or should become one about power. This is a timely perspective. In an incisive essay on the subject, Kevin Avruch makes a prediction about the concept of power in the field that is similar to the one he made about culture many years ago. "It is time we faced power but with confidence, not defensively, and made it our Other on our terms."[12]

I have written this book to help get us up to speed about power, about the interrelationships of social power and storytelling, how power, narrative, and a theory of peace intersect, and to make power our own. To do this, I show how: we will have to come to terms with the ways that power and moral discourse mutually define one another; how when we speak about justice and speak about power, we are speaking, inversely, about the same thing; and how to recognize the roots of moral authority in stories about the appropriate uses and (ab)uses of power in social life.[13] Root Narrative Theory does not just examine the stories we tell about how power leads to suffering, it reveals how justice depends on the ways in which we confront and overcome it.

Too many students of peace and conflict studies are unfamiliar with the history of debates about ideology. Most of my students at the School for Conflict Analysis and Resolution, themselves drawn from some of the most contentious zones of conflict in the world, are intimately familiar with ethnic divisions and identity politics. They know how supremacy and hegemony have wreaked havoc on the Global South and feel in their bones what it is about the West that is so infuriating. Almost all have heard of, if not read, Frantz Fanon and can understand the vital truth of his worldview without much effort. Few of them however, even those who are from the West, are familiar with the critical social theory of prior eras. Although every student can speak to the centrality of diversity and inclusion as pillars of positive peace, most see Marxism as either a kind of enduring malady that afflicts extremists in their home context or as little more than an interesting historical footnote. If they have ever thought about John Locke, they see him as a symbol of European and English cultural particularly, if not bias. The classical liberalism that their American oppressors seem always ready to appeal to, strikes them as little more than a thin cover for ethnocentrism and implicit racism, certainly not a source of ideological conviction—will fused with ideas—this even as they accede to neoliberal economic theories with grudging complacence. And most students come to the study of peace never having thought about Thomas Hobbes as anything but a bogeyman subject to Freudian projection—the very wolfman described in his theory. His imagery of "the war of all against all" only seems relevant to those with broad exposure to an international relations curriculum in which "realist" theories of a world characterized by Hobbesian anarchy are standard.[14]

I have just chosen to highlight these four thinkers, Hobbes, Locke, Marx, and Fanon to serve as placeholders for the moral authority embodied in what I call the root narratives, the emotional core of rational arguments.[15] I will call them the virtuosi, because, although they did not invent the root narratives they helped to make famous, they did use these story structures in focused and effective ways.[16] Each of the four virtuosi is intended here merely as a stand-in for a mode of thought that is in play in the open space of global affairs today, a representative that has bored so deeply into our conception of political philosophy that even as the story I tell here becomes more complicated, we, as readers, will have trouble forgetting them or what they stand for. The four virtuosi were chosen not because they are the best, but because they are so specialized. Each thinker is a representative of a form of criticism of institutional social power that has become so familiar in modern political thought that we can almost think of the virtuosi as figures of speech, each representing the whole domain of thought with which they have become associated. They are the paradigmatic critics of power.

As a critic of a certain kind of social power, each thinker has also become a kind of prophet of a certain kind of peace. If we understand peace and justice as necessary complements, peacemaking is the process of overcoming legacies of abusive power. Accordingly, each of the virtuosi is a metonymic representative of a distinctive type of potential peacemaking, each very much alive in the empirical conflicts around us today. Hobbesian thinkers dream of peace as security for the political community. Lockean peacemakers, dream of peace as liberty for the rational individuals that make up society. Marxian peacemakers dream of peace as economic equality for the people who labor with the sweat of their brow. And Fanonian peacemakers dream of peace as dignity for the oppressed peoples, who have been left outside the categories of prior politics. Each of these forms of peace are about overcoming injustice. Each is about the appropriate uses of power. Each is about realizing core values.

The "big four" root narratives are paradigmatic story structures. None of them is very likely to appear alone in living discourse on its own. When we analyze or map a conflict, we find all the forms of moral authority blending into each other in bewildering intersections of abuse and privilege. The world of moral politics is nothing if not complex, but when we focus on an interpretation of the history of power viewed through the lens of one of the four root narratives, that world becomes astonishingly simple. Root Narrative Theory is a kind of prism, separating arguments into their constituent wavelengths. Each of the four root narratives creates for us a discrete universe of political interpretations, each separate, even orthogonal to the other three, and this ideological orthogonality produces a strange effect; it is as if the world itself is different when one approaches it from the perspective of one of the root narratives.[17] If you become seduced by one of the "big four" stories of abuse of power, adopting the curious logicality of its moral authority, it will be very hard to see the injustice that you have witnessed from another perspective. Each of the root narratives is sufficient to blind most people to the vital truth of one of the other three. Although the world is complex, our stories are often not. The story structures represented by the "big four" virtuosi are enough to drive us into mindless escalations. When we are united with one of them, we are easily divided from our neighbors. This is why it is so vital to identify the root narratives clearly (and in ways we can readily remember) so that we can better help conflicting parties to see that they are playthings of the root narratives as much as they are authors of their own ambitions.

Because this is a narrative theory, I should also say a few worlds about science, certainty, and my views about how thought hooks onto the world. Although I anchor my analysis in the materialist critiques of four very different thinkers, each of whom specializes in countering the abuses of a distinct network of social power, this is a narrative theory that is attentive to the limits of a what Richard Rorty called a "correspondence theory of truth," the idea that our words correspond to things in the world. [18] This is the irony of Root Narrative Theory. I assume that no conflict can ever really be analyzed down to its objective root causes, even as I assume that the explanations that people use in making sense of moral positions in any conflict (the stories they tell) are reflections of certain material conditions that exist whether we attend to them or not. Real stories are performed, but these performances grow from recognizable root causes. We may never know the causes as they really are, but we can learn to better recognize and engage their effects. Human folly being what it is, there is no necessary connection between the problems people see and the solutions that they need. It is our duty as conflict scholars to grapple with our own fallible renditions of reality to improve the narrative ecosystems we inhabit. We construct our own conflicts, but not in a manner of our choosing. That's the best we can do.

The best use of this book is as a kind of field guide for moral politics, using it to better learn how to recognize the root narratives in empirical data. To facilitate this, I demonstrate how the "big four" critical categories have played out in the history of the analysis of conflicts and politics. I walk us through a survey of familiar thinkers and their writings from Hammurabi to Edward Said, each of which serves to ground the endless variety of interpretations that are available for moral politics in each of the root narrative categories. My goal is to empower practitioners to become better able to generate accurate portraits of the moral vocabularies of the conflicting parties they study so that they can help them to re-narrate their conflicts in terms more agreeable to their adversaries, to approach conflict from the perspective of what we might call "crises of the moral imagination."[19]

The arguments in this book may be complex but the structure of the book is simple. In the next three chapters, I lay out the argument for Root Narrative Theory, its theoretical precursors and assumptions, its basic structure and definitions, and its manifestation in the famous writings of Hobbes, Locke, Marx, and Fanon. If these kinds of arguments are not your thing, you can turn to the following four chapters, each of which serves to illustrate the uses the "big four" root narratives in the history of social thought, and the conclusion reflects on how to put Root Narrative Theory into root narrative practice.

The result is a critical theory of peace, but more importantly, a critical theory of peacemaking, predicated on the expansion of our moral imaginations and the imaginations of those we serve. My goal is to develop reliable tools for conflict analysis that make it easier for the peacemaker to helps partisans to avoid the worst and most common foibles of misinterpretation, taking steps toward the development of something like a shared understanding. This kind of practice is challenging, slow, and painstaking, but it is the only path to positive peace. We live in same world but speak different moral languages. Learning to speak with one another is no guarantee of peace, but it is its precondition.

Notes

1 I've selected these thinkers as a way to create a feeling of the breadth of the questions that were being asked in the period between and just after the two world wars of the twentieth century. The next few decades will require a similarly expansive outlook. It is always hard to get perspective on one's own epoch, but it seems fair to say that few people alive today have lived through the kind of uncertainty in great power politics that may now be emerging with the rise of authoritarian states.

2 I have always thought that it was revealing, if otherwise obvious, that the name for the organization that is most influential in the international community, The United Nations, began as a wartime institution led by the United States and England. As Dwight Eisenhower put it in his D-Day speech, "The United Nations have inflicted upon the Germans great defeats, in open battle, man-to-man." ("Transcript of General Dwight D. Eisenhower's Order of the Day"). This anglophone-led order, however multilateral it became over time, is now in transition. https://www.un.org/en/sections/history-united-nations-charter/1942-declaration-united-nations/index.html

3 Ramsbotham, *Transforming Violent Conflict*.

4 Kriesberg, "The Development of the Conflict Resolution Field."

5 Arendt, *The Origins of Totalitarianism*.

6 Bell, *The End of Ideology*.

7 Simmons, "Civil Identity and Communicative Practice."

8 Fukuyama, *The End of History and the Last Man*.

9 The study of narrative in political analysis is certainly nothing new. The various reactions to structural linguistics in France after Claude Levi-Strauss's, *The Savage Mind* became such a phenomenon, demonstrate how mature the perspective is, but there is something new in how the concept has broken into the mainstream of public consciousness. This French origin helps to explain why the concept was considered outré in mainstream social science, which was dominated by rational actor models of various kinds in the latter half of the twentieth century.

10 The analogy is to the explosion of interest in the concept of attitude and attitude measurement, beginning in sociology and then moving to psychology and political science. The idea probably caught hold at the University of Chicago, but began its meteoric rise with L.L. Thurstone's "Attitudes Can Be Measured."

11 Haidt, "The Emotional Dog and Its Rational Tail"; Haidt, *The Righteous Mind*; Lakoff, *Moral Politics*; Lakoff and Johnson, *Metaphors We Live By*. I frame Root Narrative Theory in reference to Haidt and Lakoff because I see these two perspectives as the two in the general intellectual sphere that have become the closest competitors to narrative approaches to moral conflict.

12 Avruch, *Context and Pretext in Conflict Resolution*.

13 In the word play of the term (ab)use, I have drawn heavily on two philosophical perspectives, distantly related at best, that help to speak to the dialectical definition of the concept of peace and the persistence of the presence of violence in the concept. The first of these philosophers is Judith Shklar and her efforts to revive Montaigne's conception of opposition to the vice of cruelty. As she wrote, "One begins with what is to be avoided, as Montaigne feared being afraid most of all." Shklar, *Ordinary Vices*. The other writer is the psychanalysist Julia Kristeva, in particular her early work on abjection, through which identity is formed by what we reject. Kristeva, *Powers of Horror*.

14 Waltz, *Man, the State and War.*
15 Hobbes, Locke, Marx and Fanon are useful less because the Western origin of their concepts are generative of universal categories of political thought and more because their Western origin will help to dispel illusions that the narrative resources they represent—what I call the "big four" root narratives—apply only in conflicts in peripheral parts of the world rather than in the core of the world system.
16 The goal of Root Narrative Theory is not to portray the true thoughts and meaning of the great authors, but rather to use them as illustrations of virtuoso narration in the four root narratives. In order make it easier to keep track of which version of the great narrators I draw upon in the analysis, I refer primarily to the following versions of the classic texts. Hobbes, *Leviathan*; Locke, *Second Treatise of Government*; Locke, *A Letter Concerning Toleration and Other Writings*; Marx, *Selected Writings*; Fanon, *Black Skin, White Masks*; Fanon, *The Wretched of the Earth.*
17 One practical manifestation of this effect of ideological orthogonality is the problem of reductionism, when one type of critical analysis is represented as if it were an example of another category. For example, a case of racism might be explained as if it were the result of a clash of economic interests. Reductionism is an argument that an analysist has made a category mistake. This kind of reductionism can go in any direction: dignity can be read as equality, liberty as security, etc. A further complication is that there is no final way to adjudicate between the kind of story that is appropriate to tell—the kind of power that is in play—apart from the final vocabulary and standards of evidence provided by the discursive environment. In other words, there is no ultimate test that settles the dispute about the true story. In this sense, Root Narrative Theory is consistent with skeptical theories, even though it is predicated on the ongoing existence of four forms of power in social life across history.
18 Rorty, *Philosophy and the Mirror of Nature.*
19 Throughout this book, I am trying to keep as close to the attitude toward conflict that Lederach developed in his study of imagination in conflict. It is one of the best examples of how to keep focused on peace even as we study the most divisive forms of politics. See Lederach, *The Moral Imagination.*

Bibliography

Arendt, Hannah. *The Origins of Totalitarianism.* Vol. 244. Boston, MA: Houghton Mifflin Harcourt, 1973.

Avruch, Kevin. *Context and Pretext in Conflict Resolution: Culture, Identity, Power, and Practice.* London: Routledge, 2015.

Bell, Daniel. *The End of Ideology.* New York: Free Press, 1960.

Fanon, Frantz. *The Wretched of the Earth: The Handbook for the Black Revolution that is Changing the Shape of the World.* New York: Grove Press, 1963.

Fanon, Frantz. *Black Skin, White Masks.* Translated by Richard Philcox. Revised edition. New York: Grove Press, 2008.

Fukuyama, Francis. *The End of History and the Last Man.* New York: Avon Books, 1992.

Haidt, Jonathan. "The Emotional Dog and Its Rational Tail: A Social Intuitionist Approach to Moral Judgment." *Psychological Review* 108, no. 4 (2001): 814–834.

Haidt, Jonathan. *The Righteous Mind: Why Good People Are Divided by Politics and Religion.* 1st ed. New York: Pantheon Books, 2012.

Hobbes, Thomas. *Leviathan: With Selected Variants from the Latin Edition of 1668.* Edited by Edwin Curley. Cambridge, MA: Hackett Publishing Company, 1994.

Kriesberg, Louis. "The Development of the Conflict Resolution Field." In *Peacemaking in International Conflict: Methods and Techniques*, by William Zartman and J. Lewis Rasmussen, pp. 51–77. Washington, DC: Unites States Institute of Peace, 1997.

Kristeva, Julia. *Powers of Horror: An Essay on Abjection*. Translated by Leon Roudiez. Reprint edition. New York: Columbia University Press, 1982.

Lakoff, George. *Moral Politics: How Liberals and Conservatives Think*. Chicago: University of Chicago Press, 2002.

Lakoff, George, and Mark Johnson. *Metaphors We Live By*. Chicago: University of Chicago Press, 1980.

Lederach, John Paul. *The Moral Imagination: The Art and Soul of Building Peace*. Reprint. New York: Oxford University Press, 2010.

Levi-Strauss, Claude. *The Savage Mind*. Chicago: University of Chicago Press, 1968.

Locke, John. *Second Treatise of Government*. Cambridge, MA: Hackett Publishing Company, 1980.

Locke, John. *A Letter Concerning Toleration and Other Writings*. New Edition. Indianapolis: Liberty Fund Inc., 2010.

Marx, Karl. *Selected Writings*. Edited by Lawrence H. Simon. Cambridge, MA: Hackett Publishing Company, 1994.

Ramsbotham, Oliver. *Transforming Violent Conflict: Radical Disagreement, Dialogue and Survival*. London: Routledge, 2010.

Rorty, Richard. *Philosophy and the Mirror of Nature*. Princeton: Princeton University Press, 2009.

Shklar, Judith N. *Ordinary Vices*. Cambridge, MA: Harvard University Press, 1984.

Simmons, Solon J. "Civil Identity and Communicative Practice: The Rhetoric of Liberty in the United States." In *Forming a Culture of Peace*, by Karina Korostelina, pp.165–193. New York: Palgrave MacMillan, 2012.

Thurstone, L.L. "Attitudes Can Be Measured." *American Journal of Sociology* 33 (1928): 529–554.

"Transcript of General Dwight D. Eisenhower's Order of the Day." (1944). *Our Documents*. Accessed July 19, 2019. https://www.ourdocuments.gov/doc.php?flash=false&doc=75&page=transcript.

Waltz, Kenneth N. *Man, the State and War*. New York: Columbia University Press, 1959.

2

ROOT NARRATIVE THEORY

Between social power and scales of justice

In the sociological bestseller, *Habits of the Heart*, Robert Bellah and his colleagues describe a character, Brian Palmer, a successful businessman in a large corporation who has recently decided to spend more substantive time with his family but who lacks a stable way to describe his commitment to his spouse and children.[1] They write:

> His increased commitment to family and children rather than material success seems strangely lacking in substantive justification…. Despite the combination of tenderness and admiration he expresses for his wife, the genuine devotion he seems to feel for his children, and his own resilient self-confidence, Brian's justification of his life thus rests on a fragile foundation… to hear him talk, even his deepest impulses of attachment to others are without any more solid foundation than his momentary desires. he lacks a language to explain what seem to be the real commitments that define his life, and to that extent the commitments become precarious.
>
> *(p. 8)*

This vignette and the others they describe capture something important for the study of moral politics. We see here the fragility of moral commitments in relation to available discourse and how the inability of actors to narrate their feelings in plausible ways leaves them vulnerable; their plans and values can easily fall out of alignment. We see the importance of processes of justification and the presence and absence of what the authors describe as a "language" to explain how moral commitments hook onto the world. This idea of a moral language, perhaps borrowing from Wittgenstein's philosophical investigations,[2] speaks to the centrality of narrative in moral life and what can happen when the stories we tell don't align with the values we hold dear.

Narrative provides both the conscious language that justifies actions when these actions are subject to direct reflection and the primitive and structuring symbols that work on us at the level of our moral intuitions when they are not. Khaled Hosseini, the author of the *Kite Runner,* places this dynamic in context.

> Stories are the best antidote to the dehumanization caused by numbers. They restore our empathy. Each story I hear from a refugee helps me feel, bone-deep, my immutable connection to its teller as a fellow human. I see myself, the people I would give my life for, in every tale I am told.[3]

In contrast to the suggestive literature of moral psychology and cognitive science, the sociological literature on moral reasoning demonstrates how these moral languages are not products of our first nature but rather our second, that is of political culture. Moral grammar does arise directly from biological foundations—from our moral emotions or cognitive metaphors—although it always uses these as materials to work on; it must always be recognized as the strategic product of historical struggle. For those who are not careful, this strategic dimension—we might call it ideological—is often missed in both the bio-psychological and cognitive science approach to discourse analysis, and the resulting interpretations of conflict behavior is therefore distracting and inefficient. By substituting evolutionary mechanisms for historical ones, psychological and cognitive approaches to moral reasoning run the risk of removing the ideology from ideological analysis, undermining the otherwise brilliant and productive insights they contribute. If we ever hope to transform violent conflicts, we have to look beyond emotions and family metaphors, placing the strategic development of political language—political ideas—front and center in our analyses. The moral politics of our second nature forces us to examine legacies of abusive power and how these remain with us in the master narratives of political culture.

If moral politics has to come to terms with political culture, the best place to begin is with a conceptual innovation that helped to revolutionize the study of cultural sociology in the 1980s when Ann Swidler, a leading member of the group behind *Habits of the Heart*, published her famous essay "Culture in Action: Symbols and Strategies."[4] What made Swidler's article so revolutionary was the way it shifted thinking away from culture as a source of "ultimate ends or values" (that might well be products of our conditioning experience or cognitive systems) toward culture as a means for attaining desired ends. She described culture as "more like a 'toolkit' or a repertoire from which actors select differing pieces for constructing lines of action." Culture is something we create together and then use. It is both an outcome and input to social experience. For our purposes, it's a moral toolkit not a moral foundation.

The introduction of the toolkit simile was important. It made it possible to think of culture less as a thing and more as a causal process that explained differences between types of actors, each drawing upon different cultural resources, which always had implications for morality, politics, and conceptions of the just society.

After this simile became conventional wisdom, it became unfashionable for sociologists to think in terms of the metaphor of foundations for moral reasoning. As morality is a key part of culture, it too must be thought of as a set of tools, and tools are not only useful, they are also invented by people with specific goals.

This toolkit simile, common as it is in the sociological literature, has yet to penetrate the world of conflict resolution and peace studies, nor has it shifted the broader conversation on moral politics in the popular press from the metaphor of a moral foundation; nevertheless, the potential value of thinking about moral politics in terms of moral tools as opposed to moral foundations is critical for the field of conflict resolution. Returning to the earlier version of the simile, the one used in *Habits of the Heart*, we can see how the toolkit simile might be useful:

> The main purpose of this book is to deepen our understanding of the resources our tradition provides—and fails to provide—for enabling us to think about the kinds of moral problems we are currently facing as Americans.

The Bellah group was interested in exploring how forms of commitment remained relevant for moral life in America alongside the more dominant forms of individualism. They were seeking grounds for community building, which is no less important for the conflict scholar than it was for the sociologist. Embedded and protracted conflicts are also products of parties drawing upon available cultural resources, but in ways that tend to escalate tensions rather than resolve them. If we can think about culture, especially political culture, as a toolkit and if we can better learn to use those tools—the moral languages—we will be more helpful to parties in conflict.

The sociological model is also helpful as a way to introduce a theory of narrative conflict, because the sociologist is never quick to forget the material forces implicit in the concept of social structure. If culture is the defining concept of the anthropologist, social structure is the analogue for the sociologist, a social structure most commonly imagined in relations to concrete institutions and material (extra-linguistic) forces. Bringing sociology back in to conflict resolution helps us to not lose track of how the stories we tell are always made relevant in relation to the institutional forces they describe and critique. You don't get this from the field of social psychology or cognitive science, or narrative analysis on their own. A sociological imagination is important to ensure that we don't just chase after any old kind of story that our disputants might tell, but instead look for the kinds of stories about social structure and abuse of power that produce the incommensurable worldviews and normative interpretations that engender moral conflict. As described by Barnett Pearce and Stephen Littlejohn in their seminal study, *Moral Conflict* is what happens under conditions of what Jonathan Haidt called dumbfounding—the very lack of fit between commitments and moral language that we saw in the Brian Palmer character above, but in this case in reverse.[5] In the disruptive culture wars of the 1990s people were at each other's throats but had no stable way to understand why apart from cliché. In order to overcome these dumbfounded escalations, they counseled that we need to "deal with the deep structures of the social worlds that the disputants bring into the sessions."

What are these deep structures and how can we learn to see them in the conflicts we study?[6] We know they have something to do with social institutions and the power they produce and that our interpretations of the workings of these institutions provide us with the moral tools through which to imagine a more just society. Our moral politics is the product of our political culture, itself a function of our past, collective evaluations of social power. If we knew more about the history of social power, we would have more to say about moral politics. In order to take the next step in the argument I'll need the help of two other thinkers, one another sociologist, Michael Mann, and the other a critical philosopher, Nancy Fraser. Each does particular work for the development of the argument, the first by providing us with a typology of forms of social power, and the second with a way to see how moral philosophies result from a critical analysis of the abuses of power. Together they demonstrate how the primitive moral grammar of politics operates, and how it sorts itself into four broad categories of moral authority that I call root narratives.

Michal Mann's magisterial historical sociology supplies the material elements and structural analysis that can be used for a deep structural analysis of cultural meanings. His framework for the analysis of the sources of social power will serve here as the institutional description of the elements of social power around which the ideological categories of Root Narrative Theory develop.[7] Fraser provides a complementary analysis, developed as a critical theory of justice. Her three (or in my view four) "dimensions" of justice can be thought of as ethical reactions to the abuses perpetuated by those in control of, or with special leverage over, the four forms of social power that Mann describes.[8] Put simply, from Mann, we learn what power is, and from Fraser, we learn what justice is.

Best of all, these two thinkers complement each other in a way that corrects for the errors of the other. Where Mann's materialism makes it impossible for him to recognize a realm of justice that is related to but independent of the material world of institutional means, Fraser, beginning as she does, with a left critique of what Galtung would call structural forms of violence,[9] has only recently expanded her theory to encompass critical forms of justice that become obvious from the perspective of an institutional critique like Mann's. Only recently has she considered the government as a moral antagonist, and she still has no clear way of addressing the problem of military power and the forms of justice that are required to countervail it—a problem that leads her, in her theory, to adopt awkward elements much like the Ptolemaic astronomers appeal to epicycles to preserve their paradigm from empirical anomalies.[10] Put simply, Michael Mann's theory of social power when joined to Nancy Fraser's theory of justice not only provides us with a more complete picture of how to do conflict analysis and resolution, but the tensions between the two philosophies solve problems for the other. Think of their relationship as dialectical.

What does Michael Mann have to offer peace theorists? There are many lessons in his work that I can't review here, but I will focus my attention exclusively on the introductory chapter of his three volume, *The Sources of Social Power*. Mann's description of the "four major types of power network" in that introduction, which he uses for the rest of his mammoth "history of power," provides a portrait of institutional structure—the development of concrete organizations—that avoids some of the most frequent misconceptions about social structure that had developed in the sociological, and related literatures.

Not unlike Swidler's reinterpretation of the concept of culture, Mann focused on institutions and means rather than ends or values. "I ignore original motivations and goals and concentrate on emergent *organizational power sources.*" In the place of values, he locates the motive sources of social life in four concrete networks of power: military, political, economic, and what he calls ideological. Military power is about killing the Other. Political power is about disciplining the community. Economic power is about maximizing wealth, and ideological power (not his best concept) is about communicating desire and values.

Mann is a kind of Weberian, but in his brutal materialist version of Max Weber, Mann admits that Weber's famous distinction between power and authority did not figure much in his book. Familiar with the innovations in the literature on power by the likes of Steven Lukes and Michel Foucault, Mann handled the tension between power and legitimacy by dispensing with the later notion entirely, while preserving the radical and pervasive coercive images of power presented in the radical literature of the time. It was not trendy to be soft in those days, worrying about things like moral authority. In his story, power is both "distributive and collective" and also "exploitative and functional."[11]

Mann also attempts to eviscerate the holistic imagery of the structural functionalist tradition and its influences, dismissing the language of "dimensions" of power (which are related to some false whole), the image of a "social system" (in favor of entropic fragmentation), and reductionism (no form of power is primary with respect to the others). His core image of social structure is captured in the sentence, "Societies are constituted of multiple overlapping and intersecting sociospatial networks of power." His vision of power is appealing for its materialism. It is a kind of "just the facts ma'am" approach to social analysis. There is no sentimentality here. No justice. No values. No purpose. It is all about how human beings use institutions to compel each other to obey.

For those familiar with Weber, apart from his brutal materialism, the best way to see Mann's contribution is as an adaptation and update of Weber's "Class, Status, and Party" typology for historical analysis—the so-called "three-component theory of stratification,"[12] with which Weber moved past Marxian materialism and its class primacy by introducing two other kinds of groups, status groups and parties, each treated as being of equal importance to classes—that is, not merely part of the superstructure as orthodox Marxists had insisted. What are status groups? Weber defined status groups as communities "of an amorphous kind" that are organized around particular "styles of life," each of which carries a certain kind of evaluation—what he called "status honor"—that came with associated privileges. Empirical patterns of ethnic segregation are clear examples of status differentiation as are other exclusionary patterns in informal social life. These have a material existence.

What about party? "Party" has long been considered an underdeveloped concept in Weberian analysis, somehow associated with what he called the "house of power." This is where Mann makes an enduring contribution. In Mann's theory, all social institutions represent forms of power. Class is a word for the institutions that channel economic power. Weber had presented status as the word for the institutions that channel the power of social evaluations like clubs, and families, and religious orders (without confusing them with the means of communication as Mann does). Party was how Weber began to think about state structures and their institutional forms. For Weber, parties referred to any aspect of the state in its role to influence communal action in any potential form. It is the rule making function supported by what he would elsewhere call "the monopoly of the legitimate use of physical force."[13]

Like C. Wrights Mills before him, Mann splits this party concept in two, one that he calls "political" and the other "military." Military power is the kind of power network that is used to conquer and defend territory, while political power is the kind of institutional network that is used for civil administration or to discipline those who no longer need to be conquered—those who accept the rough outline of the political community and its claim to make the laws. While the line between the two is often unclear, especially in contexts where military power has been in recent use, we get a clear sense of what "political" power is when we restrict it to apply only to the development of rules and in assigning formal rewards and penalties in relation to them. Political power is "the means of administration" that Weber refers to in his famous essay on the concept of bureaucracy. Stories of political power are populated with legislators, clerks, laws courts, and police, whereas military power is defined by its development of weaponry and the organization of deadly force. Its stories are populated by warriors, commanders, fortifiers, weapons designers, and logistics support teams. The two are often related as they appear in relation to the state, but they are different kinds of networks that play quite different roles in historical development.

With this separation of the institutional networks of the state into military and civic aspects, Mann's theory provides the scaffolding on which to build a theory of root narratives. A root narrative is defined as a way to imagine resistance against a form of social power that has been put to purportedly unjust uses, and Mann's theory provides us with a typology for the four forms of social power. Just as there are four forms of social power, there will be four root narratives.[14]

Where Mann's theory of power leaves off, Nancy Fraser's theory of justice picks up. If we take Nancy Fraser's arguments about justice at all seriously, we have to recognize that a theory of the resolution of moral conflicts could never be complete on Mann's assumptions, in which the history of power is "synonymous with a history and theory of human society itself." Indeed, Mann's materialism is distinctly amoral in its formulation. There is no room in it for anything but a purely subjective and rationalizing sense of justice. Nothing but power. Fraser provides us with a way to see how justice can act as a transcendent social force independent of mere power relations, a force of moral reflection on not just how power works—its uses—but also how it should and should not work—its abuses. Much as Emile Durkheim had described in his core image of a science of society, we need to recognize how the force of justice binds populations into patterns of concerted and intentional reaction to social forces,[15] a process that directs our attention to storytelling and narrative structure.[16]

If Michael Mann's institutionalism helps us to remember those aspects of the conflict that develop *outside the narrative*, that is whether we recognize them or not (what you might be tempted to call the facts), Nancy Fraser's critical philosophy helps us to remember that our values are only well defined when we have some form of structural injustice to confront with them. Mann teaches us what power is, and Fraser show us what we should do about it.

Nancy Fraser has been doggedly pursuing a perspective on justice and morality from a critical perspective for several decades, and her work almost exactly complements Mann's but from the other direction. Where Mann sees only organizational power in history, Fraser is primarily concerned with the meaning of justice in relation to organizational power. Where Mann would relegate all questions of meaning to a form of power he calls "ideological," Fraser begins her philosophical enterprise with a critical analysis of gender, works out the boundary of a politics of status and class based on distinct conceptions of injustice implied by each, more recently extends her perspective to include questions of the abuses of power central to classical liberalism, and is on the verge of a perspective that addresses basic questions of life and death in an anarchical world. In a sense, Fraser's intellectual journey goes backward in history. She works out the most pressing issues of justice in domains of status, which remain underdeveloped in our own time, relates these ideas to the social and economic justice—questions of the era prior to the Second World War—only then to extend the theory to the problematic of early modernity: state and sovereignty.[17]

I first encountered Fraser's work in a relatively early stage of its development in the late 1990s, when she brought her recognition vs. redistribution talk to the sociology department at the University of Wisconsin–Madison. At that time, I thought of her work in terms of its relation to Jürgen Habermas, because her concept "sub-altern counter public" was so arresting and challenging to traditional universalistic conceptions of the use of public reason and impartiality.[18] At this stage, the model she presented was a seemingly simple one. It came in the form of a two-by-two table. We all know two-by-two tables, they cross two dichotomous concepts against one another and use the resulting four cells to illustrate the implication of the conceptual cross tabulation. The issue of this discussion was how to imagine the difference between the kinds of political movements that called for justice in the form of recognition of difference from those that called for redistribution of economic resources. This is a common problem in the sociological literature, where the "new social movements" for race, gender and sexual equality are differentiated from what the German sociologist Werner Sombart called The Social Movement, namely the old social movements that fought for some form of socialism or economic reform.[19] What made these newer recognition movements different from redistribution movements was what Fraser calls "the substance of justice."

Today's social justice movements lack a shared understanding of the substance of justice. Unlike their twentieth-century predecessors, who militated mostly for "redistribution," present-day claimants couch their demands in a variety of idioms, which are oriented to competing goals. Today, for example, class-accented appeals for economic redistribution are routinely pitted against minority-group demands for "recognition," while feminist claims for gender justice often collide with demands for supposedly traditional forms of religious or communal justice. The result is a radical heterogeneity of justice discourse, which poses a major challenge to the idea of the moral balance: Where is the scale of justice on which such heterogeneous claims can be impartially weighed?[20]

What looks like a simple distinction between types of issues—economic and status-based—becomes something much more substantial in Fraser's telling. These claims to justice are crises of "understanding"; their speakers speak in different "idioms" and rely on "incommensurable ontological assumptions." Those who fight for racial justice speak a language that usurps class talk. It is as if these activists speak a different language.

Returning to Bellah, Swidler, Pearce and Littlejohn, we can see that parties to conflict, in fact, often do speak different languages, different moral languages. The conception of injustice that inspires the feminist activist to political activity has a distinct moral vocabulary from that of the union boss bargaining for wages and hours. The "logic" or style of reasoning each uses is distinct. Of course, both use the same vernacular language and formal logic, but the ways that arguments are put together to make meaningful claims are quite different. The two sides not only differ in their values; they invoke their own moral universe, using a different political storybook, based on different antagonisms, different abuses, different villains and heroes, different historical settings, and directed to different goals. Kenneth Burke would be tempted to say that these justice paradigms differ in their moral grammars.[21] The anti-capitalist and the anti-racist (in their empirically rare pure or caricatured forms) differ in their use of dramatic materials, and these form the literary and discursive material of what amount to distinctive political cultures.

Note, there is no sense here that the anti-racist and the anti-capitalist rely on different moral emotions: each may be touched at the level of fairness, pity, disgust, loyalty, or deference, to use Jonathan Haidt's categories, but these emotions are channeled into different root narratives and attached to different symbols, differing in what could be called their moral grammar. To put a Wittgensteinian spin on it, each side is playing a different language-game, not fully aware that their words mean different things and that their invoked images point in different directions. Unless these arguments are translated into the moral grammar of the other, there is little hope of commensurability and therefore little hope for positive peace—peace based on understanding.[22]

Fraser's theory has since developed from a distinction between redistribution and recognition to include what she calls representation, this last term referring to the dimension of politics. A clever reader will have noticed that her framework now looks a lot like Weber's triad, class, status and party. Fraser has developed a critical theory of justice to explain the legitimacy of the kinds of claims made by these three different camps, but as it happens, these forms of justice are each related to one of the forms of power that Weber distinguished a century ago. This means that, the various forms of Fraser's critical theory of justice differ from one another primarily in terms of the form of social power they were designed to countervail—what she calls "the substance of justice." Redistribution is the idiom of class politics, recognition that of status politics, and representation that of state or formal politics. This is precisely how I read Fraser's work, as the moral complement to the organizational analysis of the Weberian sociologist. She has developed a philosophical typology through which we can imagine the political space as divided by critical values: for redistribution, equality; for recognition, dignity; for representation, liberty, all based on a critical theory of power. As the Christian apologist Tertullian asserted, "the blood of the martyrs is the seed of the church."

There is one remaining thread on which to pull before we can end this beginning of our story. What is the idiom for a critical theory of military power—that power network that Michael Mann and C. Wright Mills hived off from Weber's conception of "party?" This distinction between military and administrative power is important for a critical theory of justice (especially for those of us who study violent conflicts), because it highlights an important lacuna in Fraser's current theory that makes it more difficult to apply the theory to cases of conflict resolution and international relations. Fraser has no "scale of justice" with which to weigh the abuses of the power of rival militaries—of those who would subject us to their mercies. She has no theory of security. No theory of refuge. If we accept her theory as complete, we will have to assume away the fact that we live in a society of sovereign states, complete with dozens of non-state actors who reserve the right to use deadly force to prove their claims to independence. We might wish this problem were not real, but unless and until the institutions of military power are abolished, the challenge of security is unavoidable.

It may be that the theory of security is lacking in Fraser's work because security is really not a liberal value (after all, it did take her some time to reverse engineer her perspective to include the idiom of classical liberalism in her framework). Unlike representation, redistribution and recognition, (which might all be related to the motto of the French Revolution *liberté, egalité, fraternité*), security represents the values of the king and the bishop.[23] It assumes that distinctions between communities will endure, that military tensions are endemic and that strategic violence is always a risk. Indeed, security is a conservative idiom, predicated on the idea that rival groups out there in the world have the means and intention to kill us (whoever we are), take our stuff, and destroy the fabric of our political community. This outcome is sufficiently horrific that it seems to be a primal motivation for political thinkers from Homer to Machiavelli and probably explains the rise of Donald Trump. It is not a comfortable space in which a modern and progressive critical theorist would move.

Aware of this problem, Fraser employs an ingenious but awkward concept: meta-disagreements that occur at the level of "second-order" questions of justice that concern who is entitled to "first-order" justice considerations. This is what I mean by the epicycle-like addition to her theory. As clever and well-argued as Fraser's position on "misframing" and "second-order meta-level questions" is, I think Mann is right to demarcate the political category from the military, and we easily see how those critical of the military power of others could generate scales of justice in the idiom of security (distinct from liberty) that would be salient and convincing to many. Accordingly, I consider security and the struggle for survival in the face of the development of the means of defense to be an independent element of a critical theory and one I will take as seriously as the others.

Perhaps it goes without saying, but now you can easily see the role our four virtuosi play in developing this theory of moral conflict and root narratives. Each of the virtuosi is the most recognizable of the specialized master storytellers of political philosophy. Each identifies the emotional core of a rational critique of a paradigm of social power: Hobbes, the critic of the abusive power of the means of defense; Locke, the critic of the abusive power of the means of administration; Marx, the critic the abusive power of the means of production; and Fanon, the critic of the abusive power of the means of socialization. With four forms of social power come four opposing values: security, liberty, equality, and dignity. Together, the analysis of four roots of social power and the root values that countervail their abuse, provide us with the base material of the four root narratives. This is the basis of Root Narrative Theory. While all of us narrate in the critical terms identified by the virtuosi, few us have ever been as clear in our analysis of the origins, abuses, and remedies for power as they have.

At this dialectical intersection of Michael Mann's theory of social power with Nancy Fraser's critical theory of justice, we have all the elements in place to describe how it is that parties to conflict so often end up speaking with incommensurable moral vocabularies. The ways that the parties establish the meaningfulness of their claims are simply different in substance. They develop political arguments using distinct moral grammars, each of which differs in the assumptions it makes about the source of social power and its attendant imaginary. As conflicting parties imagine the world in different registers, they speak past one another using languages that differ in ways they fail to understand. In the next chapter, we will explore the structure of those misunderstandings, the deep structures of our moral imaginations that we don't even understand ourselves. These categories of sensemaking and moral authority are what I call Root Narrative Theory, a framework for decoding the processes of moral reasoning.

Notes

1 Bellah et al., *Habits of the Heart: Individualism and Commitment in American Life.*
2 Wittgenstein, *Philosophical Investigations.*
3 Hosseini, "Refugees Are Still Dying. How Do We Get over Our News Fatigue?"
4 Swidler, "Culture in Action: Symbols and Strategies."
5 Pearce and Littlejohn, *Moral Conflict.*

6 This appeal to depth is resonant in many settings in which scholars are grappling with the new forms of ideology. A great example is the insightful analysis of Arlie Hochschild in her book, *Strangers in their Own Land*. (Hochschild, Strangers in Their Own Land.) She tropes on George Lakoff's cognitive metaphor theory for her analysis of "deep stories." In the language of Root Narrative Theory, the deep stories come from the system of root narratives. A deep story is one that taps into the universal story structure and articulates it with current events, politicians, and policies.

7 Mann, *The Sources of Social Power*. The most important part of the whole three volume set is the introduction to the first volume. An interested reader would find everything that I need from Mann for my argument in that introduction.

8 Nancy Fraser's philosophical work is among the most important for the development of my argument. The most critical aspect of her work is the distinction she makes between forms or paradigms of justice. Her perspective is developing over time, but the best statements are in: Fraser, "Rethinking Recognition"; Fraser and Honneth, *Redistribution or Recognition*; Fraser, *Scales of Justice*. My sense is that the perspective has more room to grow and Root Narrative Theory is one way to promote that growth.

9 Johan Galtung's signal theoretical achievement was to introduce the concept of structural violence. I understand the concept as an elaboration of a Weberian concept of class, because he uses the concept of differential life chances in his description. The two important statements he makes that differentiate structural and cultural violence occur just over two decades apart: Galtung, "Violence, Peace, and Peace Research"; Galtung, "Cultural Violence."

10 This discussion is developed in Fraser, *Scales of Justice*

11 Discussions about power have long been important in social theory, but have recently become important in peace and conflict studies as well. For a nice overview, see: Avruch, *Context and Pretext in Conflict Resolution*

12 This is one of the major typologies presented in Weber's magisterial: Weber, *Economy and Society*.

13 Gerth and Wright Mills, *From Max Weber: Essays in Sociology*. Mills is also a critical Weberian forebear to Mann in his prior division of "party" into military and political aspects. This can be found in his classic, *The Power Elite*.

14 One final innovation in Mann's work is the transformation of status to ideology (a reformulation very similar to that of Steven Lukes). This conversion of "status" into "ideology" is what I describe as the mistake that Nancy Fraser helps him to correct, but for my purposes, I will describe the four as follows: the means of defense; the means of administration; the means of production; and the means of socialization: all of them material forces.

15 Central as this insight is to constructivist thinkers, it is interesting to see how powerful the concept can be when attached to a progressive scientific agenda. The point is revived forcefully in: Haidt and Graham, "Planet of the Durkheimians, Where Community, Authority, and Sacredness Are Foundations of Morality."

16 For an interesting project that shares some of the philosophical predilections of my argument, see: Boltanski and Thévenot, *On Justification*. Like Boltanski and Thévenot, I develop a perspective on regimes of justification and I also link the regimes to classical authors. My approach differs from theirs in that I do not place as much separation between the justification regimes, instead treating them as distinct patterns of argument that overlap and interact in complex and eclectic ways. On my reading, the Boltanski and Thévenot regimes are framed as much more epistemologically distinct from one another than my root narratives. The root narratives are not so much completely separate worldviews (although their mutual orthogonality can make them feel that way), but separate wavelengths of argument. The prism metaphor is always a helpful resort.

17 This progressive character of Fraser's work is one of the aspects that I find most helpful about it. She is removing the scales from our eyes and this takes time. The process she is going through is a great example of what I think of as ideological orthogonality. When one is thinking about recognition, it is hard to think about redistribution in a coherent and clear way. The same is true for representation and what I will call refuge.

18 Fraser, "Rethinking the Public Sphere."
19 Sombart, *Why is There No Socialism in the United States?*
20 Fraser, *Scales of Justice.*
21 I will develop this sense of moral grammar in more detail in the following chapter in which I use the term in a more literal way than is typically done. I will argue that there are four basic sentences that have moral/political content, and these can be diagrammed in simple ways using the core elements: protagonist, injustice suffered, antagonist, power abused.
22 At this point it is good to keep in mind the arguments about radical disagreement and moral conflict. Ramsbotham, *Transforming Violent Conflict*; Pearce and Littlejohn, *Moral Conflict*
23 On this point, I am indebted to Reinhard Bendix, the Weberian sociologist. Bendix, *Kings or People*

Bibliography

Avruch, Kevin. *Context and Pretext in Conflict Resolution: Culture, Identity, Power, and Practice.* London: Routledge, 2015.

Barnett Pearce, W., and Stephen W. Littlejohn. *Moral Conflict: When Social Worlds Collide.* Thousand Oaks, CA: Sage, 1997.

Bellah, Robert N., Richard Madsen, William M. Sullivan, Ann Swidler, and Steven M. Tipton. *Habits of the Heart: Individualism and Commitment in American Life.* Berkeley, CA: University of California Press, 1985.

Bendix, Reinhard. *Kings or People: Power and the Mandate to Rule.* Berkeley: University of California Press, 1978.

Boltanski, Luc, and Laurent Thévenot. *On Justification: Economies of Worth.* Princeton: Princeton University Press, 2006.

Fraser, Nancy. "Rethinking Recognition." *New Left Review* 3, no. 3 (2000): 107–118.

Fraser, Nancy. "Rethinking the Public Sphere: A Contribution to the Critique of Actually Existing Democracy." *Social Text*, 25 no. 26 (1990): 56–80.

Fraser, Nancy. *Scales of Justice: Reimagining Political Space in a Globalizing World.* Vol. 31. New York: Columbia University Press, 2009.

Fraser, Nancy, and Axel Honneth. *Redistribution or Recognition: A Political-Philosophical Exchange.* London: Verso, 2003.

Galtung, Johan. "Violence, Peace, and Peace Research." *Journal of Peace Research* 6, no. 3 (1969): 167–191.

Galtung, Johan. "Cultural Violence." *Journal of Peace Research* 27, no. 3 (1990): 291–305.

Gerth, Hans H., and C. Wright Mills. *From Max Weber: Essays in Sociology.* New York: Oxford University Press, 1946.

Haidt, J., and J. Graham. "Planet of the Durkheimians, Where Community, Authority, and Sacredness Are Foundations of Morality." In *Social and Psychological Bases of Ideology and System Justification*, by John T. Jost, Aaron C. Kay, and Hulda Thorisdottir, pp. 371–401. Oxford: Oxford Scholarship. 2009.

Hochschild, Arlie Russell. *Strangers in Their Own Land: Anger and Mourning on the American Right.* New York: New Press, 2016.

Hosseini, Khaled. "Refugees Are Still Dying. How Do We Get over Our News Fatigue?" *The Guardian*, sec. Books, August 17, 2018. https://www.theguardian.com/books/2018/aug/17/khaled-hosseini-refugees-migrants-stories.

Mann, Michael. *The Sources of Social Power: A History of Power from the Beginning to A. D. 1760.* Cambridge: Cambridge University Press, 1986.

Mills, C. Wright. *The Power Elite.* New York: Oxford University Press, 1956.

Pearce, W. Barnett, and Stephen W. Littlejohn. *Moral Conflict: When Social Worlds Collide.* Thousand Oaks, CA: Sage, 1997.

Ramsbotham, Oliver. *Transforming Violent Conflict: Radical Disagreement, Dialogue and Survival.* London: Routledge, 2010.

Sombart, Werner. *Why is There No Socialism in the United States?*White Plains, NY: M.E. Sharpe, 1976.

Swidler, Ann. "Culture in Action: Symbols and Strategies." *American Sociological Review* 51 (1986): 273–286.

Weber, Max. *Economy and Society.* Edited by Claus Wittich. 2nd Vol. Berkeley: University of California Press, 1978.

Wittgenstein, Ludwig. *Philosophical Investigations.* Hoboken, NJ: John Wiley & Sons, 2009.

3

THE STORY SYSTEM

Deep structures of the moral imagination

After all of this intense philosophical reflection on social power, justice and moral grammar, it is important to stress that the point of it all is to develop very concrete and simple tools for the analysis of conflict discourse—and by conflict discourse, I mean anyone talking about conflict anywhere they happen to be speaking. Even more important than analysis, the purpose of Root Narrative Theory is to provide the student with tools for the diagnosis of conditions of radical disagreement, which can be used to help to reframe escalated and protracted conflicts and policy discussions in a way that helps conflicting parties to better hear, understand and consider each other's positions. This is what I call introducing moral complexity into the conversation.

Root Narrative Theory is intended to be used as an alternative to (perhaps in conversation with) the recent advances in moral psychology and cognitive science that have become popular with students of politics and conflict. Moral foundations theory, as developed by Jonathan Haidt and his colleagues, and George Lakoff's family metaphors approach to moral politics both help us to see why we need to think about morality as a complex phenomenon that builds on our biological capacities as well as our social experiences. Both of these approaches and those inspired by them, break down the dichotomy between reason and the emotions, highlight the importance of intuition over consciousness for moral judgment, and encourage us to be curious about values that may be unpopular in advanced, highly educated and often liberal, Western societies. These things are all also true about Root Narrative Theory as well.

What Root Narrative Theory adds that these theories lack, is a link between the history of abusive power and the structure of our moral intuitions. It's not just that one person in a conflict happens to have a strong loyalty module in his moral makeup while another has somehow been granted an aversion to harm, as Haidt sometimes suggests. Instead, the emotional circuits of both parties have been activated through vivid contact with the conflict behavior of the other party. As the victims of the horrors of abusive social power, parties to conflict continually develop new emotional associations with the data of conflict: the actors, the policies, the atrocities, the rival justifications, and the missed opportunities among other things. But these associations don't come to us unfiltered. They come to us through our reflective judgments about concrete cases—that is through stories.[1] Through political stories. We know who did what and why by matching an antagonist with a source of power and a protagonist with a form of injustice produced by it. This is the primitive grammar of the moral imagination. We might write the basic sentence of all moral politics in the form of a skeletal story like the following:

> The antagonist uses abusive power to create injustice for the protagonist.

Variations on this basic story structure provide us with the simple, linear, binary stories that demagogues employ, but also the complex, circular, and nuanced theses of the great political philosophers and theologians. The moral grammar of the political story in all its various manifestations provides us both with a way to think and a way to feel about the data of conflict. The biological mechanisms through which we feel and think about the meaning of events is always critical, but only matter insofar as they can gain access to the political world through this basic moral grammar. Even the most sophisticated among us are stuck in a social world structured by political narrative.

Root Narrative Theory assumes we see political events through the lenses of primitive story structures, the root narratives, and also that parties to conflict employ these narratives in ways that they often fail to understand. Root narratives are an important part of the analytical toolkit in that they provide the moral grammar for any given account of conflict, anchoring assumptions about the organizational means in play, the kinds of actors who matter, the historical exemplars for similar events, the ultimate goals actors bring to their actions, and even evaluations of rival descriptions likely to be offered of what actually happened. The moral grammars provide us with the conditions for the possibility of establishing the meaningfulness of our political accounts. Without them, we speak nonsense, and not even the most abstract and technical authors can escape their influence. Every technical policy argument that explains "who gets what, when, and how" in Lasswell's usage[2] only makes sense in the context of a moral grammar that also explains why we should care. Even the cynical empiricism of the international relations realist is developed in the thrall of a moral grammar, because its authors fear violent death and being at the mercy of their adversaries.[3]

There has always been something awkward in using the word grammar to describe the kind of structure I am referring to, that is since philosophers like Ludwig Wittgenstein made is unavoidable to do so. But "moral grammar" is attractive as nomenclature in the sense that it draws our attention to the fact that there is a structure behind our moral judgments that is somewhat arbitrary and cultural in the way that language is. It is annoying in the sense that we already have a clear sense of what we mean by grammar and we reserve it to describe only the formal rules of language use. Confusing at it is, the idea that there may be higher order structures in our language that steer our thinking in unknown ways is extremely helpful as a way to represent the broader concept of social structure, a structure that is entirely virtual like language yet discernable through observing the rules that people appear to obey when they make what otherwise seem to be free choices. When we think of the moral imagination, how people project themselves into a world as moral agents, the concept of a moral grammar is a natural choice for a label.

One of the best examples of the use of the concept of a moral grammar and its role in conflict appears in the book *Moral Conflict* by W. Barnett Pearce and Stephen W. Littlejohn.

> Moral conflict occurs when disputants are acting within incommensurate grammars.... In moral conflicts, new types of abilities are required—not just the ability to act skillfully within the context of one's own grammar but the ability to transcend one's own grammar, to join the grammars of others, and to weave these grammars together.
>
> *(p. 55)*[4]

For Pearce and Littlejohn, moral grammar provides us with a method for "establishing moral values" (p. 49). Just as Anne Swidler helped us to see that culture was not a foundation but rather a toolkit or a process, Pearce and Littlejohn help us to see that political morality is also best thought of as a toolkit, one that helps us to assign meaning to the ethical confusion of political life.

Sara Cobb has developed this imagery to describe how the narratives that structure our moral judgments in conflict can be developed in the cause of generating "better formed stories" that "braid" the original strands of conflicting narratives into larger wholes in which both sides are fairly represented and have legitimate future roles to play.[5] If we think about these story structures that Cobb describes with her separate strands of the braid in terms of moral grammars—ways of putting together meaningful sentences about conflict—we begin to see how we can take apart sentences in public discourse to reconstruct the narrative logic that is in play in any given conflict conversation. If we can reconstruct the form of the moral imagination that each of the parties to conflict employ, we can better imagine how the braiding process that Cobb describes can take place.

If conflicting parties do really act and imagine on the basis of incommensurate moral grammars, we first need a method through which to characterize the structure of the strands, the logic of the outrage, so that the process of interweaving can even begin. This is just what Root Narrative Theory is designed to do. It helps us to identify the presence of rival moral grammars in empirical discourse so that we can reconstruct a model (complex and contradictory as it usually is) of the moral logics that a party to conflict tends to employ. In other words, we can use Root

Narrative Theory to develop root narrative profiles of the parties in conflict that we can then use to better interact with them. What we do with these root narrative profiles is an open question, but the first step is to establish their presence and how we can come to recognize them in text. To get a sense of what a root narrative is consider the following sentence:

Foreigners use armed violence to create physical deprivation in the State.

This is a very simple statement. It does not have any specific historical content. Apart from the English etymologies of the words, the statement could apply anywhere or in any time. It is not clear what a "foreigner" is or which "State" the statement refers to. The most specific information in the sentence comes from the concept of "armed violence" and its causal influence on "physical deprivation." You can also easily see that this sentence is a variation on the theme of the sentence above that I described as the basic sentence of moral politics: *the antagonist uses abusive power to create injustice for the protagonist*. As a variation of that basic sentence, *Foreigners use armed violence to create physical deprivation in the State*, is one of the four basic root narratives. But what makes it a root narrative?

We can divide this root sentence into two major functions, which together provide enough information to create a root narrative. First, we need an antagonist function and second a protagonist function, each with a plot element and a character element. The antagonist function refers to the *Foreigners use armed violence to create* part of the sentence. The Foreigners are the character—the antagonist. The plot element is their use of *armed violence*. Armed violence is the defining form of abusive power deployed by this kind of antagonist: military power. The two elements go together and together define the antagonist function for this particular root narrative. I call this one, the Defense Narrative.

The protagonist function for the Defense Narrative refers to the *physical deprivation in the State* part of the sentence. The plot element, *physical deprivation*, is what happens as a result of the *armed violence*. It is a form of suffering or injustice. The character element, *the State*, is the protagonist that serves both as the victim of the injustice as well as the hero who will strive to overcome it. In the basic sentences of Root Narrative Theory, victims and heroes are always somehow the same person in different mode. Taken together, the form of injustice and the victim/hero character define the protagonist function in the narrative. The combination of the protagonist and antagonist function join together to form a root narrative. There are as many root narratives as there are aligned combinations of antagonist and protagonist functions, and there are as many of these as there are canonical forms of social power that are sources of distinctive forms of injustice. As I have argued above, since there are four forms of social power and four corresponding forms of injustice, there are four basic root narratives. These are represented in Table 3.1.

This all seems rather simple. In what sense is *Foreigners use armed violence to create physical deprivation in the State* really a root narrative? It is a root narrative in that it

TABLE 3.1 Primitive Sentences of the 'Big Four' Root Narratives

	Antagonist Function		*Protagonist Function*	
Root Narrative	*Character Element*	*Plot Element*	*Plot Element*	*Character Element*
	Antagonist	*Abusive Power*	*Injustice*	*Protagonist*
Defense	Foreigners	use armed violence	to create physical deprivation	in the State
Consent	Governments	use force of law	to create political coercion	of the Individual
Reciprocity	Elites	use bargaining power	to create unfair competition	for the People
Recognition	Majorities	use biased folkways	to create cultural disrespect	of the Other

elucidates the primitive moral logic that serves as the basic rationale for a whole host of more complicated statements. Here are three examples from American presidents, all of which use the logic:

> When Mexico sends its people, they're not sending their best. They're not sending you. They're not sending you. They're sending people that have lots of problems, and they're bringing those problems with us. They're bringing drugs. They're bringing crime. They're rapists. And some, I assume, are good people.[6]
>
> Yesterday, December 7, 1941 a date which will live in infamy the United States of America was suddenly and deliberately attacked by naval and air forces of the Empire of Japan.[7]
>
> This conflict started August 2nd when the dictator of Iraq invaded a small and helpless neighbor. Kuwait—a member of the Arab League and a member of the United Nations—was crushed; its people, brutalized. Five months ago, Saddam Hussein started this cruel war against Kuwait. Tonight, the battle has been joined.[8]

Each one of the speeches has a different flavor and speaks to a different context, but all use the basic moral grammar of the Defense Narrative. There are foreign actors like Mexico, the Empire of Japan, or the dictator of Iraq (antagonist character element) who send criminals, deliberately attack, or invade (antagonist plot element). The effects are some form of physical deprivation: drugs, rape, crime, loss of life, brutalization (protagonist plot element). The entity that suffers is some marker of the community protected by a state-like collective or communal entity: us, the United States, or a member of the United Nations (protagonist character element). These elements of the moral grammar vary as does the context, but they serve as cognate concepts to the basic type. The basic structure of the story changes little by substituting Mexico for Japan or Iraq. The story is set to context in time and place while using a common logical arrangement of elements. In this sense, the root narrative can be adapted from case to case and applied in an infinite number of concrete settings. The logic of its elements can be used to generate an infinite number of sentences. In this sense, the Defense Narrative is the root form of moral politics, the root of what I will call the securitarian imagination.

The full plasticity of the moral grammar of a root narrative is not immediately apparent but can be glimpsed by introducing a small number of cognate concepts; these are concepts that are substitutes for the basic plot and character elements of the antagonist and protagonist functions. They are metaphorical equivalents of the elements that tend to appear as substitutes in the empirical data of conflict stories. Table 3.2 provides a list of possible cognate concepts for the elements of the Defense Narrative. The list is not exhaustive, but suggests how plastic the root narrative is and how creative rhetors can play with it to tell unique and situated stories.

The other four root narratives work in the same way. Consider the libertarian imagination. The basic moral grammar of the sentence, *Governments use force of law to create political coercion of the Individual*, can be adapted to any context with clever concept substitutions as demonstrated by a partial list in Table 3.3.

The sentence construction of the story will vary widely from case to case, and story to story while preserving the basic logic, which can be easily implied without reference to all the functional elements of the primitive sentence. We can see this in Patrick Henry's famous speech in the build-up to the American Revolution.

> Is life so dear, or peace so sweet, as to be purchased at the price of chains and slavery? Forbid it, Almighty God! I know not what course others may take; but as for me, give me liberty or give me death![9]

TABLE 3.2 Securitarian Cognate Concepts

Antagonist Function		Protagonist Function	
Character Element	Plot Element	Plot Element	Character Element
Foreigners	Armed Violence	Physical Deprivation	The State
Minorities	Threats of force	War	The Community
Factions	Angry protest	Crime	The Tribe
Thugs	Subversion	Famine	The Nation-state
Enemies	Criminal Acts	Chaos	The World
Deviants	Intimidation	Instability	Political Apparatus
Subversives	Disruption	Paralysis	Us (flexible)
Outsiders	Insolence	Confusion	
Barbarians	Pressure Tactics		
Invaders			
Terrorists			

TABLE 3.3 Libertarian Cognate Concepts

Antagonist Function		Protagonist Function	
Character Element	Plot Element	Plot Element	Character Element
Governments	Force of Law	Political Coercion	The Individual
Kings	State Violence	Human Rights Abuses	Citizens
Tyrants	Police	Torture	Rational Actors
Dictators	Armies	Lack of Due Process	Free People
Bureaucracies	Extra-judicial Killing	Illegal Detention	Democratic governments
Total States	Authority	Domination	Universal Dignity
	Intimidation	Imprisonment	Rule of Law

Henry focuses on the most important side of the root narrative, the protagonist function: the victim/hero. He warns against the "price of chains and slavery" (protagonist plot element) and anchors his call in the contrast between the value of liberty over that of security (the opposite of death). In this example you can see how root narratives are more fundamental than political values. Values are a part of the root narrative structure, the part that provides the yardstick for measuring the injustice caused by the abusive power. The value of liberty is a metonym for the root narrative itself, an aspect of the story. In previous portions of Henry's speech, he sets the protagonist plot and character elements in richer context, but because his eighteenth century North American audience was so fluent in the grammar of the Consent Narrative, he need have said no more than these famous lines to invoke it. The antagonist function is almost superfluous for his audience. They know the villain quite well and are moved enough by simply being reminded of the root narrative by the injustice they confront together. As often happens, the protagonist function is enough to identify the moral logic of the argument.

This structure works for the root narratives behind the egalitarian and dignitarian imaginations as well. Examples of their cognate concepts are listed in Tables 3.4 and 3.5, respectively.

Based on a very simple, and indeed simplistic, structure, the root narratives provide the way for victims of social power networks to push back on power, transforming themselves from victims to heroes in the process. This is the power of the root narrative. It works on the symbolic level and recruits the moral emotions for use in practical contests of social power. The stories told can be as simple as the audience will accept or as complicated as the audience demands. Nevertheless, the moral grammar in each instance doesn't change.

Before moving to the next level of complication I should say that most people don't use a single moral logic—a single root narrative—in their evaluations. Instead they adapt bits and pieces from the larger store of existing narratives, presenting a blend or array of logics that define their own political worldview—a little bit

TABLE 3.4 Egalitarian Cognate Concepts

Antagonist Function		Protagonist Function	
Character Element	Plot Element	Plot Element	Character Element
Elites	Bargaining Power	Unfair Competition	The People
The Rich	Corrupt Bargains	Restricted Opportunity	The Proletariat
The Wealthy	Lobbying	Poverty	The Little Guy
The Establishment	Desperation	Relative Deprivation	Peasants
Bigwigs	Inside Information	Bad Deals	Workers
The Privileged	Connections	Economic Exploitation	Everyday People
Capitalism	Bribery		Folk
Markets	Monopoly		
	Clout		
	Influence		

TABLE 3.5 Dignitarian Cognate Concepts

Antagonist Function		Protagonist Function	
Character Element	Plot Element	Plot Element	Character Element
Majorities	Biased Folkways	Cultural Disrespect	The Other
Bigots	Habits	Bigotry	The Oppressed
The Masses	Prejudices	Bias	Marginalized Voices
Insiders	Ignorance	Discrimination	Ethnic/Racial Minorities
Ingroup	Insensitivity	Racism	Women
Men	Simplicity	Sexism	LGBT
Heterosexuals	Apathy	Hate	Global South
The West	Dominant Culture	Ethnocentrism	The Colonized
Supremacists	Stereotypes	Silencing	
The Mob	Chauvinism	Microaggressions	

security, a little bit liberty, etc. No one uses just one root narrative all the time. They pull on all of them to suit their taste. This heterogenous and often unconscious blend of evaluations is why any empirical representation of concrete worldviews requires that the analyst develop a profile of an array or sample of statements that a person tends to make. In this stage of the conversation, we might imagine that any given political text could be portrayed with four bars, each representing the proportion of the text that relies on the logic of one of the four forms of the imagination, securitarian, libertarian, egalitarian, and dignitarian.

We could end the story at this point, stipulating that the root narrative model provides us with a way to sort or classify all political statements into four broad categories—one for each form of injustice and abusive power. The model would be more complex than the typical spatial model that sorts political views along the dimension of left and right, or top and bottom, but still a bit less complex than actual data demand. But we can do even better. This four-category level of simplification misses the nuances of political language that the grammatical model offers through simple permutation. This is because we can gain a great deal of descriptive accuracy by simply mixing and matching the protagonist and antagonist functions of the four root basic narratives.[10]

For example, we can match the protagonist hero/victim function of the security narrative with the antagonist villain function of the equality narrative, yielding a base sentence, *Foreigners use armed violence to create unfair competition for the People*. At first glance, this may not seem like a clear story, but if you swap out the cognate concepts, the root narrative can read more like, *Minorities use unfair pressure to create restricted opportunity for the People*. (The functional nature of these primitive sentences make them a bit awkward to read). This is the root of the narrative Donald Trump promoted in his 2016 election campaign. It recognizes a group of people who are victims of unfair economic competition, *the People*, but it redirects the source of the abusive power away from big business to foreigners, people outside of the communal boundary.

As it happens, this too is a very stable structure for concocting endless variations on a primitive theme. In this case, minorities serve as a kind of representation of the Other. The actions they take and pressures they impose are unfair, even if they are only loosely linked with (and perhaps ultimately backed by) potential threats of *armed violence*. The effect of their action is to create a certain kind of harm for a consecrated group, *the People*, a group defined as always being somehow denied access to the central levers of economic decision making: the commoners. The story is general and abstract. It does not speak to any given place and time, but can be situated in any scene in which concrete particulars are identified and deployed in context. This root narrative, like the other eleven primitive combinations of these basic functions, can be given a name—I call it the Nation Narrative. It is a generative story structure about protecting those people accepted as representative of the community from being cheated by competing and unscrupulous outsiders.[11]

Table 3.6 puts the whole story system together. In each of the twelve cases, we can see how the unique combination of protagonist function and antagonist function mix to form a distinctive ideal type of story. Although the empirical origin of the four basic root narratives is a form of social power that produces a distinctive form of suffering, it is the nature of the injustice that dominates the meaning of the story. This implies that it is the protagonist function—the victim/hero—that is the most important identifier for a story type. Once you know who the victim/hero of the story is, you are able to pick out which of the four basic types of root narrative the story conforms to. The antagonist function simply differentiates among the three sub-types of the base.

Because each of the four basic root narratives serves as a universe within which creative interpretations of collective experience can be developed, it seems sensible, as I have done, to label each of the canonical or "big four" root narrative categories

TABLE 3.6 Primitive Sentences: The Full Set of Twelve Root Narratives

	Antagonist Function		Protagonist Function	
	Character Element	Plot Element	Plot Element	Character Element
	Antagonist	Abusive Power	Injustice	Protagonist
Defense	Foreigners	use armed violence	to create physical deprivation	in the State
Unity	Elites	use bargaining power	to create physical deprivation	in the State
Stability	Majorities	use biased folkways	to create physical deprivation	in the State
Consent	Governments	use force of law	to create political coercion	of the Individual
Property	Majorities	use biased folkways	to create political coercion	of the Individual
Merit	Foreigners	use armed violence	to create political coercion	of the Individual
Reciprocity	Elites	use bargaining power	to create unfair competition	for the People
Nation	Foreigners	use armed violence	to create unfair competition	for the People
Account-ability	Governments	use force of law	to create unfair competition	for the People
Recognition	Majorities	use biased folkways	to create cultural disrespect	of the Other
Liberation	Governments	use force of law	to create cultural disrespect	of the Other
Inclusion	Elites	use bargaining power	to create cultural disrespect	of the Other

as forms of the moral imagination: securitarian, libertarian, egalitarian, and digni-tarian. Although we use these four root words colloquially in much broader and less careful ways, Root Narrative Theory demands that we think of these four terms in the technical sense that is implied by Table 3.6. Security is defined against the abusive power of armed violence. Liberty is defined against the abusive power of government use of force of law. Equality is defined against the abusive power of elite bargaining power. Dignity is defined against the abusive power of ingroups exclusionary use of the *biased folkways*. I point this out because it is very easy to get caught up in the words, which are in common use, losing sight of the technical logic of the root narrative structure.

As we think about how to apply this abstract structure to concrete cases, we should remember that the relationship between "the real world" and the narrative used to portray it is far more fluid in practice than any logical person would expect it to be. We are creatures neither of heaven nor of earth. As students of framing and ideology have long argued, "the truth," "the facts," and "policy" are not the most important considerations in most political arguments. Plausibility is, which is determined by the emotional reaction a person has to the mix of moral logics that have been presented in an argument. An argument tends to be more plausible to you if its profile matches your own root narrative profile. This is not to say that truth or the real world does not matter, both in the sense of empirical regularities and consistency of moral grammar, but because, as the psychologist Jonathan Haidt says, the emotional dog wags the rational tail[12]— most people judge first and justify later. It is more important to understand a person's narrative profile (at least to get in the door) than it is to understand the technical details and conscious commitments through which she develops her specific arguments.

This Root Narrative Theory has great potential to move past existing approaches to studying political discourse because it combines the insights about the centrality of narrative, discourse, framing, and moral emotions that have developed over the past several decades with the structural analysis of institutions that were so crucial to progress in the social sciences in the nineteenth and twentieth centuries. Drawing, as it does, on a structural analysis of meaning in political argument, Root Narrative Theory provides us with a grammatical theory of political language, a way to categorize the kinds of stories people tell in a way that relates directly to the organizational environment they are trying to change. Analysis is then not just a series of endless stories, one following after another, but a structured system of argument—a story system—directed to specific types of institutional reform. Our stories point us in the direction of the substance of justice we most desire. The social world presents itself to us in terms of its root narratives.

The purpose of Root Narrative Theory is to provide peace and politics scholars and practitioners with a set of theoretically grounded tools that help them to meet participants in conflict where they are, thereby developing a framework for overcoming radical disagreement. In order to meet people where they are, we have to understand the moral logic behind their policy arguments, the points where technical and moral arguments intersect. Although this process involves all the forms of argument that are familiar to us through the study of rhetoric, I think it is most helpful to think of these processes of technical/moral linkage in terms of narrative. Through narratives of civil life, all of us blend our best empirical arguments with our favored mix of literary inflections to produce what amount to meaningful and convincing accounts in defense of our points of view. Root Narrative Theory is intended to help us make sense of these processes through a theoretically complex device that is nevertheless very easy to use. The rest of the book provides examples of how these root narratives have been used in the history of political and social thought.

Notes

1 Lara, *Narrating Evil*.
2 Lasswell, *Politics*.
3 For a very sympathetic account of how narrative is relevant in international relations see, Ronald Krebs, *Narrative and the Making of US National Security*, Cambridge: Cambridge University Press, 2015.

4 Pearce and Littlejohn, *Moral Conflict*.
5 Cobb, "Narrative Braiding and the Role of Public Officials in Transforming the Publics Conflicts."
6 Washington Post Staff "Donald Trump Announces a Presidential Bid."
7 Roosevelt, "Speech by Franklin D. Roosevelt, New York."
8 "President George Bush Speech Announcing War Against Iraq."
9 Wirt, "Patrick Henry: 'Give Me Liberty or Give Me Death!'"
10 This pattern of mixing and matching protagonist and antagonist functions corresponds with the semantic logic developed by Algirdas Greimas. This derivation can be supplied to any interested reader on request. Greimas and Porter, "Elements of a Narrative Grammar"; Greimas and Rastier, "The Interaction of Semiotic Constraints"; Greimas, *Structural Semantics*.
11 A careful reader will have already noticed that there are no perfect names for these root narratives, indeed settling on names has been one of the things that has slowed publication of the theory, the outlines of which have been clear to me for some time now. I have chosen names that I have observed in empirical practice to produce the fewest number of mistakes in coding while holding fast to the gist of the root narrative.
12 Haidt, "The Emotional Dog and Its Rational Tail."

Bibliography

Cobb, Sara. "Narrative Braiding and the Role of Public Officials in Transforming the Publics Conflicts." *Narrative and Conflict: Explorations in Theory and Practice* 1 no. 1 (December 10, 2013): 4. https://doi.org/10.13021/G8TG65.

Greimas, Algirdas Julien. *Structural Semantics: An Attempt at Method* (Daniele McDowell, Ronald Schleifer and Alan Velie, Trans.) Lincoln: University of Nebraska Press, 1983.

Greimas, Algirdas Julien, and Catherine Porter. "Elements of a Narrative Grammar." *Diacritics* 7, no. 1 (1977): 23–40.

Greimas, Algirdas Julien, and François Rastier. "The Interaction of Semiotic Constraints." *Yale French Studies*, no. 41 (1968): 86–105.

Haidt, Jonathan. "The Emotional Dog and Its Rational Tail: A Social Intuitionist Approach to Moral Judgment." *Psychological Review* 108, no. 4 (2001): 814–834.

Lara, María Pía. *Narrating Evil: A Postmetaphysical Theory of Reflective Judgment*. New York: Columbia University Press, 2007.

Lasswell, Harold Dwight. *Politics: Who Gets What, When, How*. Whitefish, MT: Literary Licensing, 2011.

Pearce, W. Barnett, and Stephen W. Littlejohn. *Moral Conflict: When Social Worlds Collide*. Thousand Oaks, CA: Sage, 1997.

"President George Bush Speech Announcing War Against Iraq." *The History Place, Great Speeches Collection*. Accessed May 2, 2019. http://www.historyplace.com/speeches/bush-war.htm.

Roosevelt, Franklin D. "Speech by Franklin D. Roosevelt, New York." Washington: Library of Congress. Accessed May 2, 2019. https://www.loc.gov/resource/afc1986022.afc1986022_ms2201/?st=text.

Washington Post Staff "Donald Trump Announces a Presidential Bid." *Washington Post*. June 16, 2015. Accessed May 2, 2019. https://www.washingtonpost.com/news/post-politics/wp/2015/06/16/full-text-donald-trump-announces-a-presidential-bid/.

Wirt, William. "Patrick Henry: 'Give Me Liberty or Give Me Death!'" In *The World's Great Speeches*, by Lewis Copeland and Lawrence W. Lamm (Eds) pp. 232–233. New York: Dover Publications, 1973.

4

CRITICS OF POWER, PROPHETS OF PEACE

Hobbes, Locke, Marx, Fanon

The Root Narrative Theory developed here is best remembered in its eponymic form: Hobbes, Locke, Marx, Fanon. These four thinkers, the virtuosi, represent the basic patterns of critique that combine in complex ways to produce the deep structures that generate the root narratives. The virtuosi represent critical perspectives in these modes, but they do not create the modes. The organizational structures they identified existed before them and after them as well, although in different form because of their writings and work. The radical claim of Root Narrative Theory is that the kinds of meaningful stories we can tell about conflict are limited by the kinds of social power there are in the world and the virtuosi are the most memorable critics of social power.

Root Narrative Theory is a structural theory, which implies that it is comprised of equivalent elements that take their meaning from the relationships between and among them, but it also has a stadial aspect, meaning that there are stages to its empirical development as well. The stages aspect helps to explain why Hobbes, Locke, Marx, and Fanon are such apt placeholders for the four critical orientations, because each of these four, taken in this order defines his problem in terms of the solution proposed by the previous member of the group.[1] Hobbes's State becomes an antagonist for Locke's liberty. Locke's liberty empowers winners on the market to exploit Marx's proletariat. The solidarity embraced by Marx's revolutionaries becomes domineering for Fanon's cultural Others.[2] In fact, the stages are best thought of not in linear form but as a circle; I often call this the "circle of power." That is to say that once we meet the end of the line with Fanon, his solution becomes Hobbes's problem in turn; Fanon's cultural rebels become factional disruptors in Hobbes's state of anarchy. The circle closes on itself, perhaps describing the current problematic of international politics under conditions of national self-determination. There are many ways to depict the circle of power, but Figure 4.1 is one of the most helpful to grasp the historical implications of the theory.

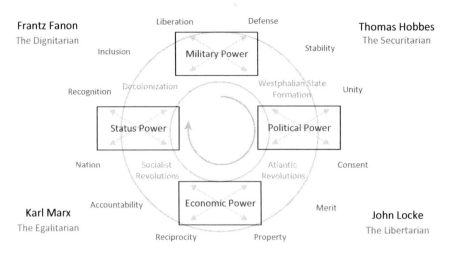

FIGURE 4.1 Root narratives in modern history

Figure 4.1, below, represents the four putative stages of the circle of power. It progresses clockwise.[3] The stages develop as political movements (in the circle) contest forms of abusive power (in the rectangles), framed in terms of the critical theorist. In each case a macro-political movement is portrayed as a contest in root narratives each associated with critical values (around the circle).

The story moves along from the era of Westphalian state formation of the late renaissance and early modern period (where Hobbes-like ideas were central), to the Atlantic Revolutions of the eighteenth century in the Americas and the vicinity of France (broadly Lockean in many cases),[4] to the socialist revolutions of the nineteenth century (Marxist as often as not), to the period of decolonization in the twentieth century, especially after the Second World War (which were Fanonian in spirit if not in letter). In oversimplified form, these four critical theories play out in rough order in macro-political transformations beginning in the seventeenth century, each dominating the scene for something like a century. Periodization in such things is folly for anything but illustrative purposes, but the theory would suggest that now that the circle has closed, we can expect our current period in which dignity squares off against equality to last until around 2050 when, the circle having closed, the model loses it predictive quality.

This historical stage aspect of the theory is a little thrilling, but beyond providing a touch of historical interpretive color, is most interesting for developing the structural aspect of the theory in that it helps to clarify how each of the four virtuosi fit together: each solves the problem posed by the solution of his predecessor and in so doing, provides us with a clear enough picture of abusive power from which to develop the full twelve category root narrative structure. We can pause for a moment to note that Figure 4.1, although a historical stage theory of macro-political developments also presents us with a values circle around the perimeter. Oddly enough, this circular presentation is much like Shalom Schwartz develops in his psychological model of basic human values, and there is some overlap between this system and his.[5] I hope it is clear why, although this system could be described as universal as well (at least in the of context of modernity and its now ubiquitous mechanisms of social power), it draws on a much different sense of how social institutions and human values intersect. Rather than assuming universal features within individual human beings, it assumes universal (or ubiquitous) features of systems of social power. It doesn't assume that all individuals are alike, rather that all systems of social stratification share structural properties. In the following, I explore how the ideas of the various virtuoso narrators played out in their writing in ways that exemplify the twelve root narratives.

Hobbes: The Securitarian

It may be difficult to accept today, when Hobbes's theories are commonly used to justify the aggressive projection of military power around the world, that Thomas Hobbes was the original Western peace theorist. He tells us this directly in his *Leviathan*:

> The law of nature and the civil law contain each other, and are of equal extent. For the laws of nature, which consist in equity, justice, gratitude, and other moral virtues on these depending, in the condition of mere nature… are not properly laws, but qualities that dispose men to peace and obedience.
>
> *(p. 174)*

And Hobbes didn't just speak about peace once or twice, he refers to peace over one hundred times in the book. When Nietzsche dismissed Hobbes's philosophy, it was precisely because Hobbes had based his views on his desire for peace. Nietzsche saw Hobbes's ideas as suitable for an English shopkeeper; as far as he was concerned, in his yearning for peace, Hobbes was incapable of seeing the value of great things that Nietzsche dreamed of for his übermensch. Hobbes may have been a peace theorist, but the problem with Hobbes's view of peace is that it is rather dismal. At its root is our desire to avoid violent death and little more.

> The passions that incline men to peace are: fear of death; desire of such things as are necessary to commodious living; and a hope by their industry to obtain them. And reason suggesteth convenient articles of peace upon which men may be drawn to agreement. These articles are they which otherwise are called the laws of nature, whereof I shall speak more particularly in the two following chapters.
>
> *(p. 78)*

In fact, if there is one thing I would have you remember about Hobbes, it is that he was obsessed with violent death and how to avoid it. That is what he means by peace, a state of affairs in which we are so afraid of the office of the head of state, that we are dissuaded from attempting to kill one another when we are tempted to do so. He tells us directly that the key to all of this is fear; "The passion to be reckoned upon is fear" (p. 88). And this imagery of fear of violent death will be central to making sense of the three ethics that define the securitarian imagination.

The securitarian frame of mind refers to a style of thought that takes for granted that the worst thing that could happen to you is that you would be physically violated by a stranger (or more likely a group of strangers) against whom you were unable to protect yourself. For the purposes of defining the category, it is not particularly important what the source of the violation might be: criminals, minority gangs, rival armies, terrorists, panicked mobs, etc. The most important thing is that whatever the source, the form of power the source brings to bear is physical force held in hands outside of the authority of the head of one's political community—the violence is somehow extra-communal. It occurs in what Hobbes described as the state of nature, and one "red in tooth and claw." In such a view, it is the job of the leader to protect the community from the private or extra-communal violence that is a constant threat, which explains why the State was instituted in the first place.

As I have been careful to say, Thomas Hobbes is only a famous representative of the securitarian imagination, not its originator. The goal is not to identify all forms of securitarian thinking as Hobbesian, nor to identify all of Hobbes's ideas as relevant for clarifying the category of justification, but to provide a clear sense of the moral grammar of the category and how rhetorical moves made in it are often accomplished. For this purpose, I will focus only on one text, we'll call it the paradigmatic text of the securitarian imagination, Hobbes's *Leviathan* of 1651, and I will pull only those themes out of it that are relevant for the broader category of securitarian thought, without straying from an honest reading of the book. Hobbesian scholars may see other themes in play in his work, but for our purposes, it is only important to see his work in relation to the deep structures of institutional power. In conversation with the three other critical nodes, this leaves us with three important themes that form his critical view: fear of violent death and protection from it; the critical importance of unity and community integrity; and the role that a powerful sovereign must play to ensure order and to promote the stability of resources, including creating the conditions for economic development; the subjects of the three securitarian root narratives: Defense, Unity, and Stability.

Defense: Foreigners *use* armed violence *to create* physical deprivation *in* the State

It is not unfair to claim that Thomas Hobbes was the first critical peace theorist, but his was a funny kind of peace. His vision was grounded in a critique of a form of power, unregulated executive force or what we might call privately held means of defense, and the characteristic emotion that animated his vision was fear. He wrote, "Fear and I were born twins. My mother hearing of the Spanish Armada sailing up the English Channel gave premature birth to me."[6] He developed this

vision of fear-based opposition to private control of the means of defense exten-
sively in his *Leviathan*, a theory developed not to realize a conception of the
greatest good—the *summum bonum*—typical since Thomas Aquinas, but to avoid
the worst thing that could happen, the *summum malum*.

This "Greatest Bad" for Hobbes, the *summum malum*, was to suffer cruel violence
at a stranger's hand, fear of which justified coercive obedience so long as it was
considered reasonable for self-preservation—a kind of gangster's bargain. "You do
what I say, and I'll make sure nothing happens to you and your little family." If the
problem was the perpetual fear of violent death, a rational solution was to create an
awe-inspiring sovereign power to protect life. This sovereign power would have
ultimate right over those who submitted to it. It was justified through a kind of
implicit social contract, implicit because those subject to it never had a chance to
negotiate its terms and sign on to its provisions. However murky the origins and
abstract the terms of such a contract, its goal was unambiguous: security, that is
collective security.

> The motive and end for which this renouncing and transferring of right is
> introduced is nothing else but the security of a man's person, in his life and in
> the means of so preserving life as not be weary of it.
>
> *(p. 82)*

Because the office of sovereign was a creature of the people's will to self-preservation, there were some limits to it. If the office holder was unable to protect
the people, the contract was not defensible. The breakdown in justification
involved the risk of "death, wounds and imprisonment," the basic bodily currency
of the securitarian imagination.

> And covenants without swords are but words, and of no strength to secure a
> man at all... if there be power erected, or not great enough for our security,
> every man will, and may lawfully rely on his own strength and art, for caution
> against all other men.
>
> *(p. 106)*

Because the security game involves not only internal dissent, but also the threat
of rival sovereign powers, the contract was also void if some other military power
was better able to protect the people from "death and bonds."

> A commonwealth by acquisition is that where the sovereign power is acquired
> by force; and it is acquired by force when men singly (or many together by
> plurality of voices) for fear of death or bonds do authorize all the actions of that
> man or assembly that hath their lives and liberty in his power... men who
> choose their sovereign do it for fear of one another, and not of him whom they
> institute; but in this case they subject themselves to him they are afraid of. In
> both cases they do it for fear, which is to be noted by them that hold all such

> covenants as proceed from fear of death or violence void; which, if it were true,
> no man in any kind of commonwealth could be obliged toward obedience.
>
> *(p. 127)*

We dismiss Hobbes as an immoral realist, but this is completely unfair. His vision was a moral vision, a denuded idealism, that could be summarized in three word-pairs: "concord, health; sedition, sickness; and civil war, death." Concord leads to the health of the state. Sedition is the sickness of the state. Civil war is the death of the state.

Unity: Elites *use* bargaining power *to create* physical deprivation *in* the State

There is little doubt that the central and animating horror of Hobbes's political imagination was the fear of violent death, and that his centrality to the political tradition of Western modernity derives from that obsession. The securitarian worldview is dominated by fear of both the external and the internal Other. Nevertheless, there are other implications of this obsession with the horrors of personal insecurity that are very much less gruesome. In fact, the securitarian imagination becomes rather sanguine when inflected with other considerations. One of the major inflections defines a story structure I call the Unity narrative that takes the protective integration of the community into a single body as a point of departure.

We often celebrate community in fanciful terms, but the securitarian first embraces the unity of community as a way to protect himself and his own from naturally divisive human nature.

> Again, men have no pleasure, but on the contrary a great deal of grief, in keeping company where there is no power able to over-awe them all.
>
> *(p. 75)*

We should note that in Hobbes, as in most examples of a securitarian orientation, the perspective assumes that all people, including the author, are unworthy or incapable of protecting another person as they would protect themselves.

> For if we could suppose a great multitude of men to consent in the observation of justice and other laws of nature without a common power to keep them in awe, we might as well suppose all mankind to do the same; and then there neither would be, nor need be, any civil government or commonwealth at all, because there would be peace without subjection.
>
> *(p. 107)*

It is this selfish and egoistic nature of mankind that provides the impulse to unite the community for Hobbes, and that selfishness has no remedy but through a kind of subjection (one might use the word submission in other examples of this category of thinking) to the central authority of the community. In the Unity narrative, it is the very "nature of men," their partisanship, that constitutes the threat to the community.

> For such is the nature of men that howsoever they may acknowledge many others to be more witty, or more eloquent, or more learned, yet they will hardly believe there be many so wise as themselves. For they see their own wit at hand, and other men's at a distance.
>
> *(p. 75)*

A final note about the concept of community as we find in the Hobbesian exemplar, although entrance into the state of security from bodily harm that only a strong state can provide is imagined as a voluntary act, once such a state is developed, it is a unity that is very difficult, if not impossible to sunder. As Hobbes put it:

> they that are subjects to a monarch cannot without his leave cast off monarchy and return to the confusion of a disunited multitude... for they are bound, every man to every man, to own, and be reputed author of, all that he that already is their sovereign shall do and judge fit to be done... for they are bound, every man to every man, to own, and be reputed author of, all that he that already is their sovereign shall do and judge fit to be done.
>
> *(p. 111)*

The Hobbesian version of the Unity narrative is particularly stark. All members are bound to one another because their well-being depends on each other. The nature of the bond is such that it conflicts with the natural, selfish tendency of all of the members of the community. Once the members of the community have recognized their own egoistic failings and entered into community with one another, it is not possible to simply exit when a chance arises. The divisiveness and querulous tendencies of human nature are too dangerous to indulge. War can be avoided, but at the cost of union. As we shall see, this narrative logic is alive in many settings that appear, at first glance, non-Hobbesian, and is one of the features of political organization from which Hobbes borrowed the most from the religious tradition that came before him.

Stability: Majorities *use* biased folkways *to create* physical deprivation *in* the State

Before moving on from Hobbes's *Leviathan*, we have one more theme to illustrate, one that is the least obvious but no less important of the three. Hobbes's securitarian imagination was dominated by bodily imagery: wounds, death, and imprisonment on the one hand, and locked doors and chests on the other. One implication of the securitarian focus on the body is that the perspective can be extended to include various other threats to the body and its health that we might called economic, or material in the sense of bodily survival and flourishing. This theme was certainly undeveloped in Hobbes, but it is there and might even be said to be hidden in plain sight. Most of this variation on the securitarian theme is hinted at in Hobbes and covered indirectly as a consequence of the main attraction.

> The only way to erect such a common power as may be able to defend them from the invasion of foreigners and the injuries of one another, and thereby to secure them in such sort as that by their own industry, and by the fruits of the earth, they may nourish themselves and live contentedly, is to confer all their power and strength upon one man, or upon one assembly of men, that may reduce all their wills, by plurality of voices, unto one will.
>
> *(p. 109)*

The themes of protecting the people from violent death and of unifying the people to overcome their selfish wills are the accents of this quotation, but the middle portions may be the most interesting. Hobbes recognizes that the point of civil society is to empower the people to nourish themselves so that they may live contentedly. There is a bare life of survival that legitimates his theory of absolutist sovereignty, but the securitarian mind stretches naturally in other directions as well. A Hobbesian is inclined to "obey a common power" in "desire and ease of sensual delight," (p. 58) over and above his fear of "death and wounds". One might imagine how this focus on the body and its ease and delight could be easily extended to concerns about economic welfare and productivity. Indeed, it is reasonable to assume that one of the foundations of a government is to ensure the economic and material welfare of the people. History would have to wait for theories of economic flourishing that took their point of departure from the liberty of individuals, but the record of history from so-called oriental despots to the occasional grain riots of Hobbes's own time made it clear that security of one's person included the ease and comfort of the body that came about when economic resources and environmental conditions were suited to promoting it.

In fact, the centrality of the economic case for security and the responsibility of the sovereign for establishing it is nowhere better exemplified than in the most famous of passages from *Leviathan*, the source of the "nasty, brutish, and short" line.

> Whatsoever therefore is consequent to a time of war, where every man is enemy to every man, the same is consequent to the time wherein men live without other security than what their own strength and their own invention shall furnish them withal. In such condition there is no place for industry, because the fruit thereof is uncertain, and consequently, no culture of the earth, no navigation, nor use of the commodities that may be imported by sea, no commodious building, no instruments of moving and removing such things as require much force, no knowledge of the face of the earth, no account of time, no arts, no letters, no society, and which is worst of all, continual fear and danger of violent death, and the life of man, solitary, poor, nasty, brutish and short.
>
> *(p. 76)*

Given stereotypes about the nature of the English people, it should, perhaps, come as no surprise that the Hobbesian line that would inflame our imaginations as one of the most famous in history would focus on the economy. Yes, the fear of violent death is central to the passage, but what really chills the modern reader to the marrow is the fact that were it not for the State we would not have all of our great stuff (food, travel, knickknacks, buildings, machinery, and cultural life). What Weber famously called "the monopoly of the legitimate use of physical force within a given territory" is also essential for economic stability. Hobbes is as much an economic theorist based on the stability guaranteed by the state as he is a theorist of the police state. Insofar as Hobbes serves as a useful model for all securitarian thinking, which I claim he does, we should expect these three themes to appear together when threats to the body politic itself are invoked, and for many liberals and progressives to rely on the Stability root narrative in times of stress.

Again, this portrait of Hobbes is intended as much to illustrate what he has to teach us about the deep structure of conflict narratives as it is about his work in itself, but these three root narratives, Defense, Unity, and Stability are all variations on the theme that Hobbes introduces to political philosophy. They define distinct threats to the community that arise from the use of violent force. Security is the concept that unites them and that defines the root narrative logic, the moral authority capable of galvanizing opposition to the abuse of social power that each opposes. They are the three themes of the securitarian imagination.

Locke: the Libertarian

Now that we have some experience in drawing out narrative themes from a great piece of political philosophy, it should be a bit easier to attempt it a second time. Much as I have done for Hobbes, I select the Locke of the *Second Treatise on Government* and not that of the *Enquiry on Human Understanding* as the best available exemplars for the libertarian form of the moral imagination, although in the last part of this section, I will draw briefly from the *Letter Concerning Toleration*.

It is a bit more important here to state plainly than it was with my use of word securitarian above, that by libertarian, I do not mean to reference the whole field of thought that often goes by that name in Anglo-American circles, one that combines a conception of free markets with open lifestyles. As with Hobbes, I define this generative logic in a negative way, as a counterweight to a form of power that comes with governing and administrative power. We might think of this interpretation of libertarianism as a category of solutions to the problems that arise once we have created a Hobbesian power that is capable of keeping us all in awe. I keep track of this loosely sequenced relationship in the development of resistance to the abusive forms of social power with the help of one of the great aficionados of the libertarian imagination, John Stuart Mill.

> To prevent the weaker members of the community from being preyed upon by innumerable vultures, it was needful that there should be an animal of prey stronger than the rest, commissioned to keep them down. But as the king of the vultures would be no less bent upon preying on the flock than any of the minor harpies, it was indispensable to be in a perpetual attitude of defence against his beak and claws.[7]

Hobbes did not seem to be overly troubled with a question that his immediate contemporaries would find obvious, if the sovereign can do whatever he likes, what is to prevent him from behaving as badly as any of his subjects? This contrast between security and liberty, between the threat of anarchy and that of tyranny remains central to any sensible conception of peace and political morality. Those of us who have been raised in liberal societies find the Hobbesian inattention to the problem positively perplexing and almost disqualifying.

In the same way that Thomas Hobbes provides us with a clear and unadulterated view on the kind of threat that animates the three securitarian root narratives, John Locke opens up a space for the root narratives of liberty, an abstract category of potential stories that unites the three narratives in a critique of government as a social power. The Hobbesian fears the mob. The Lockean fears the government. The securitarian imagination is martial, the libertarian is legal. The Hobbesian thinks about how to build a stronger state apparatus. The Lockean thinks about how to build self-regulating systems like political elections and economic markets. Neither category is more scientific or tough-minded than the other. Each is an example of the broadest category of storytelling that is capable of providing convincing accounts of what political life is and what it can become. Both root narrative categories tend to crowd out alternatives and can serve as a world of justification unto itself.

Consent: Governments *use the* force of law *to create* political coercion *of* the Individual

It probably says more about me and my upbringing in the Midwest of the United States than about John Locke himself, but I find that the second treatise is riddled with quotable material that strikes me as perfectly apt for illustrative discussion of the libertarian imagination. If my own experience is any guide, the claims made by political scientists like Herbert McClosky, and John Zaller about the strong libertarian foundation of American political discourse are spot on.

> No value in the American ethos is more revered than freedom. The rights of individuals to speak, write, assemble, and worship freely, to engage in occupations and pastimes of their own choosing, and to be secure from arbitrary restraints on their conduct are central to the nation's democratic tradition.[8]

Even more arresting is Louis Hartz's claim about the irrationally Lockean character of American political culture.

> A society which begins with Locke, and thus transforms him, stays with Locke, by virtue of an absolute and irrational attachment it develops for him. ... Surely, then, it is a remarkable force: this fixed, dogmatic liberalism of a liberal way of life. It is the secret root from which have sprung many of the most puzzling of American cultural phenomena.... There has never been a "liberal movement" or a real "liberal party" in America: we have only had the American way of life.[9]

Much like irrational Hobbesianism, which a psychologist would be tempted to describe as terror management, full of imagery of the threat of bodily harm and violent death, irrational Lockeanism (by which we actually mean commitments to the verisimilitude of libertarian root narrative cast in Lockean terms) sees the threat of arbitrary authority in every act of government. It is as if every year was 1776 and every political occasion required a fresh drafting of the Declaration of Independence.

This theme of consent is central to Locke's *Second Treatise*; indeed, it is the very core of the book. His theory, like Hobbes, invokes a mythical narrative of an implicit contract that delivers mankind from an abstract state of nature, but Locke's nature is far more friendly than is Hobbes's. In the place of "a war of all against all," Locke's transition from the state of nature is driven by the tendency of each person to overvalue their own grievances, leading to what he called "inconveniences" of various kinds in the administration of justice—think Hatfields and McCoys. The Lockean and Hobbesian views share the conceptual vehicle, the state of nature, but part ways in terms of the animating horror or *summum malum* of their respective visions. For Hobbes, the worst possible thing was to be subject to the whim of another's cruelty; for Locke it was to be deprived of one's natural liberty by a "superior power" without having provided consent.

> The natural liberty of man is to be free from any superior power on earth, and not to be under the will or legislative authority of man, but to have only the law of nature for his rule. The liberty of man in society is to be under no other legislative power but that established by consent.
>
> *(p. 283)*

In fact, political society was reducible to these contractual arrangements, any other arrangement being tyranny.

> Men being by nature all free equal and independent, no one can be put out of this estate and subjected to the political power of another without his own consent.
>
> [...]
>
> And thus that, which begins and actually constitutes any political society, is nothing but the consent of any number of freemen capable of a majority to

unite and incorporate into such a society. And this is that, and that only, which did, or could give beginning to any lawful government in the world.

(pp. 330–333)

What made Locke so attractive to the various leaders of the Atlantic Revolutions of the turn of the nineteenth century was how far Locke took his ideas—his radicalism. Once the community of individuals, its members severally deprived of their natural liberty, had entered a state of war with the usurping tyrant; the ultimate remedy was to return to the state of natural liberty, to revolve back to that natural state of affairs through what we now call a revolution.

> I say using force upon the people without authority, and contrary to the trust put in him that does so, is a state of war with the people, who have a right to reinstate their legislative in the exercise of their power... the people have a right to remove it by force. In all states and conditions the true remedy of force without authority is to oppose force to it. The use of force without authority always puts him that uses it into a state of war, as the aggressor, and renders him liable to be treated accordingly.

(p. 370)

Again, we see foreshadows of Max Weber's famous monopoly definition of the state in this excerpt. Governments have authority (as opposed to mere power) to use force by virtue of the consent of the people that they carry. When their use of force against the people begins to violate the natural terms of the contract that any free people would make with their own executive power, i.e. it violates the natural and inalienable rights of the people, the state loses its temporary monopoly and can be opposed with force. These ideas are quite current and remain a potent source of various narratives in favor of universal human rights, individual consent, and limited government around the world. We have all felt the pull of the leader who is willing to fight and die to ensure that we are "free to choose."

Property: **Majorities** *use* **biased folkways** *to create* **political coercion** *of* **the Individual**

The arguments that Locke makes in favor of the theme of consent are broadly unproblematic in the modern world. Except in the most despotic places, most people will provide at least superficial support for these libertarian principles, even if their practice breaks with them in obvious ways. Lockean liberalism has become one of the cornerstones of a master narrative of modern civilization. But there is a more controversial side to freedom as well. The mechanism through which this consensus philosophy has developed is through the institutions of commerce and trade, all of which developed to secure the property and profits of those with the capital to invest in new opportunities. Where does the defense of private property fit in this worldview?

When Thomas Jefferson first wrote, "life, liberty and property" in his rough draft of the Declaration, Benjamin Franklin is said to have substituted the recommendation to shift property to happiness, consistent with Franklin's utilitarianism, a philosophy that was already emerging at the time under the leadership of Jeremy Bentham. As with other root narratives, those stories that appeal to the moral authority of "property" can easily take on a mystical and quasi-sacred air. They serve to consecrate our otherwise secular and selfish causes with the warrant of a higher purpose. It is hard for those who see the natural goodness of private property ever to unsee it. And although support for the sacred right to own stuff seems a bit too profane for those critical of market society to fully embrace, property and the free enterprise system it supports is as central to the libertarian imagination and as sacred as is the concept of consent itself.

Locke's capacity to recognize the sacral centrality of the Property narrative is part of what, for centuries, has earned him the unrivaled title to represent this libertarian category of thought. Indeed, many wags have portrayed the *Second Treatise* as a "capitalist manifesto,"[10] and if we resist the temptation to take that association in a pejorative sense, it is not far wrong. Less than a century after the publication of the *Second Treatise*, Adam Smith would introduce us to the sanctity of the system of private property with the unforgettable image of the "invisible hand" of the market, guiding our selfish desires in prosocial directions. This association with divinity could not have been accidental. Property is one of the major categories of the modern political storybook and should not be underestimated in its civil religious pull.

Locke is our best exemplar of this sacralizing tendency of the Property narrative. He develops the very definition of political society in terms of its power to preserve property.

> But because no Political Society can be nor subsist without having in itself the power to preserve the property, and in order thereunto punish the offences of all those of that society; there and there only is political society.
>
> *(p. 324)*

Cliché as it sounds today, the loss of private property to tyranny was no small thing. It might be the muse behind Jefferson's famous opening line in the Declaration. When governments went back on their justifying promise, the people had entered a state of war.

> whenever the legislators endeavor to take away and destroy the property of the people, or to reduce them to slavery under arbitrary power, they put themselves in a state of war with the people, who are thereupon absolved from any farther obedience, and are left to the common refuge, which God hath provided for all men against force and violence.
>
> *(p. 412)*

The notion of the sanctity of property is derived from an almost material extension of one's person, much as the philosopher Hegel would describe in his complex phenomenology. A person became joined with the world through labor and he deserved to keep whatever was properly his own.

> Whatsoever then he removes out of the state of nature hath provided and left in it, he hath mixed his labour with, and joined to it something that is his own and thereby makes it his property... this labor being the unquestionable property of the laborer, no man but he can have a right to what that is once joined to, at least where there is enough and as good left in common for others.
>
> *(p. 288)*

And Locke's theory of property is tied into the proto-capitalist currents of his day. What makes the treatise something more of a manifesto for moral capitalism than for mere selfish greed-is-good acquisition is his defense of using the things that we have created in productive ways. His is a theory of private enterprise and not simply private gain.

> *God has given us things richly* I Tim. Vi. 17 is the voice of reason confirmed by inspiration. But how far has he given it us? To enjoy. As much as any one can make use of to any advantage of life before it spoils; beyond this, is more than his share, and belongs to others. Nothing was made by God for man to spoil or destroy.
>
> *(p. 290)*

In this mode of thought, a man should not sit on a trove of grain while it rots. He should not waste things that can be better used by others. But we are again in luck because God gave us money so that we could amass more wealth than we can consume, without forcing us to waste what we cannot immediately dispose of.

> This I dare boldly affirm, that the same rule of propriety [property], that every man should have as much as he could make use of, would hold still in the world without straining any body, since there is land enough in the world to suffice double the inhabitants had not the invention of money, and the tacit agreement of men to put a value on it, introduced (by consent) larger possessions and a right to them.
>
> *(p. 293)*

It is easy in a society that is so wracked by its commitment to this moral logic to poke fun at it. We are so committed to its principles and convinced by its ethical warrant that we are unembarrassed to call ourselves capitalists, and "greed is good" is something one can imagine the President of the United States saying without irony. The principles are powerful and for a reason derived from the deep structures of power. They are derived from a very principled opposition to a concrete sense of tyrannical power through which countless atrocity stories have been developed. Property is a sacralized concept in the libertarian imagination, and one that should not be discounted lightly or represented as a cover for some other motive.

Merit: Foreigners *use* armed violence *to create* political coercion *of* the Individual

The discussion of free choice and the acquisition of private property capitalized into moneyed form brings us to the third great theme of the libertarian imagination, the centrality of personal merit. The way I will present the category forces me to stretch my interpretation of Locke, as he has little to say about it directly. I will therefore extrapolate a bit with respect to Locke's own arguments to imagine what he would have said to those who developed counter narratives to his own. This is one of the best examples of showing how Root Narrative Theory is not defined or created by the virtuoso thinkers but is merely well represented by them. Luckily, we can infer what the Lockean position on these future developments might have been from his views expressed in his *Letter Concerning Toleration* of 1689.

The category of merit as a wellspring of deep stories about political life requires us to get ahead of the story, just a bit. Having lived through the great wars of religion that followed the protestant reformation, every political thinker of the seventeenth century knew how challenging it could be to encounter and accommodate cultural difference, especially when it took on ethnic dimensions like religion, language and race. After all, this was the period in which many of the great atrocities that gave birth to the modern form of what I call the dignitarian imagination were committed. Locke himself addressed this question of cultural difference in his writings on tolerance.

In that famous letter, Locke argues that the civil magistrate, i.e. the government, has no right to become involved in matters of the soul, but should constrain his interests to what he called "civil concerns" that touched only the material experience of the citizens. The soul and the opinions that arise from it should be left alone.

> Now that the whole jurisdiction of the magistrate reaches only to these civil concernments, and that all civil power, right and dominion, is bounded and confined to the only care of promoting these things; and that it neither can nor ought in any manner to be extended to the salvation of souls, these following considerations seem unto me abundantly to demonstrate.

Locke then uses the remainder of the essay to explore the implications of the limits on government to become involved in matters of belief and subjective affiliation. In one famous point of the essay he writes:

It is one thing to persuade, another to command; one thing to press with arguments, another with penalties. This civil power alone has a right to do; to the other, goodwill is authority enough.

Although Locke knew full well that any given government will be dominated by some form of group consciousness (we might say an ingroup or majority), he insisted that the individual had the right to conscience, and he could not be deprived of his right to property and the protections of civil law because of his beliefs or lifestyle. In the libertarian imagination, there are obvious ethical limits to government's authority to intervene in the sphere of private acquisition to reward group membership. For Locke and those like him, neither reward not punishment in the economic realm is justified on the basis of religious membership, and by extension we could say for linguistic or racial membership as well (and gender and sexuality fall into this category too). This is an ethic of merit and personal responsibility just as sacred to its adherents as any other civil appeal.

We can catch glimpses of how Locke might have reacted to claims for what we now call affirmative action for outgroups who had been the target of historical discrimination and abuse. In his comments in the *Second Treatise* on the native inhabitants of the Americas, which he considered to be a living example of his conceptual state of nature, we get a sense of how he sees the claims native Americans as an outgroup, just as the colonial project was gathering force.

> And thus, without supposing any private dominion and property in Adam, over all the world, exclusive of all other men, which can no way be proved, nor any ones property be made out from it; but supposing the world given as it was to the children of men in common, we see how labor could make men distinct titles to several parcels of it, for their private uses; wherein there could be no doubt of Right, no room for quarrel.... There cannot be clearer demonstration of anything, than several nations of the Americans are of this, who are rich in Land and poor in all the comforts of life.
>
> *(p. 296)*

For Locke, if the native Americans didn't know what to do with their land and couldn't discover ways to accumulate fortunes through money, then others should have the right to do so without fears that the government would step in to redistribute the fruits of production to benefit those who were unable to establish it through private enterprise. Difference should be respected, but in this framework, it is an abuse of government power to use it to speak to the state of our souls and therefore to intervene in support of redistribution along ascriptive lines. For Locke, the individualist, personal beliefs and group memberships are irrelevant as compared to our capacity to produce. It is not much of a stretch to see how this ethic of tolerance and government restraint could lead to a wide variety of creative adaptations in different circumstances like those of the neoliberal opponents of a racialized conception of the modern welfare state. The Merit narrative, is not one that will be much popular on the modern left, but it is clearly implied by the deep structural analysis of social power and perfectly consistent with a Lockean foundation.

Marx: The Egalitarian

It goes without saying that each of the exemplary thinkers I am using to illustrate the four root narrative categories has spawned vast literatures of interpretation and application. As I have repeatedly said, this role of the thinker as "founder of discursivity," although fascinating, is not how I am using the great theorists in this argument. I am less interested in what influence Hobbes, Locke, Marx or Fanon may have had than in the way that they illustrate a category of potential thought, of which each virtuoso became the most fitting modern example. In no case is this more important to state than with Marx. The Marxian literatures are vast, varied and often self-contradictory, and the often tragic political successes of Marxist philosophy have so stigmatized Marx in Anglo-American circles that it has become difficult to see the work in a balanced way. Even the mere mention of Marx can be enough to shut down open communication. With my conflict resolver hat on, I would say that this is a sure sign that we are onto a powerful and relevant conflict symbol.

Let me restate a point that I have made about both Hobbes and Locke before. They are useful for the purposes of this theory as illustrations of a focused way of thinking. Put in terms that are common in intellectual discussions today, each of the exemplary thinkers is orthogonal to the others; they are not intersectional thinkers. Instead they focus on and theoretically isolate one particular form of power, making its mechanisms legible in the social text to those of us who read them, giving us the tools to recognize power when it is in operation, and providing us with the moral warrant for criticism as we tell our own stories about the effects and abuses of power. The exemplary thinkers that I have selected in no way exhaust the range of possible versions of stories that can be told in the aspect of the root narrative that they represent. Other thinkers pick up on similar themes and provide distinctive interpretations of the same mechanisms of social power. Moreover, even when one of the exemplary thinkers has really nailed a point—somehow got it right—his ideas are only relevant insofar as they work their way through the channels of popular opinion, especially into the viewpoints of influential actors and opinion leaders. Root Narrative Theory is not a theory of the four virtuosi, but it is well exemplified by them.

The greatest danger in telling the truth about Marx as an exemplary figure for the egalitarian imagination is that reflexive critics of political Marxism will be tempted to paint all forms of the manifestation of the egalitarian imagination with the broad brush of morally polluted examples of abuses associated with figures like Joseph Stalin, Pol Pot, and Fidel Castro. Let me end this extended digression with an admonition, if you happen to be one the irrational Lockeans that Louis Hartz described who can't see anything but red when you see the name Marx, just toss in another name whenever you see his here and remember that there are many master narratives, big stories told by thinkers in an intellectual tradition, that are compatible with the larger category of the root narratives. Marxism is only the most contentious among them, and Marx's theory of history and his dictatorship of the proletariat are only examples of one of the many forms of a critique of wealth and oligarchy that are possible. Rousseau and the Populist Party of the United States are alternative choices. Whatever else we remember about it, we should recognize that the egalitarian imagination is not Marxist, even if Marx was among its greatest poets.

An example of an alternative egalitarianism might be helpful. The term "moral economy" is in common parlance mainly as a result of the influence of a famous article, "The Moral Economy of the English Crowd in the Eighteenth Century," written for the journal *Past and Present* by the English historian Edward P. Thompson.[11] Writing against what he called a spasmodic view of economic rebellion by the English peasants of the eighteenth century, he placed periodic uprisings against the ruling establishment of the period in the context of traditional conceptions of English rights—that had existed as it was said time out of mind of man—which is not dissimilar to the way the American revolutionaries saw their struggle for national independence against the British.

> We know all about the delicate tissue of norms and reciprocities which regulates the life of Trobriand islanders, and the psychic energies involved in the cargo cults of Melanesia; but at some point this infinitely-complex social creature, Melanesian man, becomes (in our histories) the eighteenth-century English collier who claps his hand spasmodically upon his stomach, and responds to elementary economic stimuli. To the spasmodic I will oppose my own view. It is possible to detect in almost every eighteenth-century crowd action some legitimizing notion. By the notion of legitimation I mean that the men and women in the crowd were informed by the belief that they were defending traditional rights and customs; and, in general, that they were supported by the wider consensus of the community.

It is difficult to find an example of what I call the egalitarian imagination as divergent from the traditional Marxist story than the English folkways argument of Thompson, both because he locates much of the energy of resistance in the moral forces of traditional culture and because he disdains what he dismissed as a "crass economic reductionism." Thompson had no theory of history and was an opponent of the dictatorship of the proletariat, but he was a great proponent of the egalitarian imagination, much as were other non-Marxist innovators from Max Weber to Barrington Moore to Bernie Sanders. The key to all of these arguments is the role they assign to the potentially destructive powers endemic to economic institutions. As Hobbes and Locke were before, Marx is merely our paradigmatic master narrator; he will be a guide through the complex moral space defined by the workings of economic power, but representative as he is, he is no more essential to its definition than would be Charles Dickens and should be thought of only as an innovator working with the material of the root narrative.

Reciprocity: **Elites** *use* **bargaining power** *to create* **unfair competition** *for* **the People**

Just as the liberal imagination of John Locke was animated in opposition to the very institutions, the organs of state power that Thomas Hobbes had celebrated as the culmination of his viewpoint, the egalitarian imagination as demonstrated by Karl Marx is founded in a critique of Locke's solution to the problem caused by the Hobbesian state. For Marx, abusive social power derives from the institutions of property, not personal property in the form of the stuff that you keep around your house, but the productive property that is essential for industrial scale economic development. Nowhere does he make the case for his vision of a world divided into haves and have nots better than in the opening lines of the *Communist Manifesto*, the dire critical analysis of capitalist society that he published with Friedrich Engels in 1848.

> The history of all hitherto existing society is the history of class struggles. Freeman and slave, patrician and plebian, lord and serf, guild-master and journeyman, in a word, oppressor and oppressed, stood in constant opposition to one another, carried on an uninterrupted, now hidden, now open fight, a fight that each time ended, either in a revolutionary reconstitution of society at large, or in the common ruin of contending classes.
>
> *(p. 158)*

The general lessons we can draw about the Reciprocity narrative in these lines are directly relevant for Root Narrative Theory. The protagonist and antagonists character elements are clearly represented here, the protagonist by the victim/hero of the oppressed as slave, plebian, serf and journeyman, the antagonist, with the oppressor as freeman, patrician, lord, and guild-master. We haven't yet seen the plot element animating the story—the injustice suffered by the protagonist or the social power wielded by the antagonist—but we already know it has something to do with class struggle. We also know that this is the story of all previous history.

This egalitarian story, the division between the rich and poor, the few and the many, is a standard form of critical analysis in most times and places. It was central to the ancient proto-Europeans and a common form of analysis in the Renaissance. Marx only provided it with the philosophical grounding and political spark to inflame the century that followed his publication with a politico-theoretical outlook from which we have not yet fully recovered. His language and social labels remain impossible to ignore.

> Our epoch, the epoch of the bourgeoisie, possesses, however, this distinctive feature: it has simplified the class antagonisms. Society as a whole is more and more splitting up into two great hostel camps, into two great classes directly facing each other: Bourgeoisie and Proletariat.
>
> *(p. 159)*

I call the perspective reciprocity, because a general lesson that can be drawn from the *Manifesto* is that one class is cheating another by exploiting them, unfairly benefitting from the work they do. Marx describes an unfair struggle for economic survival in which the rich survive only to later compete with one another. The mechanism of the injustice is what would come to be known as economic exploitation—a powerful version of cheating. As he wrote in the excerpt notes of 1844 "The death of a poor man is the worst possibility for the creditor. It is the death of his capital and the interest as well" (p. 44). This point is carried forward into our own times by one of the leading interpreters of Marx, Erik Wright, who describes the core of the perspective as anchored in a notion of antagonistic inter-dependence of material interests. Wright's illustration of the notion and how it differs from other forms of oppression is arresting.

> The crucial difference between exploitative and nonexploitative oppression is that in an exploitative relation, the exploiter needs the exploited since the exploiter depends upon the effort of the exploited. In the case of non-exploitative oppression, the oppressors would be happy if the oppressed simply disappeared. Life would have been much easier for the European settlers in North America if the continent had been uninhabited by people. Genocide is thus always a potential strategy for nonexploitative oppressors. It is not an option in a situation of economic exploitation because exploiters require the labor of the exploitation because exploiters require the labor of the exploited for their material well being. It is no accident that culturally we have the abhorrent saying, "the only good Indian is a dead Indian," but not the saying, "the only good worker is a dead worker" or "the only good slave is a dead slave."[12]

The reciprocity critique, in all its versions, relies on a sense that one party is being cheated by another by virtue of some unfair advantage—a distributive injustice. In one of the most defensive moments of the *Manifesto*, Marx and Engels accuse their critics of misunderstanding their argument about how unfair the institution of ownership of the means of production, that is large holdings of productive private property are,

> You reproach us, therefore, with intending to do away with a form of prop-erty, the necessary condition for whose existence is the non-existence of any property for the immense majority of society.
>
> *(p. 171)*

The accidents of fortune were so troubling to Marx, because he knew that, even in the fair competition for commodities that defined the liberal economics of which he was critical, when one had the advantage of a store of capital to invest, it was possible to play the game in a way that tilted it to one's advantage. He wrote, "in bourgeois society, therefore, the past dominates the present." In the Marxian version, as in all forms of a reciprocity critique, a small, economic elite is able to parlay the advantages they already enjoy into future advantage at the expense of the many who do not enjoy the same privileges. In the Marxian version of this story, the inequity leads to material suffering.

> The lower strata of the middle class—the small tradespeople, shopkeepers, and retired tradesmen generally, the handicraftsmen and peasants—all these sink gradually into the proletariat.
>
> (p. 165)

All of this exploitation of the people by the powerful can be stopped in Marx's view, and his story of a coming communism is quite similar to the kinds of stories that other egalitarians tend to tell about how a change in policy will bring about more fair conditions of economic relations.

> The distinguishing feature of Communism is not the abolition of private property generally, but the abolition of bourgeois property... the final and most complete expression of the system of producing and appropriating products, that is based on class antagonisms, on the exploitation of the many by the few.... To be a capitalist is to have not only a purely personal, but a social status in production.... Capital is therefore, not a personal, it is a social power.
>
> (p. 170)

What the reciprocity critique shares with its Hobbesian and Lockean cousins is the notion that some form of social power has been abused. The moral warrant for taking political action to oppose that social power then derives from the nature of that abuse, and all the stories told in this idiom tend to share some form of that moral warrant. What makes Marx such a useful paradigm for illustrating this root narrative is his clear sense of both the nature and operation of the power (what we might call the empirical warrant of his critique) and the nature of the injustice that derives from its operation (the moral warrant that defines the abuse). As he wrote in his *German Ideology* of 1845:

> This alienation, to use a term which the philosophers will understand, can be abolished only on the basis of two practical premises. To become an intolerable power, that is, a power against which men make a revolution, it must have made the great mass of humanity propertyless, and this at the same time in contradiction to an existing world of wealth and culture.
>
> (p. 121)

Marxism floundered because the world in which "the great mass of humanity" became propertyless never fully materialized, but he had helped posterity to recognize an "intolerable power" in the form of a bourgeois property that created value through free exchange on markets that would be difficult for all of us to forget.

Marx saw the class structure as a kind of state of war from which escape into a thoroughly regulated economy would prove a solution: "In depicting the most general phases of the development of the proletariat, we traced the more or less veiled civil war, raging within existing society." But the civil war of the classes has not been without its transformations. Given our experience with the Marxist states that did emerge, it might be surprising to point out that many of the market correcting agenda items of the *Communist Manifesto* have become part of our modern welfare states. Consider: progressive incomes taxes, inheritance taxes, national banking systems, regulated utilities, environmental management, and public education. All of these were called for in the *Manifesto* on the grounds of class equity. Such is the power of the root narrative.

Nation: Foreigners *use* armed violence *to create* unfair competition *for* the People

One thing that makes Marx a bad representative of the egalitarian imagination is the fact that he explicitly stood against two of its most potent, populist variations. He only really told reciprocity stories and warned against the other two egalitarian root narratives. Where John Locke does seem to advocate for all three aspects of the libertarian imagination, Marx is markedly less flexible, a trait that would play out in the thought and actions of his adherents.

Marx was no populist. Nevertheless, even though Marx was laser focused in his analysis on the origin of exploitation in the actions of the few—the bourgeoisie— he was clearly aware of another major category of concern for the egalitarian, how unfair competition can be attributed to those who live outside the boundaries of the community, how exploitation can be projected on those who are not us: onto the Other. I do want to stress that this concern about unfair, sectional exploitation and abuse of economic power by the adversaries of the collective is not a natural Marxist mode. Socialists are not natural nationalists. One might even call it heretical to Marxism to make the association between the two insofar as he spent quite a bit of time inoculating his followers from the nationalist temptation. Having said this, we have to recognize how important a sense of loyalty and popular solidarity remains for even the Marxian version of the egalitarian imagination. Marx simply extended his notion of the nation to the whole of the world proletariat, but even in this creative rearticulation of the Nation narrative he did not alter its primitive moral logic. Those outside the moral community are national enemies of the proletariat just as they are often enemies of the People in cruder forms of the story structure.

The first clear signs of Marx's engagement with the notion of egalitarian solidarity and its uses appears in his 1844 *Toward a Critique of Hegel's Philosophy of Right*; it emerges when he begins to formulate his concept of the proletariat. If you can let go of all the symbolic baggage that has been heaped on this term since his use of it, the proletariat is a helpful way to think of the People brought together as a people, all sharing the same rights and responsibilities, defined against the depredations of the elite few. The distinctiveness of the People as proletariat does not arise so much from what they are as from what they oppose. Marx is clear about his hopes for what will define them—opposition to class oppression—but aware that the energy that binds them, enthusiasm for the collective, has a sectarian tendency. The proletariat is a vision of the nation as global collective, a universal nation, but his dream of universal unity implies the need for international conflict that would last until global integration could be achieved.

He addressed this nationalist tendency of the egalitarian mindset directly in his critique of Hegel, framing the issue in distinctively international, if not global, terms.

> The only emancipation of Germany possible in practice is emancipation based on the theory proclaiming that man is the highest essence of man. In Germany emancipation from the Middle Ages is possible only as emancipation at the same time from partial victories over the Middle Ages. In Germany, no brand of bondage can be broken without every brand of bondage being broken.... The emancipation of the German is the emancipation of mankind.... When all the inner conditions are fulfilled, the day of German resurrection will be announced by the crowing of the Gallic Cock.

The national identity of the proletariat was something that even Marx recognized could not be entirely ignored "in practice." He had hope for the great mass of people in the world to organize against the "intolerable power" organized at the level of the world market, but there was something in the heart of the proletarian idea, that is in the egalitarian imagination, that continued to rely on the nation—the community boundary—for its definition. Marx was desperately concerned to ensure that the community of the future be defined in global terms, but he was so concerned to defend against nationalism because the logic of the category of egalitarian moral thought presses so readily against this universalism. It tends to locate the extra-national "Other" as one of the three great agents of cheating, competition, and exploitation just as Accountability locates the government, or "the one," as the economic adversary and Reciprocity locates it in the elite, or "the few." Egalitarian thinking is naturally inflected in the direction of nationalism (or group consciousness more generally). This natural tension with a more inclusive philosophy can be overcome, as Marx tried to do, but it is a constant temptation of the egalitarian to blame the immigrant as readily as the businessman when economic expectations are dashed. This is the populist underbelly of egalitarian thought.

By the time of the 1848 revolutions and his collaboration with Engels on the *Manifesto*, Marx had worked this problem through to his own satisfaction. They wrote:

> All previous historical movements were movements of minorities, or in the interest of minorities. The proletarian movement is the self-conscious, independent movement of the immense majority in the interest of the immense majority.... Though not in substance, yet in form, the struggle of the

proletariat with the Bourgeoisie is at first a national struggle. The proletariat of each country must, of course, first of all settle matters with its own bourgeoisie.

(p. 168)

But the "immense majority" would only develop in tension with the tendency of working-class parties to organize in cultural, sectarian, and national blocs.

The Communists do not form a separate party opposed to other working-class parties. They have no interests separate and apart from those of the proletariat as a whole. They do not set up any sectarian principles of their own, by which to shape and mold the proletarian movement.... In the national struggles of the proletarians of the different countries, they point out and bring to the front the common interests of the entire proletariat, independently of all nationality.

(p. 169)

There is a reason that all the "the other working class parties" tended toward particularism. It is endemic to the perspective. As much as Marx inveighed against a nationalist conception of egalitarian resistance to economic oppression, the subsequent history of Marxist movements, as well as most forms of populism, beginning already with the Bonapartism of Marx's own day, have relied on some version of a "we are being cheated by them" story. The most famous argument to describe this tendency was Benedict Anderson, who targets Marxist predictions directly as a point of departure for his own theory of nationalism.

Perhaps without being much noticed yet, a fundamental transformation in the history of Marxism and Marxist movements is upon us. Its most visible signs are the recent wars between Vietnam, Cambodia and China. These wars are of world-historical importance because they are the first to occur between regimes whose independence and revolutionary credentials are undeniable, and because none of the belligerents has made more than the most perfunctory attempts to justify the bloodshed in terms of a recognizable Marxist theoretical perspective. While it was still just possible to interpret the Sino-Soviet border clashes of 1969, and the Soviet military interventions in Germany (1953), Hungary (1956), Czechoslovakia (1968), and Afghanistan (1980) in terms of— according to taste—"social imperialism," "defending socialism," etc., no one, I imagine, seriously believes that such vocabularies have much bearing on what has occurred in Indochina.... Such considerations serve to underline the fact that since World War II every successful revolution has defined itself in national terms.[13]

John Mearsheimer and other international relations realists would argue that this nationalist tendency is a function of the logic of security that inevitably organizes the society of states—shifting the argument from one root narrative category to another—and there is surely something to this, but the communist revolutions that provided Anderson his opening imagery were moved by a critique of capitalist exploitation—an egalitarian justification—as much as they were by security concerns. The Vietnamese people were animated as much by economic competition with the Cambodians as they were by protection of life and limb, and vice versa. The analytical structure of Root Narrative Theory provides us with a way of seeing the links between the economic criticisms of Marxist movements and their approaches to state formation. Both are variations on a common egalitarian narrative.

If we take the arguments of the communist revolutionaries in China, Vietnam and Cambodia seriously—which is not the same thing as giving in to their revolutionary perspectives—we can see how the egalitarian imagination continues "in practice" to rely on an "us vs. them" point of view, where the them is defined in sectarian terms, dividing the People from the proletariat and the broader egalitarian cause. In this aspect, the egalitarian imagination is always haunted by "the subversive"—what Stalin would immortalize as "the Enemy of the People." This equality-within-community-boundaries point of view may sit in uncomfortable tension with other universal perspectives on liberation from abusive power, but it appears to occupy a stable position in the space of root narratives. Marx saw this right away. This is why he so fervently preached that "the working men have no country." If they would win the world, they would have to overcome their natural tendencies to cut themselves off from it.

Accountability: **Governments** *use* **force of law** *to create* **unfair competition** *for* **the People**

I have chosen my paradigmatic thinkers so that the model I am proposing is defined in the tightest and most parsimonious way I can produce. For every Thomas Hobbes, there is a Hugo Grotius. As I said above, many critical thinkers other than Marx would draw their moral authority in opposition to the "intolerable power" of a wealthy elite and the abusive tendencies of oligarchical power. This was common since the time of Aristotle. Marx is useful to illustrate Root Narrative Theory because he was able to position his critique against the Lockean liberal notions that animated the theories of political economy and free trade that were still developing in his day. He helps to explain why so much conflict in the twentieth century was over the nature of the social system, socialism and capitalism, and why "socialist" remains one of the most damning political labels in America today.

As useful as Marx is to illustrate the reciprocity form of the critique of exploitation, he is less useful in clarifying the two other variations of the ethic, Marx meets Frantz Fanon and Marx meets Thomas Hobbes. Although these variations on the egalitarian imagination were less than critical for Marxists as they attempted to carve out a space for institutional checks on the stratifying tendencies of laissez-faire market society, later egalitarian thinkers, especially those who were less than comfortable in pillorying the capitalist system of commodity exchange itself, would work in modes other than the ethic of reciprocity. Easy as it is to see "the exploitation of the many by the few," it is also possible to imagine ways that the many could be exploited by the one, i.e. the government, or by the Other, i.e. foreigners and people outside the authoritative political community. The fact that exploitation could be something perpetrated by those who hold the reins of power over the monopoly of the legitimate means of violence is enough to establish its own category of critique, one that I call the Accountability narrative.

The Accountability narrative is best defined in opposition to the abuses of economic power that arise from the use of state power, i.e. law, the courts, the police, and the general bureaucracy that runs the affairs of the state. This is the lair of John Stuart Mills's "King of the vultures," because although it is quite possible for an aristocracy to unfairly benefit from the labor and activities of the great mass of the people, it is also quite easy for the King and his court to do so as well. Marx did not believe that the state was a foundational power. He saw it as a "superstructure" for the economic "base," which was structured by the overall "mode of production." But we see clear signs in Marx that the theme of government corruption was central to even his own egalitarian imagination.

Marx was the very model of what we refer to as an economic reductionist. True, his writings are full of complex and suggestive philosophical speculation that makes us think that Marx, himself, was able to see the richness of human life, especially in speculative communism, and to recognize the cultural nuances and the importance of literature, but he has written enough on the ways in which all of these things are mere products of economic relations that one is tempted to take him literally as well as seriously. Most later versions of stories told as accountability stories treat the state as an independent entity with its own logic and rhythms, which can lead to abusive exploitation of the people through taxation, but for Marx, under capitalism the state had become little more than a passthrough for capitalist interests. Even rendered in this way, we get a full sense of how powerful the government corruption theme can be for Marx. This from *The German Ideology*.

> To such modern private property corresponds the modern state which has been gradually bought by property owners through taxes, has fallen entirely into their hands through national debt, and has become completely dependent on commercial credit they, the bourgeois, extend to it in the rise and fall of government bonds on the stock exchange. Being a class and no longer an estate, the bourgeoisie is forced to organize itself nationally rather than locally and give a general form to its averaged interest. Through the emancipation of private property from the community, the state has become a separate entity beside and outside civil society. But the state is nothing more than the form of organization which the bourgeois by necessity adopts for both internal and external purposes as a mutual guarantee of their property and interests.

(p. 154)

Most of the class stories of the twentieth and twenty-first century that are developed as accountability stories will portray the state as a power that often acts on its own against private capital, but the imagery of an exploitative state is a stable feature of the broader cluster of arguments. As Marx wrote, "The executive of the modern State is but a committee for managing the common affairs of the whole bourgeoisie" p. 161.

Apart from Marx's view that the forces of capital had conquered the state and turned it to their own uses, it is not clear how he would have viewed a state power that could not be reduced to a creature and effect of economic interests, but there are some passages in Marx in which the corrupt power of state officials in what he saw as particular historical transitions were portrayed. These speak to the more general and stable category of accountability as an egalitarian root narrative that many other critics of power often employ. One of these passages appears in his *The Eighteenth Brumaire of Louis Bonaparte* in which he describes the fall of the French Second Republic and the rise of a military commander, Louis Bonaparte, after a coup.

> This executive power with its enormous bureaucratic and military organization, with its extensive and artificial state machinery, with a host of officials numbering half a million, besides an army of another half million, this appalling parasitic body, which enmeshes the body of French society like a net and chokes its pores, sprang up in the days of the absolute monarchy.
>
> *(p. 198)*

Speaking about the corrupt Bonapartist government he wrote of its aimless and venal structure of authoritarian rule, appealing mainly to the peasants.

> [The peasants'] representative must at the same time appear as their master, as an authority over them, as an unlimited governmental power that protects them against the other classes and sends them rain and sunshine from above.
>
> *(p. 200)*

This condemnation of absolutist French rule in the mid–nineteenth century could easily serve as the model for the kind of rhetoric that many contemporary critics of corrupt governments develop even now. Marx saw his ideas as part of his materialist theory of history, but the Accountability narrative is available in all times and places to those who see the government clerk and the petty bureaucrat using their position to enrich themselves.

Fanon: The Dignitarian

It is a bit of a relief to finally come to the Frantz Fanon section of the book. To be sure, the rhetorical examples of Hobbes, Locke, and Marx are as useful for understanding conflict and the opportunities for peace as is Fanon's, but they are thinkers of yesterday, where Fanon is the thinker of our own time. True, the abuses that define our canonical values, security, liberty, and equality, remain as much a challenge as the abuses of identity that Fanon identified, but nothing is so characteristic of the past seven decades as is the dignitarian imagination.

As a sociologist trained to see Max Weber's insights in everything, my word for the form of power against which Fanon inveighed was the power of social status, not status attached to economic or political position, but status, per se, liberated from those contexts and attached only to what we might call a style of life or lifestyle. It is an aesthetic power with influence over our tastes that comes from social closure, the ability to exclude people from participation and from identification with a set of daily practices. The kinds of practices that best capture the unique form of power that the dignitarian resents and opposes are not those that we would associate directly with the three other categories of social critique, especially the economic or egalitarian mode.

The arena in which status circulates is what we might call cultural. Therefore, the Fanonist imagination is an inherently cultural/political imagination. This is why Fanon is a much better representative in this category than is someone like Antonio Gramsci or Pierre Bourdieu, because although Gramsci and Bourdieu were responsible for helping many later critics to recognize the abusive power of seemingly innocent cultural practices, they were unable to liberate themselves from the Marxist problematic. Their theories were hybrids of the egalitarian and dignitarian modes, whereas Fanon reveals the problem directly, thereby avoiding the risk of reducing the category of cultural violence to economic exploitation—the classic Marxist foible. Indeed, this was the major intellectual struggle in Marxist circles as the problems of status abuse became impossible to ignore with the rise of Italian Fascism and German National Socialism. Writers like Max Horkheimer, Theodore Adorno, Walter Benjamin and others that we associate with the Frankfurt School wrestled with Weberian insights with respect to majority culture lifestyles, anti-Semitism, and the ways that culture and consumer tastes could be made to serve the cause of economic exploitation. Even the use of the term socio-economic status (a conceptual blend of class and status) in the mainstream sociology of the twentieth century fell prey to the confusion of influences that Fanon would dissolve.

As the dignitarian imagination developed over the course of the twentieth century, usually nestled in a Marxist critique of some kind, its differentiating feature became apparent. Where egalitarians saw economic structure as the defining challenge for black people and other marginalized groups, the dignitarian saw clearly how the most vexing problems were instead the networks informally managed by the dominant groups in society. The cultural establishment surely benefitted from its political connections and wealth, but the source of injustice it promoted was the pattern of association itself and the invidious values that were attached to that pattern. As is true of all people, members of the ingroup were engaged in informal activities—lifestyles—that were granted prestige and deference, while those in the lifestyles and cultural habits of the various outgroups were denigrated. Systematic invidious evaluation, had a tendency to destabilize self-concept, producing a crisis of identity.

The lifestyle (and I balk at using this term because it seems so innocuous; I mean something much deeper here) of the outgroup was the thing that gave a person's life meaning. The networks of personal association that define a lifestyle could touch on very profound sources of identification like religion, sexuality and family structure, or less deep but perhaps equally meaningful topics like food, forms of dress, favored forms of art, and leisure activities, but in almost all cases these differences became political when they were differentiated enough to be designated as ethnic. Fanon was the theorist who exploded on the scene when the abuses of patterns of ethnic association had become intolerable with the colonial expansion of Europe. Fanon did not invent the form of critique that he would develop better and in a more focused way than others, but he became the voice of the zeitgeist when the category of cultural violence became a recognizable and intolerable power all its own. And the Fanonist moment has not yet passed.

The logic of inclusion and outgroup recognition for racial minorities that burns in the pages of Fanon was as well represented for the category of gender by Simone de Beauvoir with her *Second Sex* and would later be extended to the categories of sexual orientation and gender identity by Judith Butler's *Gender Trouble*. Edward Said would make a career, a movement and a new word out of his examination of Christian status abuse of the Muslim world in his *Orientalism*. Indian authors were important innovators in this tradition as well. Authors like Gayatri Chakravorty Spivak would extend this "inexorable logic" to explore the cultural plight of what she called the subaltern, and Homi Bhabba would demonstrate how destabilizing the whole process was for social categories in general, which he argued were becoming necessarily hybrid.[14] All of these authors and countless others worked in a context in which military, political and economic power were given, but they all became innovative because they isolated the feature of social power that previous thinkers had either ignored or confused: they documented the abuses of ingroup status, white, male, straight, European, cishet, Christian, married, etc. In this sense the most recent forms of political critique have opened up a space for peacemaking that most previous thinkers were unable to even clearly see. As much as we have a need to ensure physical security, to protect citizens from their governments, and to develop systems of fair economic cooperation and competition, today's peacemakers are moved to include women, to recognize indigenous rights, and to overcome the barriers of racism and ethnocentrism. The field of struggle in each of these cases always touches on the areas exemplified by Hobbes, Locke and Marx, but is not reducible to them. It is culture. It is representation. It is lifestyle. Let's put it another way; the struggle is to preserve a way of life.

Recognition: Majorities *use* biased folkways *to create* cultural disrespect *of* the Other

At the heart of the Fanonist imagination is the concept of recognition. We remember Fanon more for his advocacy of violence as a means of overcoming European hegemony, but what stands out is not his prescriptive project but his diagnostic critique. Fanon understood what Tocqueville was getting at when he wrote

Under the absolute government of a single man, despotism, to reach the soul, clumsily struck at the body, and the soul, escaping from such blows, rose gloriously above it; but in democratic republics that is not at all how tyranny behaves; it leaves the body alone and goes straight for the soul.

(p. 255)[15]

The dignitarian imagination is a creative rejection of the systematic abuse of the soul. And just as Locke derived his vision from a critique of Hobbes's solution, and Marx derived his from a critique of Locke's, so Fanon derives his vision from a critique of the Marxian vision of universal solidarity. For the member of the minority or the outgroup, the folks defined as the Other, the People and their preferences are the source of the abusive power; democracy itself is the source of the soul's sickness. We see this abusive power immediately in the following introductory passages from Fanon's *Black Skin, White Masks*.

Blacks are men who are black; in other words, owing to a series of *affective disorders they have settled into a universe* from which *we have to extricate them.* The issue is paramount. We are aiming at nothing less than *to liberate the black man from himself.*

The white man is trapped in his whiteness. The black man in his blackness. We shall endeavor to determine the tendencies of this double narcissism and the motivations behind it… only a psychoanalytic interpretation of the black problem can reveal *the affective disorders responsible* for this network of complexes.

That is where we would like to position ourselves. We shall attempt to discover the various mental *attitudes the black man adopts in the face of white civilization.*

We believe *the juxtaposition of the black and white races* has resulted in *a massive psycho-existential complex.* By analyzing it we aim to destroy it.

we are witness to the desperate efforts of a black man striving desperately to discover *the meaning of black identity. White civilization and European culture* have imposed an existential deviation on the black man. We shall demonstrate furthermore that what is called *the black soul is a construction by white folk.*

There are few short pieces of prose that capture so much about the political mood of an era as does Fanon's introduction to his *Black Skin, White Masks*. The implications of the analysis were not just predictive of political currents but remain at the forefront of our current quest for peace. I have highlighted those lines that require extra attention so that we are sure to capture what is distinctive about the dignitarian mode of the moral imagination with respect to its cousins.

The first thing to notice is a rather obvious point; the origin of the harm is what Max Weber called the status group. This is a subtle point. It is not the class structure or the political structure that is the source of the Fanon's suffering. It is the racial structure, which happens to employ political and economic resources to maintain itself. To get a sense of what that means, consider what is left over after you have removed abuses of power that derive specifically from either control over the lawmaking power of government or differential access to the property system. What remains is the differential evaluation and exclusion of certain kinds of people for who they are. What is left over are the ascribed characteristics of people, the things that are almost written on their bodies and from which they cannot escape. These are forms of identity at the ground of this form of the moral imagination.

This is an obvious but crucial point, because it helps to establish the dignitarian root narrative. Note that Fanon identifies "white civilization," "European culture," and the "juxtaposition of the black and white races" as the source of the abuses that forced him to write a book "that no one asked me to." At the root of Fanonian rage is not insecurity, lack of freedom, or economic inequality, although these things all come with a racialized status structure. At the root of his rage is disrespect. His hatred is a product of hate.

To understand institutionalized racism (or any other form of institutionalized prejudice or intolerance) as racism it is important to examine what form of the institution is that could be defined by its incorporation of ascriptive characteristics. This is where it becomes important to adapt Michael Mann's theory of social power institutional networks. Recall that Mann saw society as structured by social power that was channeled into means and not ends. He identified four kinds of power networks that he adapted from Max Weber's trio: class, status and party. In this case, Mann was wrong to break with Weber's status concept. His adaptation moved his theory away from the adequate typology of institutionalized means rather than toward it. The source of Fanonian suffering is not the mass media or the systems of representation, per se, but rather the representations of the aesthetic value of groups in it and the patterns of association that take place in voluntary and largely informal associations. In the dignitarian imagination, the personal is necessarily political.

The second defining theme in Fanon's introduction is the causal importance of "affective disorders." What Fanon had the courage to do in this book, was to place emotional sickness at the heart of politics. Fanon was born and raised in Martinique, a French dependency, and his intellectual development was always shadowed by the alienating experience of coming to Paris as an outsider who could in some sense never come inside. At the time, a radical critique was one that targeted economic, not cultural abuse. He was well aware that the political conjuncture he faced had little room for the kind of analysis that he would propose. Politics was about other things. It was about the wars of the great men. It was about the revolutions that freed mankind from tutelage. It was about the struggle for world communism. It was not about the psychological complexes that kept the races separate from one another in a garish hierarchy. It was this racial hierarchy that he knew marginalized him as a human being and cast him outside the human family. That is what plagued him. His suffering must have felt like a kind of horror, and he wrote *Black Skin, White Masks* to narrate that horror. His personal trauma, motivated by a Freudian therapeutic model, led to a theoretical analysis of the abuses of the cultural structure that is now quite familiar.

It is important to recognize that Fanon places the problem of racism in a psychological context rather than an economic or state political one. This is because those other modes of thinking about power and resistance are still somehow more obvious to us, even as the problems of psychological trauma have upended our politics the world over. The trauma he experienced was that, as a black man, he had no real basis for stable identification; he had no legitimate voice. He was rendered as a savage, an object, something less than fully human. His only hope was to pass in white society and hope that he could become a lesser version of the ingroup that he hoped to join. This was, and is, a general problem, an institutional problem. It is about Weberian status.

Now, it is much easier than then to see why this problem is a problem that has political dimensions, but even today, we tend to dismiss the affective source of the malady. This is why Fanon is so critical. He insists on the problem of group dignity. He recognizes that the "affective disorders" are "responsible for this network of complexes" that define the plight of the black man. His punctuation of the analysis does not begin with the affective disorder, but once the disorder has been established, it has to be addressed in order for the society to heal. The emotional and psychological side of the challenge of difference is a central feature of Fanon's analysis that is not trivial. We all know the child's rhyme that says, "sticks and stones can break my bones but words will never hurt me." Fanon disagrees. He sees these words—and the broader world of group representations—as a "massive psycho-existential complex" that has to be analyzed so that it can be destroyed. The urgency that Fanon feels in this quest is as pointed as that Marx felt in the most strident passages of the *Manifesto*. This psychological complex (and others like it) is a problem of world historical proportions.

In an anniversary celebration to Fanon's influence, philosopher Cornel West provides a sense of how profound and clarifying this insight into massive psycho-existential complex is:

> Frantz Fanon, to me, is a soulmate. He helped sustain me in so many others because he is the most profound revolutionary theorist of empire, of anti-colonial struggle. He is also one of the greatest courageous intellectuals of the twentieth century in telling the truth. And the condition of truth is always to allow suffering to speak.... Let's look at for me what is most important about his theories... what [this inferiority complex] really means... to try to convince them that they are less moral, less beautiful, less intelligent, less human, and most importantly to keep fear at the center of their souls.[16]

Those who study identity often begin with later psychological approaches like the social identity theory of Tajfel and Turner,[17] which provides rigorous empirical support for the tendency of people to form invidiously valued groups out of minimal and trivial conditions, but it is the psychoanalytic traditions and reactions to them like those of Fanon, Simone de Beauvoir and Erik Erikson[18] that provide a clear sense of the depth of identification processes and how these can become attached to politically relevant considerations. The essence of Fanon's approach (insofar as it is appropriate to attribute essence to the ideas of an existentialist philosopher) is the link between group difference and its psychological effects. The set of complexes that result from colonialism are such that the black man becomes an agent of his own subordination. His identification with white civilization causes him to make a fetish of whiteness and to denigrate himself. Only by overcoming this enemy within can the member of the misrepresented group hope to overcome the violence that derives from adverse representations of his group. This requires assertion from the members of the subordinated group and recognition from the other.

One final thing to note about the category of thinking that I call the Recognition narrative is that although it deals with particular cultural exclusions, it can be generalized to a principle, the principle of dignity, to become a universal norm. This is what Fanon called his "new humanism." Although there are calls in many versions of recognition stories for remedial symbolic treatment to make up for past abuses, there is great potential for this attention to asymmetric group recognition to become a norm applicable to all people in any place. Fanon's introduction does not dwell on this aspect of the perspective, but we see it clearly in later parts of the book.

> Colonial racism is no different from other racisms. Anti-Semitism cuts me to the quick; I get upset; a frightful rage makes me anemic; they are denying me the right to be a man. I cannot dissociate myself from the fate reserved for my brother.

> *(p. 69)*

What Fanon says of racism, others have said of sexism, heterosexism, the cultural aspects of colonialism and any other form of group differentiation one can imagine. The logic is the same. Contact with a dominating group in which outgroup members are not treated as potentially equal members leads to invidious comparisons and abusive representations. These representations can be subtle, but they all tend toward a kind of supremacist cultural abuse, which is good neither for the ingroup nor the outgroup. As Thomas Jefferson lamented about race and slavery in the United States, "but, as it is, we have the wolf by the ear, and we can neither hold him, nor safely let him go."

Liberation: Governments *use* force of law *to create* cultural disrespect *of* the Other

As with the various arguments in favor of redistribution along cultural lines, there is an important analytical distinction to make between arguments in support of recognition and those that target not the aesthetic biases of the culture but the aesthetic biases of the government itself. These stories are what I will lump under the Liberation narrative. The differentiating characteristic of these arguments is their focus on the injustices that derive from government actions that jeopardize the physical safety and political rights of the members of underrepresented groups based on their group status. As with the Recognition narrative, this ethic is more about sticks and stones than it is about names that can hurt. In fact, because the issues addressed in questions of liberation touch on physical violence and life and death struggles, they are often the first to rise to the surface in ascriptive struggles. Liberation narratives are the most commonly offered by members of the #BlackLivesMatter campaign and it also is why we speak about the movement to liberate African Americans as the civil rights movement. In the first case, it is the injustice of bias in policing and the unjust killing of black people by the police that marks the story. In the second, it is the history of lynching and the absence of basic police protections that provided impetus to the movement and moved its leaders to accuse the government of not protecting the basic civil rights of black people. Both of these movements are framed as liberation stories.

If the Recognition narrative is what you get when a Fanonian meets a Marxist—when a multiculturalist meets an egalitarian—liberation is a murkier territory defined by the arguments that emerge when a Fanonian meets a Hobbesian, concerning the risk of violent death and the state's inability to protect certain kinds of people from it. The territory is murky because the boundaries of the community that the Leviathan was contracted to protect is always unclear. As Benedict Anderson argued, what differentiates one national community from another is always, on some level, an act of the imagination, and it never becomes particularly concrete.

In terms of the philosophy of Frantz Fanon, the Liberation narrative appears more in his *Wretched of the Earth* than in *Black Skin, White Masks*. In his opening section of that book that he called "On Violence," Fanon explained why it was that the colonized group demands dislocation of the national order.

> National liberation, national reawakening, restoration of the nation to the people or Commonwealth, whatever the name used, whatever the latest expression, decolonization is always a violent event.
>
> We have seen how the government's agent uses a language of pure violence. The agent does not alleviate oppression or mask domination. He displays and demonstrates them with the clear conscience of the law enforcer and brings violence into the homes and minds of the colonized subject.
>
> The violence which governed the ordering of the colonial world, which tirelessly punctuated the destruction of the indigenous social fabric and demolished unchecked the systems of reference of the country's economy, lifestyles, and modes of dress, this same violence will be vindicated and appropriated when, taking history into their own hands, the colonized swarm into the forbidden cities. To blow the colonial world to smithereens is henceforth a clear image within the grasp and imagination of every colonized subject.

The logic of this perspective centers on the problem of colonial violence. Fanon is famous because he inverted this logic into a program for confronting it. Under conditions of colonial violence, the Hobbesian contract was never effectively established for the outgroup, a condition that quickly becomes intolerable.

In most cases, there is some link between a demand for basic civil rights and a remedy for economic exploitation, but there is a substantive difference between what happens when Fanon meets Marx and when Fanon meets Hobbes. In this latter case, fundamental questions are in play about the nature of the boundaries of the political community itself. Will Kymlicka describes the logic of this ethic with the concept he calls "self-government rights."

> Self-government rights. In most nation states, the component nations are inclined to demand some form of political autonomy or territorial jurisdiction, so as to ensure the full and free development of their cultures and the best interests of their people. At the extreme, nations may wish to secede, if they think their self-determination is impossible with the larger state.
>
> (p. 27)

Although the demand to secede is what Kymlicka calls an extreme position on this interpretation, it does speak to the ultimate goal of a liberation story. Because secession is such an extreme case, especially for non-ethnic forms of group difference like gender, sexual orientation, disability etc., liberation is not a perfect label for this root narrative. Even in the case of ethnic conflict, the demand for basic civil protections from violence often stops short of a call for full separation, but the extreme serves as a defining boundary for the norm. All of these examples are liberation stories, even when they restrict their demand to equal protection of the laws for targeted outgroups.

A powerful example of a restricted call for liberation can be found in Martin Luther King's "Letter from a Birmingham Jail." Because of the dramatic salience of the events of the 1950s and 1960s, we tend to remember the anti-segregation focus of the American Civil Rights Movement (an inclusion story), but the history of lynching and police violence were always central to the movement and its rhetoric at its origins.

> We have waited for more than 340 years for our constitutional and God given rights. The nations of Asia and Africa are moving with jetlike speed toward gaining political independence, but we still creep at horse and buggy pace toward gaining a cup of coffee at a lunch counter. Perhaps it is easy for those who have never felt the stinging darts of segregation to say, "Wait." But when you have seen vicious mobs lynch your mothers and fathers at will and drown your sisters and brothers at whim; when you have seen hate filled policemen curse, kick and even kill your black brothers and sisters.[19]

The Liberation narrative is always in some way about official and sanctioned persecution. We can see how this logic was employed to establish a link between the plight of the oppressed and the actions of the state in language of the Dyer Bill, an anti-lynching measure that passed the U.S. House of Representatives but could not get past a Senate filibuster in 1922. In section 2, the logic of liberation and the need for protection of basic civil rights (a liberation story) is clear.

> That if any State or governmental subdivision thereof fails, neglects, or refuses to provide and maintain protection to the life of any person within its jurisdiction against a mob or riotous assemblage, such State shall by reason of such failure, neglect, or refusal be deemed to have denied to such person the equal protection of the laws of the State.[20]

This primordial concern for physical protection across racial lines in the American civil rights movement continues to animate calls for racial justice, as a quick search of the Twitter feed on #BlackLivesMatter reveals, and liberation is a root narrative applicable to any marginalized status group. Any group can fear for the physical safety of its members or can accuse the state of failing to provide equal protection. Examples of violence toward gay people, the use of rape in war and the internment of minority groups on suspicion of subversion are all examples of cases in which this ethic is commonly mobilized.

Inclusion: *Elites* use *bargaining power* to create *cultural disrespect* of *the Other.*

When people speak about institutionalized racism, they are often telling inclusion stories. Their accounts tend to focus on the discriminatory aspects of the leading institutions of private and civil life like industry, and education, providing examples of inclusion by detailing the forms of exclusion. Arguments that draw their power from what are ultimately psychological and cultural forces are translated into other institutional arenas. The stakes become material. Race, or gender, or sexual orientation, or language use, become economic issues. As these institutions are deployed to promote the status interests of the dominant group, they become issues of limits placed on equal opportunity and they offer a way to fight neoliberalism outside of the context of the various forms of populism described in the egalitarian section. This often leads to empirical accounts that demand intrusion into these self-organized processes to remediate the abuse of what we might call status-conditioned economic power.

Whatever one can say about the Inclusion narrative, it would be hard to say it was central to the philosophy of Frantz Fanon. Inclusion tends to assume the integrity of the political community and seeks to make it more just by allowing those who have been excluded from economic and educational institutions to better flourish in them. Fanon's vision was of the more radical kind in that he planned for separation and supersession. Nevertheless, we can see traces in his work of the racially conscious economic critique that is characteristic of the Inclusion narrative. We know the presence of the ethic when difference is posited as the reason why liberal institutions will prove insufficient to promote racial justice. As with the Reciprocity narrative, formal freedoms will not be enough to overcome the forces of discrimination. These sentiments scream from the pages of *The Wretched of the Earth* whenever they appear.

> The colonial world is a world divided into compartments. It is probably unnecessary to recall the existence of native quarters and European quarters, of schools for natives and schools for Europeans; in the same way we need not recall apartheid in South Africa. Yet, if we examine closely this system of compartments, we will at least be able to reveal the lines of force it implies. This approach to the colonial world, its ordering and its geographical layout will allow us to mark out the lines on which a decolonized society will be reorganized.
>
> *(p. 37)*

Although the plan for Fanon is not integration into the political and economic world of the oppressor, the "system of compartments," ethnic exploitation in economic and education affairs serves to "mark the lines" of the coming reorganization.

Lest we forget, the challenge for the dignitarian is to overcome the conqueror, who comes from outside and introduces forms of group-targeted economic exclusion. In its inclusion variations, the focus of the abusive relationship with this colonial other is primarily economic.

> It is neither the act of owning factories, nor estates, nor a bank balance which distinguishes the governing classes. The governing race is first and foremost those who come from elsewhere, those who are unlike the original inhabitants, "the others."
>
> *(p. 40)*

And in a move that is typical of many inclusion stories, the story adapts to even major changes in political organization. In Fanon's account, he tells of the ways that the old caste system is re-instantiated even after the colonial power has been forced out, with black people becoming exploiters of other black people on racial grounds. This style of critique points to the challenge of overcoming entrenched systems of status domination as they play out in the economic sphere.

> The former colonial power increases its demands, accumulates concessions and guarantees and takes fewer and fewer pains to mask the hold it has over the national government. The people stagnate deplorably in unbearable poverty; slowly they awaken to the unutterable treason of their leaders. This awakening is all the more acute in that the bourgeoisie is incapable of learning its lesson. The distribution of wealth that it effects is not spread out between a great

many sectors; it is not ranged among different levels, nor does it set up a
hierarchy of halftones. The new caste is an affront all the more disgusting in
that the immense majority, nine-tenths of the population, continue to die of
starvation. The scandalous enrichment, speedy and pitiless, of this caste is
accompanied by a decisive awakening on the part of the people, and a growing awareness that promises stormy days to come.

(p. 166)

And in what is perhaps the worst aspect of all, the old caste is replaced by a new
one in which a native bourgeoisie build its new status position in the larger global
economic system, suggesting that even political liberation is not enough and that
some form of inclusion in global economic relations is necessary.

The bourgeois caste, that section of the nation which annexes for its own profit
all the wealth of the country, by a kind of unexpected logic will pass disparaging
judgments upon the other Negroes and the other Arabs that more often than
not are reminiscent of the racist doctrines of the former representatives of the
colonial power. At one and the same time the poverty of the people, the
immoderate money- making of the bourgeois caste, and its widespread scorn for
the rest of the nation will harden thought and action.

(p. 167)

Although Fanon concentrates his energy on the racialized colonial struggle of
the twentieth century, further insight into the dynamics of the dignitarian critique
is provided by the political scientist, Donald Horowitz, in his *Ethnic Groups in
Conflict*. What is so helpful about Horowitz's research and argument is that it serves
to generalize the problem of invidious group distinctions, at least to all ethnic distinctions. A piece that he adds is the tendency for a set of binary distinctions to
develop around the ethnic divide across almost every boundary of ethnic relations,
sorting people into what are often described as "advanced" as distinct from
"backward" groups. The advanced groups are not only seen to possess material
advantages, they are also seen to enjoy traits in their culture that would continue to
provide them with advantages in future competitions. This divide in supposed
cultural advantages and disadvantages, spurious as it may be, is often cited to justify
the need for explicit remedies beyond Lockean processes of free competition to
deal with between-group inequalities. The crushing universality of the phenomenon makes it clear that the dignitarian imagination and its literary products will
long remain a central part of the peacemaker's toolkit.

To be backwards is, first and foremost, to feel weak vis-à-vis advanced groups.
The Assamese, remarks Myron Wiener, see themselves as so weak that they do
not believe they could compete with the Bengalis, asserted to be superior in
skills and motivation, in a free labor market. Likewise, a leader of a backward
group in Bihar told Weiner that members of his group are "not very bright.

They have limited intelligence so they cannot do well in school," just as Telanganas told him they were "no match for the Andhras." The same was said by Karens, who felt they could not keep up with the more "sharp-witted" and "aggressive" Burmans. Backward groups in general feel at a competitive disadvantage as they compare their imputed personal qualities with those imputed to advanced groups.

(p. 167)[21]

This intersection of cultural and economic/consensual processes lead to a variety of complicated interpretations of inter-group equity in actual empirical data. This kind of complexity in invidious distinctions is not specific to ethnic differences but could be extended to any number of other ascriptive group boundaries. The ubiquity of economically-relevant, group-differentiating traits points to the complexity of inclusion stories. On the one hand, economically-relevant cultural privilege can lead to a story about the injustices that arise from it, or it can lead to a justification for the presence of the disadvantage. After all, why should a backward or non-competitive group be rewarded for having those traits? What marks an argument as a member of this ethic is that cultural privilege is portrayed as an illegitimate product of history, often of political conquest and repression. It is something that is to be overcome. There are few areas of political thought that remain as fraught as this one and counterarguments proliferate, but at the same time, few arguments remain as important for moving toward a condition of peace. The distributional effects of cultural difference are critical for any anti-supremacist agenda.

This chapter demonstrated how the logics of Root Narrative Theory were present in the big four virtuoso narrators, Hobbes, Locke, Marx, and Fanon. The next four chapters of this book will provide illustrations of the "big four" root narrative categories, dividing each of the four into their three corresponding divisons. These sections will explore various ways that the root narratives manifest in history. Since the scope of Root Narrative Theory is any political statement made anywhere in the world and at any time, the universe of possible examples is infinite. In these illustrations I do my best to draw on famous and well circulated statements and arguments that should be familiar to a broad audience. The purpose is to show how just about any political argument can be characterized by its use of the twelve logics of Root Narrative Theory.

Notes

1 There is a problem with stage theories of social process. They are often taken too literally rather than as gross abstractions of processes that play out in different rhythms and sequences. It is easy to imagine that a theory as broad as this one can only ever hope to provide the broadest historical generalization about when the different root narratives were at their peak in structuring organizations and energizing social movements. I should also say that even though the circle of power describes how the root narratives seemed to sequence in the early modern period, there is no reason why they should have to unfold in this way.

2 All excerpts from this chapter come from standard texts for the four virtuosi that are available in English. Hobbes, *Leviathan*; Locke, *Second Treatise of Government*; Locke, *A Letter Concerning Toleration and Other Writings*; Marx, *Selected Writings*; Fanon, *Black Skin, White Masks*; Fanon, *The Wretched of the Earth*.
3 Whenever I present this work, people tend to think of Chuck Tilly and his approach to historical macro-sociology. This is not far wrong, and Tilly did review a much earlier version of my thinking on this topic for a conference celebrating the fiftieth anniversary of C. Wright Mills's *Power Elite*. Much as I have tried to incorporate Tilly's ideas into this framework, nothing much but the general attitude toward the use of sociological concepts in history comes through.
4 Stearns et al., *World Civilizations*.
5 There is plenty to read on Schwartz's agenda. Schwartz and Bilsky, "Toward a Universal Psychological Structure of Human Values."; Schwartz, "Universals in the Content and Structure of Values"; Schwartz, "Beyond Individualism/Collectivism"; Schwartz, "A Theory of Cultural Values and Some Implications for Work". As I have argued above, the major difference between Schwartz's theory of Basic Human Values and the Root Narrative Theory is that in the latter, values come from narratives of abusive social power, not from the nature of individuals. The difference is subtle but critical, because the values of Root Narrative Theory have to be understood in terms of social relations rather than individual characteristics. Nevertheless, the root narratives are universals in that power, in its various forms, is the same across human history and geography. This could make Root Narrative Theory attractive to universalists who recognize the appeal of symbolism, emotion, and framing in politics.
6 Shand, *Central Works of Philosophy*.
7 Shand, *Central Works of Philosophy*.
8 McClosky and Zaller, *The American Ethos*.
9 Hartz, *The Liberal Tradition in America*.
10 McPherson, *Political Theory of Possessive Individualism*.
11 Thompson, "The Moral Economy of the English Crowd in the Eighteenth Century."
12 Wright, *Class Counts*.
13 Anderson, *Imagined Communities*.
14 Spivak, "Can the Subaltern Speak?"; Bhabha, *The Location of Culture*.
15 Tocqueville, *Democracy in America*.
16 West, "Fanon's Legacy in Contemporary African-American Thought."
17 Tajfel and Turner, "An Integrative Theory of Intergroup Conflict."
18 I have already spoken about Fanon and Beauvoir, but the concept of identity as we now use it probably has as much to do with the psychoanalysis of Erik Erikson as with anyone else. Erikson, *Childhood and Society*.
19 King, "Letter from a Birmingham Jail."
20 U.S. Congress. *Proceedings and Debates*.
21 Horowitz, *Ethnic Groups in Conflict*.

Bibliography

Anderson, Benedict. *Imagined Communities*. New York: Verso, 1983.
Bhabha, Homi K. *The Location of Culture*. London: Routledge, 2012.
Congressional Edition. U.S. Government Printing Office, 1922.
Erikson, Erik H. *Childhood and Society*. New York: W. W. Norton, 1963.
Fanon, Frantz. *Black Skin, White Masks*. Translated by Richard Philcox. Revised edition. New York: Grove Press, 2008.
Fanon, Frantz. *The Wretched of the Earth: The Handbook for the Black Revolution That Is Changing the Shape of the World*. New York: Grove Press, Inc., 1963.
Hartz, Louis. *The Liberal Tradition in America*. New York: Harvest, 1955.

Hobbes, Thomas. *Leviathan: With Selected Variants from the Latin Edition of 1668*. Edited by Edwin Curley. Cambridge, MA: Hackett Publishing Company, 1994.

Horowitz, Donald L. *Ethnic Groups in Conflict*, Updated Edition with a New Preface. 2nd ed. Berkeley: University of California Press, 2000.

King Jr., Martin Luther. "Letter from a Birmingham Jail," (April 16, 1963) http://mlk-kpp01.stanford.edu/index.php/encyclopedia/encyclopedia/enc_letter_from_birmingham_jail_1963/.

Locke, John. *A Letter Concerning Toleration and Other Writings*. New Edition. Indianapolis: Liberty Fund Inc., 2010.

Locke, John. *Second Treatise of Government*. Cambridge, MA: Hackett Publishing Company, 1980.

Marx, Karl. *Selected Writings*. Edited by Lawrence H. Simon. Cambridge, MA: Hackett Publishing Company, 1994.

McClosky, Herbert, and John Zaller. *The American Ethos: Public Attitudes toward Capitalism and Democracy*. Cambridge, MA: Harvard University Press, 1984.

McPherson, C. B. *Political Theory of Possessive Individualism: Locke to Hobbes*. Oxford: Clarendon Press, 1962.

Mill, John Stuart. *On Liberty*. Edited by Elizabeth Rapaport. Cambridge, MA: Hackett Publishing Company, 1978.

Schwartz, Shalom H. "A Theory of Cultural Values and Some Implications for Work." *Applied Psychology* 48, no. 1 (1999): 23–47.

Schwartz, Shalom H. "Beyond Individualism/Collectivism: New Cultural Dimensions of Values." In *Cross-cultural Research and Methodology Series, Vol. 18. Individualism and Collectivism: Theory, Method, and Applications* by U. Kim, H. C. Triandis, Ç. Kâğitçibaşi, S.-C. Choi, and G. Yoon (Eds), pp. 85–119. Thousand Oaks, CA: Sage Publications, 1994.

Schwartz, Shalom H. "Universals in the Content and Structure of Values: Theoretical Advances and Empirical Tests in 20 Countries." In *Advances in Experimental Social Psychology, Vol. 25*, by Mark P. Zanna (Ed.), pp. 1–65. Amsterdam: Elsevier, 1992.

Schwartz, Shalom H., and Wolfgang Bilsky. "Toward a Universal Psychological Structure of Human Values." *Journal of Personality and Social Psychology* 53, no. 3 (1987): 550.

Shand, John. *Central Works of Philosophy: The Seventeenth and Eighteenth Centuries*. Montreal: McGill-Queen's University Press, 2005.

Spivak, Gayatri Chakravorty. "Can the Subaltern Speak?" In *Can the Subaltern Speak? Reflections on the History of an Idea*, by Rosalind C. Morris, pp. 21–78. New York: Columbia University Press, 1988.

Stearns, Peter N., Michael Adas, Stuart B. Schwartz, and Marc Jason Gilbert. *World Civilizations: The Global Experience*. Vol. 2. New York: HarperCollins, 1992.

Tajfel, Henri, and J. C. Turner. "An Integrative Theory of Intergroup Conflict." In *The Social Psychology of Intergroup Relations*, by W. G. Austin and S. Worchel (Eds), pp.33–47. Monterey, CA: Brooks/Cole, 1979.

Thompson, Edward P. "The Moral Economy of the English Crowd in the Eighteenth Century." *Past and Present* 50 (1971): 76–136.

Tocqueville, Alexis de. *Democracy in America*. New York: Harper Perennial, 1966.

U.S. Congress. *Proceedings and Debates of the 2nd Session of the 67th Congress of the United States of America*. February 3, 1922. Washington, DC: U.S. Government Printing Office, 1922.

West, Cornel. "Fanon's Legacy in Contemporary African-American Thought." Princeton: Princeton University. Frantz Fanon Foundation.

Wright, Erik Olin. *Class Counts: Comparative Studies in Class Analysis*. Cambridge: Cambridge University Press, 1997.

IMAGINING SECURITY

Defense, Unity, Stability

The Defense narrative

The securitarian imagination is a form of moral politics that builds on the simple story that the community is threatened by violence and physical harm. In its most primitive form it is captured by the sentence: *Foreigners use armed violence to create physical deprivation in the State*. The defining feature of a security narrative is this notion of *physical deprivation in the State*. Anything that creates such suffering, killing, sexual violence, vandalism, starvation, and even collective demoralization fits the narrative model and demands redress in the form of protection.

The first and perhaps most important version of the securitarian imagination is the Defense narrative, in which the political leader draws her moral authority from her ability to protect the nation from hostile foreign elements—from the Other who does not belong. Although the root narrative is so powerful and natural that it is often written off as either paranoia or simple common sense, it is a story structure through which to describe the traditional first duties of the leader: to protect the people from violent death and other depredations. Important as this protection can be in domestic affairs, it the staple of international politics. Defense is a narrative form appropriate to the condition of intercommunal division, especially when these divisions are hardened into national boundaries. As the poet Percy Bysshe Shelley put it:

> Nations had risen against nations, employing the subtlest devices of mechanism and mind to waste, and excruciate, and overthrow. The great community of mankind had been subdivided into ten thousand communities, each organized for the ruin of the other.[1]

This condition of intercommunal division powers the Defense narrative, even as the sometimes–ephemeral boundaries of communities and nations flow and change.

Timeless in its appeal and building on theological predicates, we can see the story structure at work as early as the book of Isaiah:

> For the breath of the ruthless is like a storm driving against a wall and like the heat of the desert. You silence the uproar of foreigners; as heat is reduced by the shadow of a cloud, so the song of the ruthless is stilled.[2]

We can see it in ancient South Asian sources as well, like the *The Arthashastra* of Kautilya

> A reckless king will easily fall into the hands of his enemies. Hence the king shall ever be wakeful.[3]

We see it in the French Revolution, in which one of the most fearsome of the radicals and the first president of the Committee on Public Safety remarked, "let us be terrible so the people will not have to be,"[4] an indication that he understood the tensions that securitarian rhetoric placed on democratic practice. We can also see the narrative alive in modern politics, as in this revealing episode reported in the *New York Times* about an evangelical woman who explained her support for Donald Trump in 2016 even amid damning audio evidence of him condoning sexual assault: "'We weren't looking for a husband,' she said. 'We were looking for a body guard.'"[5]

To put the Defense narrative in deep yet modern context, I thought it would be appropriate to analyze portions of Edward Gibbon's *The Decline and Fall of the Roman Empire.* [6] As a work of history, his is a defense story with enough depth, prestige, and historical investment that it can help to portray how natural the mode of reasoning is for moral politics, especially in the West and the Anglosphere. This book, published in the same year as the Declaration of Independence and Adam Smith's *The Wealth of Nations,* [7] may provide some of the most vivid imagery with which the social imaginary of the securitarian is furnished.

Gibbon famously described history as "little more than the register of the crimes, follies, and misfortunes of mankind," and his massive and imaginative history of Roman decline speaks to the uneasy place of the value of security in the modern era. Security is something obvious and unspoken, even perhaps a necessary condition for peace, but it is the peace of the securitarian thinker consumed by the threat of predation. These predators are imagined to come at the community from various angles, some internal and some external, but there is always something intensely foreign about them—they don't ever really belong. Somehow the imagery of the barbarian and his vicious appetites—and mind you every culture seems to have this image—invades even the most sensible account of threats to life and limb. These stories are commonly filled with images of violent death, rape, murder, fire, lawlessness, and hatred.

Gibbon is master of this mode, elevating the form into magisterial art. Among my favorite of examples is this passage describing the political habits of the

Thuringians, allies of Attila the Hun as he passed through modern day France just prior to the final fall of Rome in the fifth century. It sets the scene as an example of the Defense narrative vivid as any I have seen.

> They massacred their hostages, as well as their captives: two hundred young maidens were tortured with exquisite and unrelenting rage; their bodies were torn asunder by wild horses, or their bones were crushed under the weight of rolling wagons; and their unburied limbs were abandoned on the public roads, as a prey to dogs and vultures. Such were those savage ancestors whose imaginary virtues have sometimes excited the praise and envy of civilized ages.

Murder, rape, torture, desecration, and the capricious and sadistic whims of the savage; these are among the admonishing plot elements of a typical defense story. When in a pinch, you can always be sure that you are in the presence of a Defense narrative when you can identify a villain in the text who can be portrayed as a violent predator who has no respect for your civilization or for your values—today this would most commonly be a terrorist. The trick is to look for the ways the author describes EVIL. Of course, I don't mean the living presence of malevolence, but instead EVIL as an acronym, when appeals are made with emotional, vivid, intense, and literary language. EVIL accounts provide us with a sense of moral clarity and channel narrative intuition.

We can get inside the narrative by its choice of words. The word "prey" is an important one. It refers to the abusive power of the antagonist, the capacity for predatory violence. In the passage, the victims are passive, "hostages" and "captives," innocent "maidens," and are "civilized." Their attackers are filled with "unrelenting rage." Their chosen means of violence are brutal: "wild horses," "the weight of rolling wagons." Their effects are inhuman, "massacred," "bodies torn asunder," left to be eaten by "dogs and vultures." These are all helpful elements of the meaning system of the Defense narrative. It is not enough that violent death and cruelty are present. We need an element of EVIL, of them coming to attack us, demanding we organize for defense. Most important of all, once the players and scene have been set and disbelief suspended, the animating story is not merely an emotional reaction, it has become a logical argument with prescriptive power.

Gibbon's story works so well because he uses images in predictable combination to effortlessly elicit a sense of the dangerous world outside the British Empire— Sauron threatening the Shire—and this world stood as a challenge to the growing power and destiny of the British people. The narrative is indirect and catches the reader in the subjunctive mode; Gibbon attacks no specific contemporary group of savages but implicates all of them past, present, and future. A story about the past, his story has implications for moral choices in the present. The reader fills in the details, interpellating himself in the pages of the story. Gibbon's terms merely foreshadow, through analogy, an impending collapse of the eighteenth-century global project, which influences the way we think about the very concept of security and predatory forces.

The savage nations of the globe are the common enemy of civilized society; and we may inquire with anxious curiosity whether Europe is still threatened with a repetition of those calamities, which formerly oppressed the arms and institutions of Rome. Perhaps the same reflections will illustrate the fall of that mighty empire and explain the probable causes of our actual security.

This imagery is echoed in contemporary use by the famous and moving speech of President George W. Bush on the evening of the September 11 terrorist attacks.

The pictures of airplanes flying into buildings, fires burning, huge structures collapsing, have filled us with disbelief, terrible sadness and a quiet, unyielding anger. These acts of mass murder were intended to frighten our nation into chaos and retreat. But they have failed. Our country is strong. A great people has been moved to defend a great nation.[8]

In Bush's excerpt, the threats are present and concrete. Unlike Gibbon, Bush speaks of a gathering predatory threat that confronts us today, demanding our vigilant opposition, and yet the moral logic of the Defense narrative is on clear display in both examples. Notice again the presence of violence, "fires," "structures collapsing," "mass murder." Again, we see unconventional and perhaps uncivilized means of violence, "airplanes flying into buildings," and showing how the Other fails to respect the rules of engagement. The motives are insidious, "intended to frighten us into chaos and retreat." On the opposite side of the story, expressions of hope suggest future victory of a "great people" a "great nation" who have engaged the predators with "quiet, unyielding anger," a subtle but meaningful contrast with Gibbon's "unrelenting rage." It is easy to mock these devices, but they are well deployed in the right moment, and they are the basis of the moral authority of the root narrative. Neither Gibbon nor Bush was stale or ineffective in his historical moment, and both can remain moving to those for whom the root narrative is a convincing and salient part of their narrative profile. George Bush hits the notes his audience wanted to hear in his song of social suffering, much like Gibbon had done in drafting his best seller—still in print—about the barbarian threats to empire. There are countless ways to tell the same kind of story that Gibbon and Bush tell in these examples, but the moral logic we see in these passages remains a constant.

Examples of stories structured by the Defense narrative are quite easy to find in history, and some are uncannily moving. We might have the cultural resources available today to dismiss Gibbon and Bush as narrow partisans merely rationalizing their colonial projects, but when the threat of insecurity assails you from an outsider you truly fear and despise, the moral logic of defense is a siren song hard to wax one's ears to. In our time, the prototypical Other is the Nazi movement and Adolph Hitler. Any number of recent examples of defense logic could be adduced from contemporary discourse in which we speak of "appeasement" and "Munich." We remain traumatized by World War II. But to get a full sense of the power of the moral grammar of this root narrative, we can find few better examples than Winston Churchill and his speech to Parliament on June 4, 1940, just ten days before the fall of Paris to Nazi troops.

> We are assured that novel methods will be adopted, and when we see the originality of malice, the ingenuity of aggression, which our enemy displays, we may certainly prepare ourselves for every kind of novel stratagem and every kind of brutal and treacherous manœuvre. I think that no idea is so outlandish that it should not be considered and viewed with a searching, but at the same time, I hope, with a steady eye… I have, myself, full confidence that if all do their duty, if nothing is neglected, and if the best arrangements are made, as they are being made, we shall prove ourselves once more able to defend our island home, … Even though large tracts of Europe and many old and famous States have fallen or may fall into the grip of the Gestapo and all the odious apparatus of Nazi rule, we shall not flag or fail. We shall go on to the end. We shall fight in France, we shall fight on the seas and oceans, we shall fight with growing confidence and growing strength in the air, we shall defend our island, whatever the cost may be. We shall fight on the beaches, we shall fight on the landing grounds, we shall fight in the fields and in the streets, we shall fight in the hills; we shall never surrender.[9]

How do we know that this is a defense story? I probably don't need to tell you how, but we see the formal elements here clearly enough. We could code this passage even if we had never heard of this war and knew nothing of the context. First there are obvious signals, "invasion," "defend our home," etc. The threat of violent death and submission goes without saying, and the threatening forces are uncivil and unbounded by the means of fair play: "novel methods will be adopted," "no idea is so outlandish," "novel stratagem." The motives of the enemy are also clear and dark, "brutal", "treacherous," "odious," displaying "malice" and "aggression." Like Bush, Churchill refers to the strength that the violence of the other produces in us, demonstrating the unity of the victim/hero element of the protagonist function. His repetition of his resolve to fight at the beginning of the closing sentences of the peroration have become one of the most famous examples of anaphora but work so well because they signal how the aggression of the Other has only made us strong. This is a critical part of the narrative's moral logic. Our moral force derives from the strength we generate together to fight and defend our home. This is why the concept of "duty" is also an important element of Defense narrative grammar. When the political community (imagined as it may be) is threatened by uncivilized and violent aggression, we have no choice but to commit ourselves to its defense—those who do not are cowards and ingrates. Churchill conveys this as if it were a fact of nature.

All of these elements taken together serve to make this one of the best examples of the form. Before passing from it, I would like to say a word about the root narrative approach to conflict data that marks it as different from George Lakoff's metaphor theory of moral politics. Where Lakoff would see elements of what he calls "strict father morality" in Churchill's speech, I see the moral logic of institutional critique. The Defense narrative and all its supporting elements, violence, barbarism, strength, duty might be described in Lakoff's terms, but their origin is not only in how the brain works through clustering metaphors, but how it works to use those metaphors in the face of the impending abuses of social power—the power of the Other to devastate with predatory violence. The Defense narrative is a rational reaction to a specific form of institutional threat. It is the threat that is posed by the military capabilities of an aggressive Other. If a political community truly does face such an adversary, the moral logic of the narrative is not only a vestige of an earlier way of thinking, but a sensible use of human reason. In other words, by exploring an institutional analysis of the Defense narrative, we see the origin of strict father morality in historical terms. We can see why some people adopt this version of a strict father morality and why it is so hard to convince them to abandon it. In a world filled with predatory foreign powers, we should expect the development of many strict fathers (and mothers). Dysfunction emerges when the story structure is applied to inappropriate cases. A Defense narrative solution that is applied to a Dignity narrative problem is likely to prove ineffective.

The threat of the foreigner, the outsider and the Other is a structuring element of the ethic of defense. It is always there, if occasionally implicit. Root narratives seldom stand alone, blending and building on other ethics in their pictures of the world. There are liberal, consensual and individualized forms of the idiom. Indeed, Hobbes's version of the defense narrative was highly individualistic and had no explicit conception of nation to define it, relying instead on the general problem of privatized violence for personal safety. But there is a way in which the securitarian imagination naturally inclines to the needs of the nation over those of the individual, leveraging the existential threat to usurp private rights.

Powerful as they were in context, these excerpts from Gibbon, Bush, and Churchill are not the only way that the Defense narrative presents in empirical data. Often, the interpretive and moral elements are buried in technical accounts within the scholarly arguments of authors purportedly committed to value neutral explanations and predictions. Consider this infamous passage from Samuel Huntington's "Clash of Civilizations" article in Foreign Affairs magazine.

> In Eurasia the great historic fault lines between civilizations are once more aflame. This is particularly true along the boundaries of the crescent-shaped Islamic bloc of nations from the bulge of Africa to central Asia. Violence also occurs between Muslims, on the one hand, and Orthodox Serbs in the Balkans, Jews in Israel, Hindus in India, Buddhists in Burma and Catholics in the Philippines. Islam has bloody borders.[10]

Unlike both Gibbon, who was writing with color and panache for a less cautious audience than is typical for American political science writing, or Bush and Churchill, who were preparing to react to unthinkable foreign policy disasters,

Huntington's article is written in a dispassionate and largely technical style. A great majority of it has no codable content, which is to say that it would be hard to claim that those passages were written in the spirit of one of the twelve moral grammars of Root Narrative Theory. Nevertheless, this one passage does have such content, betraying the securitarian mindset and the steering value of the Defense narrative so that the whole article appears in a different light, which is the very reason we remember it so well. This is typical of technical arguments. The value commitments that drive the research questions behind the technical answers tend to be buried in dispassionate prose, ensconced in the introductions, discussions, and conclusions of scholarly arguments.

This passage in Huntington's article was so powerful precisely because it reframed the technical logic of the preceding arguments (the empirical warrant for belief) in terms of the moral logic of the Defense narrative. It put the technical analysis into context. This repositioning of his analysis, projecting into the space of the Defense narrative, was far more powerful than if he had simply ranted about the threat and lingering evil posed by Muslim nations. Restraint is a key element of the scholarly form, which signals care and seriousness. Because his story did not feel emotionally charged and unfair critics and fans alike responded to his story as something important, but they never forgot his well-placed literary sorties: "crescent-shaped," "bulge of Africa," "bloody borders."

The point is not to demonstrate that Huntington was a writer dominated by security concerns, that is clear enough, but that even the most technical accounts are only intelligible and interesting because they participate in the context of moral conversation. They bring left and right brain together. It is hard to portray a careful thinker like Huntington in the perpetual thrall of his moral emotions. His arguments surely draw on his moral intuitions, but over the course of a lifetime of disciplined reasoning, the cold moral logic of claims begins to overwhelm the hot cognitions of the moment. Narrative form dominates and channels emotion to its own ends. For Huntington, as for all of us who write about politics and peace, our technical accounts are only intelligible when situated in relation to a root narrative structure, which puts such accounts in moral context.

Even our most technical and scholarly accounts are meaningful if and only if we can somehow hook them onto social values, and social values cannot be separated from the history of social power and our interpretations of it. We can only decide why we should care about technical arguments by situating them in the space of justice, relative to a moral grammar, and this is only possible in the narrative mode. Empirical social science provides us with empirical warrants for adhering to our beliefs, but the choice of moral grammar provides just as important a moral warrant, where values and reflective judgment drive the process of reasoning. The bottom line is that even the most technical arguments of social science can be described in terms of their root narrative structure. The structure supplies them with their reason for being, with their meaning. In this sense, social science theories (even those told by the most gimlet-eyed economist) are simply more complicated and less emotional stories about the adverse effects of social power. All politics is moral politics. We can see this clearly in Ken Waltz's famous *International Theory of Politics*:

> The state among states, it is often said, conducts its affairs in the brooding shadow of violence. Because some states may at any time use force, all states must be prepared to do so—or live at the mercy of their militarily more vigorous neighbors. Among states, the state of nature is a state of war. This is meant not in the sense that war constantly occurs but in the sense that, with each state deciding for itself whether or not to use force, war may at any time break out. Whether in the family, the community, or the world at large, contact without at least occasional conflict is inconceivable; and the hope that in the absence of an agent to manage or to manipulate conflicting parties the use of force will always be avoided cannot be realistically entertained. Among men as among states, anarchy, or the absence of government, is associated with the occurrence of violence.[11]

> (p. 102)

Even in Waltz's realist account, we see values on clear display. Because other "states may at any time use force" against us, we need to be prepared to use force too. Why? Because if we are not prepared we will be at their mercy. Why is this a bad thing? Because it just is bad and you know it, too. He doesn't have to explain because it is so obvious. The abuse of power need not even be stated. We have already read about it in Gibbon. This is where the story lands at what Richard Rorty called its "final vocabulary," where it hits bottom and can go no deeper.[12] Waltz's theory of international politics is an abstract account of how the world works, but it works according to the logic of the Defense narrative. We don't question why we do not want to "live at the mercy" of the Other. We simply don't want to and that's that. The very possibility casts us under "the brooding shadow of violence."

I think of this point—the values basis of international relations realism—as among the most important of the book, because the international relations realists, like Kenneth Waltz, are important examples of how moral reasoning transitions from fast, superficial, and intuitive modes into slow, thorough, and reasoned ones. It would be hard to find a more disciplined and abstract thinker than Kenneth Waltz, but even his ideas are predicated on the moral intuitions guided by narrative structure. All of his theories are built with this narrative toolkit, not directly on emotional foundations. We don't know how he came to his conclusions about his premises, but we can assume that he stuck with them after decades of careful reflection on the subject. It wasn't all post hoc rationalization after an emotional outburst.

Waltz didn't invent his premises, he stood on the shoulders of giants, and the most important of Waltz's giants was Thomas Hobbes and his analysis of vulnerability under structural conditions of anarchy. In the preface to the 2001 edition of his 1959 classic *Man, The State, and War*, Waltz wrote:

> Moreover, conflict is shown to lie less in the nature of men or of states and more in the nature of social activity. Conflict is a by-product of competition and of efforts to cooperate. In a self-help system, with conflict to be expected, states have to be concerned with the means required to sustain and protect themselves. The closer the competition, the more strongly states seek relative gains rather than absolute ones.[13]

There is little sign of moral emotion in this argument and we are apt to mistake it for a merely technical statement, even though it offers a moral prescription as clear as any we might find in a highly emotional speech like Churchill's that we saw above. The critical hinge is the line "states have to be concerned with the means." This is a prescription for action. On what is it based? A settled horror of the alternatives to self-help, i.e. military devastation and pleas for mercy.

The moral foundations of our political judgements are therefore not the emotions themselves, but rather the emotionally laden symbols that have been activated by the world's greatest political storytellers. Another way to say this is that the moral foundations of our political views are structured by root narratives, which provide us with the templates for the stories we tell when we stand on the shoulders of giants like Hobbes, Locke, Marx, and Fanon (or Kenneth Waltz, Milton Friedman, John Kenneth Galbraith, and Gunnar Myrdal). Their moral reasoning has become our moral intuition.

> Practical men who believe themselves to be quite exempt from any intellectual influence, are usually the slaves of some defunct economist. Madmen in authority, who hear voices in the air, are distilling their frenzy from some academic scribbler of a few years back.[14]

The philosopher, theologian and economist and political scientist, among others, have provided us with our "voices in the air," which appear to us as our own and private conscience, as the emotional connections for our rational arguments. Any of you still tempted to rely primarily on social intuitionist theory to code for moral content in documents should at least accept that Haidt seems to have been influenced by voices in the air himself in generating his liberty code. The biological assertions in favor of liberty as a moral foundation are much weaker than the others and he formulated it as a way to explain the rise of an active social movement, precisely when the libertarians, whom we will discuss below, were making a comeback in practical politics. But liberty is not a primal moral emotion, it is the evaluative component of a story structure defined in opposition to an institution we call government. True, in escalated conflicts, we are highly imbalanced and emotionally-biased narrators, but the fault, dear reader, is not in our glands but in our systems.[15]

The Unity narrative

The Defense narrative may be the most archaic source of political stories. It plays on our primal fears of violent death and our willingness to hand over our security to a strong man who would protect us. The Unity narrative is also central to the securitarian mindset, but it is of a very different character, and has to be approached with more care in analysis because it tends to emphasize attitudes that appear to many of us to be unambiguously good, even though there is as much potential for abuse of the perspective as there is of the Defense narrative.

We can represent the story structure of the Unity narrative with the sentence, *Elites use bargaining power to create physical deprivation in the State.* The protagonist function is the same as it is for the Defense narrative, but the antagonist function has changed. Now the threat to our material well-being is the clout of elites within our own community. The antagonists are borrowed from the egalitarian imagination. An easy way to think about these villains in unitarian terms is as faction leaders causing mischief within the body politic. Where the Defense narrative posits enemies around every corner and valorizes martial strength, the Unity narrative is very sensitive to dissent, promoting selflessness, commitment to a larger purpose, and duty to the political community.

Indeed, the presence of the word "community" may be the best indicator in conflict data that the communicator is employing the Unity narrative. Community is the indicator that marks the protagonist victim/hero of the story. While there is significant overlap between the basic logic and imagery of the Defense narrative and what George Lakoff has called "strict father morality" the Unity narrative often emphasizes the appealing features of his "nurturant parent morality." Where the Defense narrative emphasizes the controlled use of violence, the Unity narrative demands that we remove its causes. Where defense encourages dominance, unity encourages understanding. Where defense thinking is often used to justify war, unity thinking is the most natural idiom through which to justify peace.

We can see the positive feeling often present in the Unity narrative in some famous examples from ancient and medieval European history. Cicero used the structure when he wrote, "There is no more sure tie between friends than when they are united in their objects and wishes.[16] St. Thomas Aquinas used the story structure when he wrote, "Now the welfare and safety of a multitude formed into a society lies in the preservation of its unity, which is called peace."[17] It is true that peace is the goal of the Unity narrative, but violent death remains its foil. This helps to explain why so many peace thinkers obsess about dark and chilling images. These are always somehow haunting the story. More than in any of the other eleven root narratives, the Unity narrative places the accent on the positive, on the protagonist and on hope, but the threat to unity is never forgotten and is easily disinterred. It is selfishness. Uncivil ambition. The lust for power. *Libido dominandi.* Even original sin. The ancient historian Thucydides captures this force in one of the most memorable passages of his story of civil war.

> Indeed it is generally the case that men are readier to call rogues clever than simpletons honest, and are as ashamed of being the second as they are proud of being the first. The cause of all these evils was the lust for power arising from greed and ambition; and from these passions proceeded the violence of parties once engaged in contention.[18]

And such is the character of the Unity narrative that as desirable and bright are the prospects of its object, there is something inherently unattainable about it, often inducing a nostalgia that is rarely present in the other root narratives as this passage from Genesis demonstrates.

> And the Lord God said, Behold, the man is become as one of us, to know good and evil: and now, lest he put forth his hand, and take also of the tree of life, and eat, and live for ever: Therefore the Lord God sent him forth from the garden of Eden, to till the ground from whence he was taken. So he drove out the man; and he placed at the east of the garden of Eden Cherubims, and a flaming sword which turned every way, to keep the way of the tree of life.

My chosen point of entry into the political varieties of Unitarian thinking are the speeches of Abraham Lincoln. Lincoln is so important for me because his example has always struck me as sort of a mystery, not the part he played as the great emancipator, freeing the African American slaves, but the role he played in support of the Union. Consider this famous letter that Lincoln wrote to Horace Greeley on August 22, 1862 in which he defended his decision not to free the slaves, which he would eventually do on January 1 of the following year.

> As to the policy I "seem to be pursuing" as you say, I have not meant to leave any one in doubt. I would save the Union. I would save it the shortest way under the Constitution. The sooner the national authority can be restored; the nearer the Union will be "the Union as it was." If there be those who would not save the Union, unless they could at the same time *save* slavery, I do not agree with them. If there be those who would not save the Union unless they could at the same time *destroy* slavery, I do not agree with them. My paramount object in this struggle *is* to save the Union, and is *not* either to save or to destroy slavery. If I could save the Union without freeing *any* slave I would do it, and if I could save it by freeing *all* the slaves I would do it; and if I could save it by freeing some and leaving others alone I would also do that. What I do about slavery, and the colored race, I do because I believe it helps to save the Union; and what I forbear, I forbear because I do *not* believe it would help to save the Union.[19]

This passage is certainly full of codable moral content, but what is the moral logic at work in it? Lincoln is rather clear that he is not considering the rights of the slaves as a group to justify his position (a Liberation narrative). In fact, this is a perfect example of how a writer pivots from one root narrative to another. Where Greeley had attacked Lincoln in an editorial to his New York Tribune expressing how many of his supporters were "sorely disappointed and deeply pained by the policy you seem to be pursuing with regard to the slaves of rebels," Lincoln makes it clear that whatever policy he might choose employs a different moral logic. He assails the threat to national security posed by the rival elites in the South.

What mattered to Lincoln was "the Union" not slavery—unity not libera- tion. Contrary to his critics, his policy draws its meaning from a securitarian not a dignitarian imaginary. This is part of what makes Lincoln less appealing to contemporary progressives than he once was. Traveling to visit the Antietam battlefield (the battle that gave Lincoln the conviction to risk emancipation) my wife (who was not born in the United States) asked me, "but why was the Union so important anyway? Why didn't he just let the South go and save himself the trouble?" As I thought about the problem, I had no good answer. Unlike Lincoln, I had not cultivated as deep a commitment to the Unity nar- rative as he had. The argument had always made sense to me intuitively, but when questioned about it directly, I was morally dumbfounded. Union was good because that defined the political community that I knew, America, but I had no good reasons for it as I did for fighting slavery and ethnic oppression. I suspect that I am not alone in this.

Although it is clear to many of us living today why it is morally unacceptable to enslave people on the basis of their race, it can be harder to argue why it is critical to preserve a specific political community, especially when it is not under current threat of dissolution. In fact, many people my age are more likely to be suspicious of unitarian thinking and its link to insidious illiberal agendas than they are to its inherent virtues. After Benedict Anderson it is harder to imagine nation as a natural community.

The threat posed by the Unity narrative becomes clear as we consider it in contrast to its defining alternative, the Consent narrative. Where unity stresses the duty of individuals to sacrifice for the whole, for the social body, consent demands that the social body respect its constituent parts, the real bodies. One of the great defenders of the Consent narrative in opposition to various forms of unitarian thinking was the philosopher Karl Popper. In his book *The Open Society and its Enemies*, written in 1945 after consultation with the economist and arch libertarian Friedrich Hayek, Popper launched an attack on the logic of collectivism and its "totalitarian ethics," which he blamed for the cataclysm of World War II.

> From the point of view of totalitarian ethics, from the point of view of col- lective utility, Plato's theory of justice is perfectly correct. To keep one's place is a virtue. It is that civil virtue which corresponds exactly to the military virtue of discipline.[20]

Popper assails the collectivist mentality at what he took to be its root, the anti- democratic worldview of the first philosopher, Plato and his founding unity story. This critique, though quite different in ideological focus from the Frankfurt School Marxists, Max Horkheimer and Theodore Adorno, who condemned the entire project of European modernity in their *Dialectic of Enlightenment*, [21] nevertheless shared its "a pox on both their houses" style. Popper would attack collectivism at the foundations of Western rationality to demonstrate how vital the liberal enter- prise truly was.

Plato had argued that society should be thought of as a single organism and that the best definition of justice involved each part of that body doing his duty to serve the interests of the whole. Put another way, Plato was *the* proto structural functionalist. As with most powerful stories, the narrative force of Plato's story is carried by the character of its villain, whose name was Thrasymachus, which could be translated to mean fierce fighter. Thrasymachus played the role in Plato's narrative of a person whose only moral position was individual self-interest. Unlike the similar arguments of modern political realists in international relations theory today, Thrasymachus's worldview cannot be readily described as securitarian in terms of the Defense narrative described above. Instead, his is a brutal kind of individualism, that of the tyrant much like the Prince that Machiavelli would envision almost two thousand years later. Using his clever storytelling skills, Plato develops his collectivist conception of moral order in contrast to the obviously partial perspective on justice that Thrasymachus put forward, captured in Thrasymachus's phrase "justice is the advantage of the stronger."

Popper's argument in *The Open Society* is important because it helps to demonstrate the differential nature of the two root narratives. Plato's collectivism (and the various anti-democratic systems that might derive from it) can only be fully understood against the contrast of an individualist worldview. The antagonist of the Unity narrative is borrowed from egalitarian thought, the primary contrast that demonstrates the potential abuses of individual liberty. The Unity and Consent narratives as roots for moral systems come into focus when the dysfunction of the one is contrasted with that of the other. Where Plato portrays individualism as disunity, in Popper's view, Plato's moral universe destroys the individual in defense of imaginary unity.

> For the cogs in the great clockwork of the state can show "virtue" in two ways. First, they must be fit for their task, by virtue of their size, shape, strength, etc.; and secondly, they must be fitted each into its right place and must retain that place. The first type of virtues, fitness for a specific task, will lead to a differentiation, in accordance with the specific task of the cog. Certain cogs will be virtuous, i.e. fit, only if they are ("by their nature") large; others if they are strong; and others if they are smooth. But the virtue of keeping to one's place will be common to all of them; and it will at the same time be a virtue of the whole: that of being properly fitted together—of being in harmony. To this universal virtue Plato gives the name "justice". This procedure is perfectly consistent and it is fully justified from the point of view of totalitarian morality. If the individual is nothing but a cog, then ethics is nothing but the study of how to fit him into the whole.[22]

(p. 103)

If Popper's read on Plato's philosophy is less than charitable, we should remember that moral politics plays out in real time, not in our memory of it. The fascist forces responsible for so much bloodshed and suffering in the Second World

War were only then being routed as Popper wrote. It was relatively easy to see any line of thinking they espoused as rotten to the core. And fascists were certainly unitarians. Consider how this Platonic imagery and the elements of the Unity narrative are on display in the writings of Julius Evola, one of the leading voices of right-wing extremism in Europe. In his *Revolt Against the Modern World*, published in 1934, he wrote:

> To remain limited by national characteristics in order to dominate on their basis other peoples or other lands is not possible other than through a temporary violence. A hand, as such, cannot pretend to dominate the other organs of the body; it can do so, however, by ceasing to be hand and by becoming soul, or in other words, by rising up again to an immaterial function that is able to unify and to direct the multiplicity of the particular bodily functions.[23]

(pp. 75–76)

And Evola's unitarian thinking, which would be powerful to anti-liberals after the war was in line with ideas that had given rise to it like Benito Mussolini's *The Doctrine of Fascism*. You might be tempted to recoil in horror when reading the following passage. Instead, try to look at it openly for the unitarian themes, perhaps even substituting the words justice or union for fascism.

> To Fascism the world is not this material world which appears on the surface in which man is an individual separated from all other men, standing by himself and subject to a natural law which instinctively impels him to lead a life of momentary and egoistic pleasure. In Fascism man is an individual who is the nation and the country. He is this by a moral law which embraces and binds individuals and generations in an established tradition and mission, a moral law which suppresses the instinct to lead a life confined to a brief cycle of pleasure in order, instead, to replace it within the orbit of duty in a superior conception of life.[24]

We have to remember, hard as it may be, that fascism was a form of moral politics. It had a moral logic to its appeals. Note how Mussolini derides the pettiness of individualistic pleasures and emphasizes the importance of duty rather than rights. These are standard securitarian themes. We see similar themes in the work of the philosopher Carl Schmitt, who was aligned with and sympathetic to the Nazi cause. He published the following lines in his *The Concept of the Political* published in 1932.

> As a polemical concept against such neutralizations and depoliticizations of important domains appears the total state, which potentially embraces every domain. This results in the identity of state and society. In such a state, therefore, everything is at least potentially political.[25]

Schmitt was extreme in his eradication of the individual and celebration of the "total state," but his thinking owes much to the Unity narrative. Indeed, Schmitt is remembered for his artful reframing of politics as an us vs. them contest for survival. Absolute unity in service of the Defense narrative.

We know where this version of collectivism led, and it is hard not to judge all possible versions of the Unity narrative against the fascist example as Popper has done, but the dangers of individualist thinking have been attacked just as often. If we take Plato's character, Thrasymachus, as an example of rampant individualism, an egoist untroubled by his privilege and unconcerned about potential abuses of it, the virtue of unity becomes again apparent. A good example is that point of the Republic in which Thrasymachus concedes to Socrates that his view of justice is in fact the definition of injustice.

> "Suppose a city, or an army, or pirates, or thieves, or any other group of people are jointly setting about some unjust venture. Do you think they'd be able to get anywhere if they treated one another unjustly?"
>
> "Of course not."
>
> "What if they didn't treat one another unjustly? Wouldn't they stand a much better chance?"
>
> "They certainly would."
>
> "Yes, because injustice, I imagine, Thrasymachus produces faction and hatred and fight among them, whereas justice produces cooperation and friendship, doesn't it?"
>
> "Let's say it does," he said. "I don't want to disagree with you."
>
> "Thank you, my friend. Now, another question. If it's the function of injustice to produce hatred wherever it goes, then when it makes its appearance among free men and slaves, won't it make them hate one another and quarrel with one another, and be incapable of any joint enterprise?"
>
> "Yes it will."[26]
>
> *(Plato, p. 32)*

This whole passage of dialogue, along with much of the surrounding material in it, could be coded as an example of the Unity narrative, which illustrates how creative and open ended this aspect of the securitarian mindset can be. There is an infinite number of ways to present the logic and, as with the other root narratives, it can be used with respect to an endless array of actual policy prescriptions or empirical events. The narrative form is flexible and adaptable to any context, and any and each of the twelve manifestations of the root narratives is a container large enough to explain entire worlds, all the while ignoring the implications of the others. We can clearly see what is wrong with Thrasymachus's argument, and we suspend our critique of fascism as we make our judgment. As with each of the root narratives, the Unity narrative is as powerfully liberating as it is ominous.

But if we are to be truly open to discovering the ethic of unity in conflict data, we also have to be attentive to the way it appears in arguments in favor of institutions other than the state, often in forms that are critical of state supremacy. Some of these expressions are not particularly deep in a philosophical sense, while touching us to the core in the spirit of the moment. Rodney King, a victim of Los Angeles police violence in 1992, is a powerful example, "People, I just want to say, you know, can we all get along? Can we get along?"[27] Unity in a nutshell.

Other examples are developed on the basis of more reflection and emotional distance. An example is the sustained philosophical sociology of Amitai Etzioni, who helped to push the development of the approach called communitarianism. Defending his perspective against critics who cast it in a negative light (often framed from a Consent narrative counterpoise), he argues:

> Community can be defined with reasonable precision. Community has two characteristics: first, a web of affect-laden relationships among a group of individuals, relationships that often crisscross and reinforce one another (as opposed to one-on-one or chain-like individual relationships); and second, a measure of commitment to a set of shared values, norms, and meanings, and a shared history and identity – in short, a particular culture.[28]

Not merely a social science perspective, Etzioni's philosophy is a clear example of how one can extend technical arguments into the moral domain; he shows in a detailed way how consent is counterpoised to unity. We learn how close this conception of community is to the larger perspective of securitarian thought in Etzioni's defense of communitarianism. In his *The Moral Dimension*, he engaged this tension head on.

> A responsive community is much more integrated than an aggregate of self-maximizing individuals; however, it is much less hierarchical and much less structured and "socializing" than an authoritarian community. We need to reject the Hobbesian notion that individuals must subordinate their basic rights as a prerequisite for security. Threats to security are not so high as to require that we all yield to the Leviathan to shield us. Nor can we build on the Lockean notion that all rights are vested in individuals, who may or may not wish to delegate some of these rights, on the basis of their deliberations, to a community. *Individuals and community are both completely essential, and hence have the same fundamental standing.* [29]

Much as predicted by Root Narrative Theory, Etzioni explores the deep structural contrast between Hobbesian and Lockean thinking siding with both even as he places a strong accent on the securitarian side of the ledger. He develops the meaning of community by placing it in contrast to notions of individual consent. His ideas develop in line with Greimasian logic, drawing their meaning from logical, semiotic contrasts. Etzioni's thought is developed at that precise intersection of critical thought that divides the securitarian and libertarian imaginations, developing his ideas in a non-reductionist way that respects both points of view in their essence. The way he navigates this contrast likely serves as part of an explanation for the prominence of his work. Etzioni makes our contrasting assumptions clear to us.

I would be remiss if I did not provide an example from a ubiquitous figure in the discussion of the balance between communitarian and individual values, Alexis de Tocqueville. Many of his statements and political claims, especially those that we tend to cite, fall into the unity category. Here is an example from his discussion of juries, which points out the danger of individual egoism (and in its sexism may also harken back to that famous passage in Genesis about the Garden of Eden):

> The jury teaches each man not to retreat from responsibility for his own actions; a manly disposition, without which there is no political virtue. It vests each citizen with a sort of magistracy; it makes all feel that they have duties to fulfill toward society and that they enter into its government. By forcing men to get involved in something other than their own affairs, it combats individual egoism, which is like the rust of societies.[30]

While we find none of the ominous threat of Julius Evola in this passage or even the apocalyptic grandeur of Abraham Lincoln, many of the characteristic elements of the Unity narrative are here: duty, responsibility, commitment and larger purpose. Like Etzioni we remember Tocqueville for his ability to master contrasting ideals. He demonstrates the value of unity by immersing himself in the logic of consent only to arrive at a devasting critique of individualism, thereby defining the value of unity in contrast. His arguments in *Democracy in America* reveal the inner logic of both ethics, just as they were coming into clear focus in the West.

Many authors today find it difficult to navigate these contrary positions, but Tocqueville provided a model that many Americans still consider to be the most profound commentary of American mores to this day. The natural tension between the two root narratives may supply us with the reason why. We also see this contrast on clear display in the sub-title of one of the most successful Tocquevillian books in recent memory by Robert Bellah and his colleagues, *Habits of the Heart*. The subtitle is "Individualism and Commitment in American Life." Here we see the keywords of the two root narratives contrasted to great effect. Bellah's morality speaks to us through the grammar of the Unity narrative.[31]

If the ethic of unity is present in the justifications of smaller and non-authoritarian communities of commitment, we can also see its logic in play to make sense of relationships in the international domain. There is no more natural idiom through which to speak about peace between nations. Among the three criteria that Alfred Nobel included in his will to specify the Nobel Peace Prize, the most decisive among the three was what he described as that part of the prize that would be given to "the person who shall have done the most or the best work for fraternity between nations." This "fraternity" to which he referred is straight out of the Unity narrative playbook.[32]

The perspective also made its way into the founding documents of the post-World War II world order, especially those having to do with the new institutions developed to govern the more inclusive global community. A good example is the preamble of the United Nations Charter.[33] As is typical of such documents, the structure of a preamble is rather prescribed, but Article II is almost entirely structured by the logic of the ethic of unity.

1. The Organization is based on the principle of the sovereign equality of all its Members.
2. All Members, in order to ensure to all of them the rights and benefits resulting from membership, shall fulfil in good faith the obligations assumed by them in accordance with the present Charter.
3. All Members shall settle their international disputes by peaceful means in such a manner that international peace and security, and justice, are not endangered.
4. All Members shall refrain in their international relations from the threat or use of force against the territorial integrity or political independence of any state, or in any other manner inconsistent with the Purposes of the United Nations.
5. All Members shall give the United Nations every assistance in any action it takes in accordance with the present Charter, and shall refrain from giving assistance to any state against which the United Nations is taking preventive or enforcement action.

We see indicators throughout: the sense of membership, the importance of duty and peaceful means, and the need to remain loyal to the whole. The preamble demonstrates how when it was necessary to imagine a new world order after World War II, it was the providence of the Unity narrative that guided and inspired the leadership, an extraordinarily common moral logic used in a wide variety of settings and to remarkably divergent ends.

To round out our discussion of the typical usages and natural appeals of the Unity narrative, I will end with a brief discussion of one of the most prominent positive examples of the Unity narrative from the Western corpus, which closely parallels Plato's admonishing of Thrasymachus. This is the collection of writings in favor of voting for the Constitution of the United States known as the Federalist Papers. The most famous in this regard is the Number 10, written by James Madison on November 23, 1783—the "mischiefs of faction" essay. It begins much as Plato's argument had developed with a clear demonstration of EVIL.

> Among the numerous advantages promised by a well-constructed Union, none deserves to be more accurately developed than its tendency to break and control the violence of faction. The friend of popular governments never finds himself so much alarmed for their character and fate, as when he contemplates their propensity to this dangerous vice. He will not fail, therefore, to set a due value on any plan which, without violating the principles to which he is

attached, provides a proper cure for it. The instability, injustice, and confusion introduced into the public councils, have, in truth, been the mortal diseases under which popular governments have everywhere perished; as they continue to be the favorite and fruitful topics from which the adversaries to liberty derive their most specious declamations.[34]

We are clearly in the presence of the Unity narrative. The antagonism that sets the narrative is on clear display here in the figure of "the violence of faction." It is a "dangerous vice" which is cause for "alarm" and "contemplation." It is a securitarian concern not unlike Plato's. Many great thinkers seem to gravitate to the notion of unity and the greatness of the community that arises from it.

This form of anti-factional, securitarian thinking has ever since been an important part of the American political tradition, even as the official ideology of the country is Lockean liberal. Again, Abraham Lincoln is one of the figures who places this contrast in more clear relief. As context for Lincoln's political Unitarianism in the letter in support of the Union cited above, consider another speech that captures this sort of crisis thinking more directly, the "Seventh of March Speech" by the Massachusetts Senator Daniel Webster.

Sir, I am ashamed to pursue this line of remark. I dislike it, I have an utter disgust for it. I would rather hear of natural blasts and mildews, war, pestilence, and famine, than to hear gentlemen talk of secession. To break up this great government! to dismember this glorious country! to astonish Europe with an act of folly such as Europe for two centuries has never beheld in any government or any people! No, Sir! no, Sir! There will be no secession! Gentlemen are not serious when they talk of secession.[35]

What is adversary? The prospect of secession. Disunity. Webster's remarks have none of the subtlety that are typical of the Federalist papers. The way this excerpt works is to highlight the Unity narrative in contrast with the Stability narrative discussed below. Webster would prefer to risk hazards that are usually considered even more vexing than the dissolution of unity, "war, pestilence, and famine" than to abandon unity. Put another way, the Unity narrative is explicitly more important to Webster than the Stability narrative. We see here the power of the root narrative and how it crowds out other ways of thinking, even as it recognizes them and uses them for dramatic effect.

Notably, this same speech is where Webster uses a line that will come to embody the ethic of unity in American political discourse, "I wish to speak to-day, not as a Massachusetts man, nor as a Northern man, but as an American." Echoes of this line reverberated over the centuries. Recall one of the most powerful political moments of the twenty-first century, when Barack Obama presented himself to the world in the 2004 Democratic National Convention keynote address, "There's not a black America and white America and Latino America and Asian America; there's the United States of America."[36] If we wonder why that speech catapulted an unknown state senator to the presidency four years later, we might ponder the narrative force of the Unity narrative and its ability to speak to pressing issues across the ages.

Unity in the face of racial division was as relevant in Obama's time as it was in Webster's, and the primary moral grammar that rendered interpretations of that division meaningful remained unity. As Lincoln put it in his first inaugural address on March 4, 1861.

> The mystic chords of memory, stretching from every battle-field, and patriot grave, to every living heart and hearthstone, all over this broad land, will yet swell the chorus of the Union, when again touched, as surely they will be, by the better angels of our nature.[37]

This is unity at its finest.

The Stability narrative

Securitarian thinking comes in three quite different varieties. We have already seen how dramatically different the Defense narrative can be from the Unity narrative. Where one stresses strength and power, military capacity and vigilant commitment to duty, the other stresses love and commitment, interdependence, roots, history and selflessness. The Stability narrative with its ethic of order is different from the other two, yet again. Its focus is the threat posed not so much by selfishness, but rather by interdependence itself, especially of the interdependence of the masses, which, if unregulated can lead to chaos, crime, disorder, and devastation. In this sense, it is the People themselves who are the antagonists in the Stability narrative, and it is the leader who can discipline them, as the paternal representative and embodiment of the collective, who serves as the protagonist. In its primitive form, the story is, "*majorities use biased folkways to create physical deprivation in the State.*" In the Stability narrative, the People—the commoners—behave as they always do, relying on tradition and sometimes outmoded folkways, leading to massive coordination problems and disaster; the leader—the shepherd—is the person who can break through these habits to produce order.

To get a sense of the historical depth of the appeal of the Stability narrative, consider this extended transcription from the Code of Hammurabi, inscribed in the eighteenth century BC, taken from the early portion of the text.

> Hammurabi, the prince, called of Bel am I, *making riches and increase*, enriching Nippur and Dur-ilu beyond compare, sublime patron of E-kur; who *reestablished* Eridu and purified the worship of E-apsu; who conquered the four quarters of the world, made great the name of Babylon, rejoiced the heart of Marduk, his lord who daily pays his devotions in Saggil; the royal scion whom Sin made; who *enriched* Ur; the humble, the reverent, *who brings wealth to* Gish-shir-gal; the white king, heard of Shamash, the mighty, who again *laid*

the foundations of Sippara; who *clothed the gravestones* of Malkat with green; *who made* E-babbar *great*, which is like the heavens, the warrior who guarded Larsa and *renewed* E-babbar, with Shamash as his helper; the lord who *granted new life* to Uruk, who *brought plenteous water* to its inhabitants, raised the head of E-anna, and *perfected the beauty* of Anu and Nana; shield of the land, who *reunited the scattered inhabitants* of Isin; who *richly endowed* E-gal-mach; the protecting king of the city, brother of the god Zamama; who *firmly founded the farms* of Kish, crowned E-me-te-ursag with glory, *redoubled the great holy treasures* of Nana, *managed the temple* of Harsag-kalama; the grave of the enemy, whose help brought about the victory.[38]

How are we to render the moral grammar of this document? How does its author make meaningful statements about public affairs and moral politics? The overarching moral of these lines is something like, rulers are responsible for economic development and resource stability and paternal care of the people who live in their territories. I have highlighted those parts of the document that point to the moral politics of the Stability narrative in italics. Hammurabi speaks of "making riches and increase," and brags about having "reestablished Eridu," the sacred city. He "enriched" the city of Ur. He "clothed the gravestones." He "granted new life" to the city of Uruk, in part by bringing "plenteous water to its inhabitants." And so on, and so on. The Code also spends a great deal of its time in later sections on economic contracts and questions of family and household organization. It is a document written by a conqueror and defender of the people, but one who draws his legitimacy from his capacity to stabilize, organize and develop the material foundations of society, its economic life. Hammurabi was a general, but he portrays himself as a governor. He prides himself for having "brought about the well-being of the oppressed."

This is the final form of the securitarian worldview. It secures our material interests and prevents the mass of us from preying on the commons in a way that leads to disorder and anarchy. As the Athenian leader and poet Solon put it; "The winds stir up the sea. But when no wind agitates it, the sea is, of all things, most just."[39] The ethic of stability emerges for those who seek to balance the needs of the whole community against the disorganized actions of its many individual members. The *summum malum* of the perspective is anarchy and economic disaster. Its villains are impersonal forces of chaos and people who do not get with the program—the wayward children of paternal empire. Its great heroes are patriarchs, strongmen, humanitarians, traditionalists and innovators, organizers, and practical actors. Hammurabi celebrates his achievement in making Babylon great again. His is the securitarian face of economic development.

This ancient use of the Stability narrative is consistent with the Wittfogel Thesis presented in his book *Oriental Despotism*, first published in 1957. The book might better have been named *The Hydraulic Society* to avoid the ethnocentric assumptions that made his theory attractive then and suspect now, but it presents the Stability narrative in clear form. In an attempt to explain how the demands of large-scale water management projects (think of the river Nile) gave power to paternalistic governments in agricultural civilizations, Wittfogel reasoned that the demands associated with managing a vast productive resource like a water supply provided an opportunity for central authorities to concentrate political power in a way that could be justified as serving the well-being of the whole of the community.

> If irrigation farming depends on the effective handling of a major supply of water, the distinctive quality of water — its tendency to gather in bulk — becomes institutionally decisive. A large quantity of water can be channeled and kept within bounds only by the use of mass labor; and this mass labor must be coordinated, disciplined, and led. Thus a number of farmers eager to conquer arid lowlands and plains are forced to invoke the organizational devices which—on the basis of pre-machine technology—offer the one chance of success: they must work in co-operation with their fellows and subordinate themselves to a directing authority.... The majority of all hunters, fishermen, and rainfall farmers who preserved their traditional way of life were reduced to insignificance, if they were not completely annihilated.[40]

The core idea is simple; living with others poses risks that can arise from uncoordinated actions and these risks often provide those who can contain them with opportunities to justify their authority. As with the two prior presentations of the securitarian root narrative, this is a broad arena of political interpretation with innumerable points of connection to institutions and events. All of these points of articulation are knit together by the core imagery of threats to the basic human needs of the community: scarcity, famine and impoverishment. If the problem is economic insecurity, the solution is often economic organization. The solution is the Stability narrative. The point here is not to ascertain the validity of Wittfogel's thesis, but to classify it as an example of sophisticated storytelling in this mode. The people "subordinate themselves to a directing authority" on moral terms. There are both instrumental and ultimate considerations in play, but this is moral politics.

I begin the discussion of this root narrative with what might be thought of as a less than progressive example in order to help the reader to recognize the darker side of a moral perspective that will be quite appealing in other cases. The Stability narrative is often employed to justify caretaking for the poor, humanitarian interventions in the face of catastrophe, prosocial engagements in support of economic growth, and philanthropy in general. Tellingly, one of the most commonly used prosocial presentations of the Stability narrative is the concept of harmony. For all of the people to act in accordance with the collective as if they were all part of a larger ensemble of voices is perfectly consistent with the logic of stability. Of course, the use of the harmony concept in the Confucian tradition provides ample opportunities to recognize the Stability narrative in countless non-Western arguments.

> The Master said, the junzi acts in harmony with others but does not seek to be like them; the small man seeks to be like others and does not act in harmony.[41]

Although committed communities filled with gentlemen who act in harmony are very helpful supports for stability, there is no better guarantor than the big man, what Machiavelli called the Prince, and his power to order and stabilize the collective is among the most essential, if awful, of the powers that a human being can wield. To recognize a stability story, the analyst has to become sensitized to both the appealing and the atrocious presentations of the value system. There are many examples of both.

Let me hammer this point through with another excerpt from the philosopher Carl Schmitt, this time from his *Political Theology*. This book is famous for his concept he described as "the exception", a concept with which he opens that book, "sovereign is he who decides the exception" (p. 5). By the exception, Schmitt meant a general crisis under which the rules and laws that define daily life are necessarily suspended.

> The exception, which is not codified in the existing legal order, can at best be characterized as a case of extreme peril, a danger to the existence of the state, or the like. But it cannot be circumscribed factually and made to conform to a preformed law. It is precisely the exception that makes relevant the subject of sovereignty, that is, the whole question of sovereignty. The precise details of an emergency cannot be anticipated, nor can one spell out what may take place in such a case, especially when it is truly a matter of an extreme emergency and of how it is to be eliminated.[42]
>
> *(pp. 6–7)*

The paternalism of the Stability narrative can be jarring to many and is often a cause for pushback against it, but Schmitt taps directly into the strict father side of the moral grammar in a way that helps to explain why so many people over such long stretches of history have used the story structure to justify authoritarian rule. Stated in negative terms, the goal is to overcome the horrors of anarchy. Stated in positive terms, it is to enrich the people, protecting their physical bodies from harm and a father would do for a child.

What marks this story structure as distinct from the Defense narrative is that there is often no external enemy asserted or implied in the Stability narrative. The cause of the suffering is disorganization itself, perhaps just as the result of coordination or vision. Wherever we see calls for a strong leader, we can be confident that the Stability narrative is not far away.

Nowhere is this right-of-center appeal clearer than with respect to issues of crime and civil disorder. It is in this area that governments have deployed the Stability narrative as their claim to rule more than any other. and it is very common to see it used in relation to problems of crime. This is clear all over the world today, but is commonly indicated by references to the phrase "law and order," which is different in important ways from the Consent narrative indicated by the phrase "the rule of law."

If the phrase law and order is a clear indicator of the Stability narrative, no politician was better associated with it than President Richard Nixon, who made this phrase a centerpiece of his presidential campaign in 1968—so much so that it became a code word for racism. His speech to the Republican National Convention that year serves as a good illustration of the use of the Stability narrative in relation to the crime issue.

> As we look at America, we see cities enveloped in smoke and flame. We hear sirens in the night. We see Americans dying on distant battlefields abroad. We see Americans hating each other; fighting each other; killing each other at home. And as we see and hear these things, millions of Americans cry out in anguish. Did we come all this way for this?[43]

The durability of the root narrative in the area of crime crosses party lines and applies in almost any setting you might look for it. One good example of this is the 1994 Crime Bill signed that year by President Bill Clinton. In this signing speech, Clinton also deftly associates stability with a threat to freedom.

> If the American people do not feel safe on their streets, in their schools, in their homes, in their place of work and worship, then it is difficult to say that the American people are free.[44]

But the Stability narrative has many other uses that have little to do with crime itself. Far to the left of these law and order appeals, we can refer back to the work of the English economist, E.P. Thompson and how it can be applied to economic life as illustrated in his now classic study of bread riots in early modern England. There, Thompson argued that these "riots" should be thought of less as the spontaneous and mechanical reaction of a hungry population and more as an illustration of moral outrage; the masses agreed to obey insofar as the leader promised to secure their livelihoods and acted in good faith to do. Violations of the contract were cause for rebellion. This stability story is what defined the moral economy of the period.

> While this moral economy cannot be described as "political" in any advanced sense, nevertheless it cannot be described as unpolitical either, since it supposed definite, and passionately held, notions of the common weal – notions which, indeed, found some support in the paternalist tradition of the authorities; notions which the people re-echoed so loudly in their turn that the authorities were, in some measure, the prisoners of the people. Hence this moral economy impinged very generally upon eighteenth-century government and thought, and did not only intrude at moments of disturbance. The word "riot" is too small to encompass all this.[45]

There is little by way of the justification of authoritarian power here, but the excerpt and the concept of the moral economy Thompson develops are framed with the characteristic imagery of contemporary versions of the Stability narrative: peasants rioting to protect their rights to basic human needs, paternalistic leaders rushing to assure them of these rights, and an "unpolitical" politics that served as a motive for violent conflict. The logic of the ethical thinking that underpins the narrative category is simple, the people as a community should be protected from economic anarchy and famine. It is the sovereign's responsibility to prevent this, and he is only sovereign if he can do so. Such ideas are of great antiquity, we can see them already in the Old Testament as in this passage from Genesis 47:14.

> Wherefore shall we die before thine eyes, both we and our land? buy us and our land for bread, and we and our land will be servants unto Pharaoh: and give us seed, that we may live, and not die, that the land be not desolate.

Stability can result from paternalistic rule, but many other institutions and philosophies can be associated with it as well. One of the surprising advantages to using the logic of Root Narrative Theory to explore the meanings of ideas is that it helps to explain the peculiar genius of history's most riveting thinkers. On the one hand we have the radical specialists like Hobbes, Locke, Marx, and Fanon, who were able to take a trenchant insight in institutional abuse and spin it into a complete worldview. On the other hand, as we saw above with Alexis Tocqueville, there are thinkers whose insight is located at the intersection of two radical currents, explaining the value of one by taking the other into serious consideration—Tocqueville explained how modern individualism could only be sustained in an environment structured by community and commitment.

Adam Smith is a figure like that as well, drawing inspiration at the intersection of the Stability and Consent narratives. Smith was able to develop a conception of stability resulting from processes of unrestricted and self-interested exchange that demonstrated how the freedom of the masses (traditionally understood as a primal threat to resource stability) can ironically lead to stability, economic efficiency, and wealth on a scale never before imagined. Paradoxically, stability would be affirmed by a certain kind of anarchy: the liberty to "truck, barter, and exchange." In this sense, Smith is a philosopher of stability, even as he celebrates the new freedoms of the eighteenth-century enlightenment.

> As every individual, therefore, endeavours as much as he can both to employ his capital in the support of domestic industry, and so to direct that industry that its produce may be of the greatest value; every individual necessarily labours to render the annual revenue of the society as great as he can. He generally, indeed, neither intends to promote the public interest, nor knows how much he is promoting it. By preferring the support of domestic to that of foreign industry, he intends only his own security; and by directing that industry in such a manner as its produce may be of the greatest value, he

intends only his own gain, and he is in this, as in many other cases, led by an invisible hand to promote an end which was no part of his intention. Nor is it always the worse for the society that it was no part of it. By pursuing his own interest he frequently promotes that of the society more effectually than when he really intends to promote it.[46]

This spectacular intervention highlights a rather surprising feature of modern liberal society in which free markets and a laissez-faire approach to economic management by the state has become associated with the very notion of economic order: disorder as the foundation of order. Like Tocqueville, Smith is a master of paradox. Through a powerful effort of the ideological imagination, he helped to convince powerful actors that the forces of individual self-interest are themselves the best protection of the stability and growth of the public interest—the doctrine of the invisible hand thereby becomes a less than obvious example of the Stability narrative, one of the most surprising and counter-intuitive in Western literature. After Smith, countless conservatives and securitarians have learned to love this liberal idea.

Another famous example of the effects of individualism on resource stability points to market failure more than market success: that made by Garrett Hardin for *Science* magazine in 1968 called the "Tragedy of the Commons." Hardin's article became famous, in part, because it provided an argument built on the rational actor assumptions of neoclassical economic thought that appealed to the fears of leading thinkers at a time when soaring world population confronted many with existential anxiety. Population growth appeared to be a threat to economic stability on a global scale, an insight that owed more to Thomas Malthus and his gloomy projections about population explosion than to Adam Smith and his sanguine predictions about the virtues of a self-regulating market. Hardin tells a story about social peril in which collective resources, available space, clean air and water, etc., are at risk when left to the individual and unregulated choices of the masses. He tells a stability story.

The rational herdsman concludes that the only sensible course for him to pursue is to add another animal to his herd. And another; and another.... But this is the conclusion reached by each and every rational herdsman sharing a commons. Therein is the tragedy. Each man is locked into a system that compels him to increase his herd without limit—in a world that is limited. Ruin is the destination toward which all men rush, each pursuing his own best interest in a society that believes in the freedom of the commons. Freedom in a commons brings ruin to all.[47]

This Malthusian turn speaks to both the power and the flexibility of the Stability narrative. In this version, the rational actions of the uncoordinated masses lead to general ruin. The only solution to such a problem must come from outside or above. The general moral warrant for all of these economic claims derives from the ability of the storyteller to project an institution as capable of protecting a community from instability with respect to the necessary conditions of life. Because policies can be projected onto any story structure, economic theory becomes a securitarian battleground, often with libertarian and egalitarian overtones. The dismal science is only dismal insofar as it deals with basic human needs, which when unsecured lead to dire circumstances.

One of the best written and influential examples of the political versatility of the Stability narrative in the economic domain is the 1944 book by the Viennese economic historian, Karl Polanyi, *The Great Transformation*. [48] The book is a magisterial examination of the causes of the great wars of the twentieth century, placing the blame on what he called the "self-regulating economic system," directly challenging Adam Smith's stability story, in which unregulated markets were framed as the very sources of stability and growth.

As with many thinkers on the left, Polanyi's argument might be classified in many passages as more consistent with the egalitarian imagination than the securitarian, but the main thrust of his argument speaks to the social dislocations caused by market forces and the danger these pose to individual self-respect, community relations, national political stability, and even great power conflict. His arguments consistently point to the "catastrophe" brought about by the self-regulating market system. He identifies the catastrophe early in English history as the Tudor and Stuart kings attempted to protect the people from the emerging enclosure system that handed over common lands to private interests in order to increase the scale of production, boosting sales in distant markets.

> We recall our parallel between the ravages of the enclosures in English history and the social catastrophe which followed the Industrial Revolution. Improvements, we said, are, as a rule, bought at the price of social dislocation. If the rate of dislocation is too great, the community must succumb in the process. The Tudors and early Stuarts saved England from the fate of Spain by regulating the course of change so that it became bearable and its effects could be canalized into less destructive avenues.

Polanyi sees the development of the catastrophe again in the passage of an obscure law to protect labor from 1795 known as Speenhamland, which he argues contributed to the degradation of labor in England despite its bad intentions.

> Speenhamland precipitated a social catastrophe. We have become accustomed to discount the lurid presentations of early capitalism as "sob-stuff." For this there is no justification. The picture drawn by Harriet Martineau, the perfervid apostle of Poor Law Reform, coincides with that of the Chartist propagandists who were leading the outcry against the Poor Law Reform. The facts set out in the famous Report of the Commission on the Poor Law (1834), advocating the immediate repeal of the Speenhamland Law, could have served as the material for Dickens's campaign against the Commission's policy. Neither Charles

Kingsley nor Friedrich Engels, neither Blake nor Carlyle, was mistaken in believing that the very image of man had been defiled by some terrible catastrophe.

He then describes how the expansion of the market system, interacting with movements for social protection pushed the civilization of the nineteenth century to the collapse of the two world wars of the twentieth century. His use of the word "catastrophe" is a telling mark of his securitarian perspective.

From these two angles, then, we intend to outline the movement which shaped the social history of the nineteenth century. The one was given by the clash of the organizing principles of economic liberalism and social protection which led to deep-seated institutional strain; the other by the conflict of classes which, interacting with the first, turned crisis into catastrophe.

Finally, he makes it clear that the moral force and analytic power of his argument is quite different from that typical of Marxist interpretations, substituting the suffering caused by cultural degradation for economic exploitation.

Not economic exploitation, as often assumed, but the disintegration of the cultural environment of the victim is then the cause of the degradation. The economic process may, naturally, supply the vehicle of the destruction, and almost invariably economic inferiority will make the weaker yield, but the immediate cause of his undoing is not for that reason economic; it lies in the lethal injury to the institutions in which his social existence is embodied.

Progressive economics often tends to focus more on the vulnerabilities left open by economic organization than the opportunities that can be generated by it. On the left, scarcity conscious and a focus on adversity is a common feature of economic thinking.[49] A pointed example of how the Stability narrative can be adapted to novel economic adversities comes from the U.S. case and Franklin Delano Roosevelt's most important and enduring innovation, the signing of the Social Security Act on August 14, 1935.

Today a hope of many years' standing is in large part fulfilled. The civilization of the past hundred years, with its startling industrial changes, has tended more and more to make life insecure. Young people have come to wonder what would be their lot when they came to old age. The man with a job has wondered how long the job would last. This social security measure gives at least some protection to thirty millions of our citizens who will reap direct benefits through unemployment compensation, through old-age pensions and through increased services for the protection of children and the prevention of ill health. We can never insure one hundred percent of the population against one hundred percent of the hazards and vicissitudes of life, but we have tried

> to frame a law which will give some measure of protection to the average citizen and to his family against the loss of a job and against poverty-ridden old age.[50]

Did you ever wonder why this economic program was called Social Security? Why not something else like the Economic Equality Act? After all, that was an outcome it tended to produce. But Roosevelt made an argument for equality cast in terms of security. This was no accident for such a savvy political operator. Powerful as class-based arguments were in that era, Roosevelt knew that his strongest claim to legitimacy came from the perception that he could take action to fight the Great Depression brought on by the stock market crash of 1929. It was more important for him to be seen fighting disorder than for him to be seen fighting the rich. Therefore, it was rather natural for him and his allies to frame this landmark economic program in securitarian terms. In this line of thought, old age insurance—pensions for all working people—is good in that it protects an aging population from material want and physical suffering. Roosevelt thereby could represent himself as a kind father of the people much like Hammurabi had done. Nothing like a pension will produce that effect, and insofar as the appeal of the Republican Party rests on the foundation of security, the fact that Social Security was a program that was more about economic security than economic fairness made it hard for his critics ever to undo.

Given the securitarian foundation of his appeal, it should come as little surprise that Roosevelt was often vilified as a paternalistic tyrant who used the powers of government to capitalize on a crisis, but if FDR took securitarian liberties in the wake of the Great Depression, so did most of his predecessors to a greater or lesser degree. The following example from the Great Recession of 2008–2009 is an illustration of the Stability narrative that should remind us now of Carl Schmitt's "state of the exception," much as FDR's example had to those on the mid-century supporters of laissez-faire.

On September 7, 2008 as the banking system of the United States began to fall apart in response to the collapse of leading investment banks, the Secretary of the Treasury, Henry Paulson issued this memo, one that Schmitt would surely have interpreted as the emergence of the true sovereign in the period of crisis.

> The four steps we are announcing today are the result of detailed and thorough collaboration between FHFA, the U.S. Treasury, and the Federal Reserve. We examined all options available, and determined that this comprehensive and complementary set of actions best meets our three objectives of market stability, mortgage availability and taxpayer protection. Throughout this process we have been in close communication with the GSEs themselves. I have also consulted with Members of Congress from both parties and I appreciate their support as FHFA, the Federal Reserve and the Treasury have moved to address this difficult issue.[51]

I hope it is clear how consistent this language is with the Stability narrative. Paulson is taking action in the interest of "market stability, mortgage availability and taxpayer protection." He has collaborated with the relevant executive agencies to develop his plan, but the Members of Congress and the GSEs, the [Government Sponsored Enterprises] were merely consulted. As much as the tone of the document reflects calm and professionalism, it was the closest thing to the announcement of martial law—albeit a special and restricted form—that I can recall in modern American politics. Everything was in play in that moment of the exception and the Stability narrative was driving the innovators.

This state of exception to the stability generated by God's invisible hand was jarring enough that then President George W. Bush was forced just after the 2008 election to come to New York City's Federal Hall, the first capital of the nation, where George Washington had been sworn in as president, to speak in defense of the system on which stability in the modern world was founded: capitalism.

> The benefits of free market capitalism have been proven across time, geography, and culture. Around the world, free market capitalism has allowed once impoverished nations to develop large and prosperous economies. And here at home, free market capitalism is what transformed America from a rugged frontier to the greatest economic power in history.[52] November 14, 2008.

We should remember here the counterintuitive nature of Adam Smith's "invisible hand" stability story, which is intellectually fragile in that it projects stability onto a system of what amounts to ordered anarchy. To those outside the faith of free markets and the alchemy of the Scottish Enlightenment, it is far from obvious why government inaction would lead to greater economic stability. In 2008, this fragility was revealed as if for the first time. To hear George Bush advocate for the future viability of capitalism as if it were not a foregone conclusion was more jarring than any event I can remember in my lifetime, far more intellectually disorienting than the terrorist attacks of 9/11.

If free markets are an unlikely candidate to play the protagonist in a stability story, other familiar institutions are more so. Humanitarian causes are a natural fit for securitarian arguments and stability stories. I remember one example of this kind that was common as I came into political consciousness, the results of the famine in Ethiopia that took place in the early 1980s. Like most Americans raised in the 1970s I didn't know much about Africa and the various histories and internal privileges that defined it. I had little idea that Ethiopia was one of the wealthier and developed countries in the region. It was in no way obvious to me that the problem of famine could be exacerbated by civil war and human rights violations. I was therefore not ready to bring libertarian logic to bear in response to the crisis coverage. Instead, the most compelling way for me to think about the problems in Ethiopia—my way of seeing—was through the stability lens. The problem was one of resource stability that could be addressed by philanthropic action. The moral logic I applied to my thinking about Ethiopia was humanitarian, structured by the Stability narrative, not the paternalistic kind of stability supported by Hammurabi, but the kind that derives from a sense of shared responsibility for those who are in need because of disorders that might be beyond anyone's control.

Humanitarian causes are often framed as stability stories, which feel different from either defense or unity stories, even as they do much of the same work. The animating horror of a stability story is death, pain, and material want. The problem is to deploy resources in a coordinated way to help those who need them. Stability stories are about basic human needs. In most cases, a laissez faire approach is counterintuitive. Governments seem better positioned to intervene in a crisis. But in the international arena, there is no single state that has authority to play that stabilizing role. Into this gap stepped the non-governmental organization: the NGO.

We see this story embodied in countless humanitarian causes from The International Red Cross, to Doctors Without Borders, to the International Campaign to Ban Land Mines to the Intergovernmental Panel on Climate Change. The goal of each of these civil society organizations is to provide a coordinated and sensible approach to resource crises, caused by some kind of neglect, lack of leadership, or inappropriate use or distribution of resources. In none of these cases is the stabilizing force a government, per se, but the moral logic the organizations deploy remains the same; coordinated action is needed to protect human life. And once the moral logic is made flesh (in the form of an institution) it tends to perpetuate itself. This language from an Oxfam advertisement is a great example of what to look out for in humanitarian stability stories.

> The humanitarian situation is rapidly deteriorating. With the next rainy season already late in some areas, there are growing concerns that it will get much worse, driving communities deeper in crisis across the region. We cannot wait for these rains to fall. There is a small window of opportunity to avoid the worst and we must take action now. We urgently need to increase our humanitarian response to get food and clean water to those who are facing starvation.[53]

This is a stability story. There is no appeal to Pharaoh. There is no sovereign to step into the "state of the exception." But there is crisis, and the international non-governmental organization system has been developed as a way to address humanitarian crises outside the authority of the system of states. As in this example, philanthropy is a kind of syncretic blend of securitarian and libertarian impulses, but the security theme and its urgent sense of duty and self-sacrifice dominates.

There are so many uses of the Stability narrative in political life that it is hard to suggest that it fits with any clear ideology of the left or the right, but the inherent paternalism of the story structure marks it as an ultimately conservative way of thinking. Therefore, as a fitting cap to this discussion of the presentation of stability stories in the history of the European conversation, it is hard to do better than to look to the classic font of modern conservative thought, Edmund Burke's *Reflections on the Revolution in France*. There, Burke provides a mixed profile, as all authors do, that lurches between various forms of securitarian, and occasionally libertarian justifications, but his central focus is on the evils of instability posed by the French Revolution and its metaphysical attachment to the rights of man.

> The Assembly, their organ, presents them with the farce of *deliberation*— which is done with as little decency as liberty. They behave like actors before a riotous audience at a fair; they act amidst the tumultuous cries of a mixed mob of ferocious men and of women lost to shame, who... direct, control, applaud, explode them, and sometimes mix and take their scats among them, domineering over them with a strange mixture of servile petulance and proud, pre-sumptuous authority.... This assembly, which overthrows kings and kingdoms, doesn't even *look like* a grave legislative body.... Like the evil principle, they have a power to subvert and destroy, but none to construct anything except machines to create further subversion and destruction.[54]

Attacking the mode of thought of the revolutionaries, their hypocritical appeals to liberty, their mode of conduct, their pretensions, and their merely destructive critical attitudes, Burke invokes the muse of stability throughout his argument, and as children of the French Revolution, Burke is still speaking to us. As we remember Burke's warning, it is easy to understand why leaders in non-Western contexts might be wary of giving up on a securitarian mindset for liberal promises, fitting with the since-disputed story that when Premier Zhou Enlai was asked his opinion of the events of 1789, he replied "it's too soon to tell." As Burke reminds us, radical disagreement is often predicated on a clash between conservative fears and liberal aspirations, between the securitarian and the libertarian imaginations. It is to these, in their various incarnations, that we now turn.

Notes

1 Shelley, *The Works of Percy Bysshe Shelley in Verse and Prose*.
2 *The Bible*, Isaiah 25:4–5.
3 Radhakrishnan and Moore, *A Source Book in Indian Philosophy*.
4 Mayyasi, *Call to Virtue*.
5 Peters and Dias, "Shrugging Off Trump Scandals, Evangelicals Look to Rescue G.O.P."
6 Gibbon and Trevor-Roper, *The Decline and Fall of the Roman Empire, Volumes 1 to 6*.
7 Smith, *The Wealth of Nations*.
8 Bush, "Statement by the President in Address to the Nation."
9 Churchill, "We Shall Fight on the Beaches."
10 Huntington, "The Clash of Civilizations?"
11 Waltz, *Theory of International Politics*.
12 Rorty, *Contingency, Irony, and Solidarity*.
13 Waltz, *Man, the State and War*.
14 Keynes, *General Theory of Employment, Interest and Money*.

15 Haidt has been very clear that the liberty moral module is less well conceived than his others, and that he developed it because the Tea Party philosophy struck him as an anomaly. Haidt's caution is clear on his website MoralFoundations.org. Of course, from the perspective of Root Narrative Theory, the Tea Party and the statements of its members are less an anomaly than training data. The sad part about this example of inappropriate extrapolation is that less careful followers of Haidt simply include liberty among his list of moral emotions.
16 Douglas, *Forty Thousand Quotations, Prose and Poetical.*
17 Aquinas, *On Kingship.*
18 Thucydides, *History of the Peloponnesian War.*
19 Lincoln, "Abraham Lincoln Papers."
20 Popper et al., *The Open Society and Its Enemies.*
21 Horkheimer and Adorno, *Dialectic of Enlightenment.*
22 Popper et al., *The Open Society and Its Enemies.*
23 Evola, *Revolt against the Modern World.*
24 Mussolini, "The Political and Social Doctrine of Fascism."
25 Schmitt, *The Concept of the Political.*
26 Plato, *The Republic.*
27 "Rodney King."
28 Etzioni, "Communitarianism."
29 Etzioni, *The Moral Dimension.*
30 Tocqueville, *Democracy in America.*
31 Bellah et al., *Habits of the Heart.*
32 Nobel, "The Will of Alfred Nobel."
33 United Nations, "Preamble to the Charter of the United Nations."
34 Madison, "The Federalist No. 10."
35 Webster, "The Seventh of March Speech."
36 "Watch Barack Obama's 2004 Keynote Speech to Democratic National Convention | The Independent."
37 "Inaugural Addresses of the Presidents of the United States."
38 "Hammurabi."
39 Schurmann, *Broken Hegemonies.*
40 Wittfogel, *Oriental Despotism.*
41 Eno, "The Analects of Confucius."
42 Schmitt, *Political Theology.*
43 "Address Accepting the Presidential Nomination at the Republican National Convention in Miami Beach, Florida | The American Presidency Project."
44 "Making Communities Safer – William J. Clinton."
45 Thompson, "The Moral Economy of the English Crowd in the Eighteenth Century."
46 Smith, *The Wealth of Nations.*
47 Hardin, "The Tragedy of the Commons."
48 Polanyi, *The Great Transformation.*
49 Perlman, *A Theory of the Labor Movement.*
50 Roosevelt, "Statement on Signing the Social Security Act."
51 "Statement by Secretary Henry M. Paulson, Jr. on Treasury and Federal Housing Finance Agency Action to Protect Financial Markets and Taxpayers."
52 "George W. Bush: The President's Radio Address."
53 Oxfam, "Ethiopia Food Crisis."
54 Burke, *Reflections on the Revolution in France.*

Bibliography

"Address Accepting the Presidential Nomination at the Republican National Convention in Miami Beach, Florida | The American Presidency Project." Accessed August 7, 2019.

https://www.presidency.ucsb.edu/documents/address-accepting-the-presidential-nomina tion-the-republican-national-convention-miami.

Aquinas, Saint Thomas. *On Kingship: To the King of Cyprus.* Aeterna Press, 1982.

Bellah, Robert N., Richard Madsen, William M. Sullivan, Ann Swidler, and Steven M. Tipton. *Habits of the Heart: Individualism and Commitment in American Life.* Berkeley, CA: University of California Press, 1985.

The Bible, New International Version. London: Hodder & Stoughton, 2015.

Burke, Edmund. *Reflections on the Revolution in France, and on the Proceedings in Certain Societies in London Relative to That Event. In a Letter Intended to Have Been Sent to a Gentleman in Paris. / By the Right Honourable Edmund Burke.* Cambridge: Cambridge University Press, 2011.

Bush, George W. "Statement by the President in Address to the Nation." September 11, 2001. Washington, DC: The White House. Accessed July 17, 2018. https://georgew bush-whitehouse.archives.gov/news/releases/2001/09/20010911-16.html.

Churchill, Winston. "We Shall Fight on the Beaches." June 4, 1940. The International Churchill Society. https://winstonchurchill.org/resources/speeches/1940-the-fi nest-hour/we-shall-fight-on-the-beaches/.

Douglas, Charles Noel. *Forty Thousand Quotations, Prose and Poetical: Choice Extracts on History, Science, Philosophy, Religion, Literature, Etc. Selected from the Standard Authors of Ancient and Modern Times, Classified According to Subject.* Garden City, NY: Halcyon House, 1917.

Eno, Bob. "The Analects of Confucius," n.d., 159.

Etzioni, Amitai. "Communitarianism." In *The Encyclopedia of Political Thought,* 2014, 620–625.

Etzioni, Amitai. *The Moral Dimension: Toward a New Economics.* New York: The Free Press, 1988.

Evola, Julius. *Revolt against the Modern World.* Inner Traditions International Rochester, Vermont, 1995.

"George W. Bush: The President's Radio Address." Accessed July 18, 2018. http://www. presidency.ucsb.edu/ws/index.php?pid=84857.

Gibbon, Edward, and Hugh Trevor-Roper. *The Decline and Fall of the Roman Empire, Volumes 1 to 6.* Reprint edition. London: Everyman's Library, 2010.

"Hammurabi." Accessed July 18, 2018. https://history.hanover.edu/courses/excerpts/ 211ham.html.

Hardin, Garrett. "The Tragedy of the Commons." *Science* 162, no. 3859 (December 13, 1968): 1243–1248. https://doi.org/10.1126/science.162.3859.1243.

Horkheimer, Max, and Theodore W. Adorno. *Dialectic of Enlightenment.* New York: Continuum, 1989.

Huntington, Samuel P. "The Clash of Civilizations?" *Foreign Affairs* 72, no. 3 (1993): 22–49.

"Inaugural Addresses of the Presidents of the United States: from George Washington 1789 to George Bush 1989." Text. Accessed December 1, 2012. http://avalon.law.yale.edu/ 20th_century/froos2.asp.

Keynes, John Maynard. *General Theory of Employment, Interest and Money.* London: Penguin Books, 2016.

Lincoln, Abraham. "Abraham Lincoln Papers: Series 2. General Correspondence. 1858–1864: Abraham Lincoln to Horace Greeley, Friday, August 22, 1862." Clipping from Aug. 23, 1862*Daily National Intelligencer,* Washington, DC." Online text. Washington, DC: Library of Congress. Accessed July 17, 2018. https://www.loc.gov/resource/mal.4233400/?st=text.

Madison, James. "The Federalist No. 10", *The Federalist Papers,* November 23, 1787. Accessed July 17, 2018. http://web.csulb.edu/~jlawler/Course%20DW/Federalist_10.htm.

"Making Communities Safer – William J. Clinton." Accessed August 7, 2019. https:// www.clintonlibrary.gov/museum/permanentexhibits/communitiessafer/.

Mayyasi, Kim A. *Call to Virtue: Republics of Character from Rome to 1776*. Minneapolis: Hillcrest Publishing Group, 2016.

MoralFoundations.org. Accessed July 17, 2018. http://moralfoundations.org/.

Mussolini, Benito. "The Political and Social Doctrine of Fascism." *The Political Quarterly* 4, no. 3 (n.d.): 341–356. https://doi.org/10.1111/j.1467-923X.1933.tb02289.x.

Nobel, Alfred. "The Will of Alfred Nobel." November 27, 1895. *The Nobel Prize*. Accessed July 17, 2018. https://www.nobelprize.org/alfred_nobel/will.

Oxfam. "Ethiopia Food Crisis." Oxfam International. Accessed July 18, 2018. https://www.oxfam.org/en/emergencies/ethiopia-food-crisis.

Perlman, Selig. *A Theory of the Labor Movement: Reprint of 1928 Ed*. Macmillan, 1949.

Peters, Jeremy W., and Elizabeth Dias. "Shrugging Off Trump Scandals, Evangelicals Look to Rescue G.O.P." *The New York Times*, April 26, 2018, sec. U.S. https://www.nytimes.com/2018/04/24/us/politics/trump-evangelicals-midterm-elections.html.

Plato. *The Republic*. Cambridge: Cambridge University Press, 2000.

Polanyi, Karl. *The Great Transformation: The Political and Economic Origins of Our Time*. Boston: Beacon Press, 1944.

Popper, Karl R., Alan Ryan, and E. H. Gombrich. *The Open Society and Its Enemies: New One-Volume Edition*. With a new introduction by Alan Ryan and an essay by E. H. Gombrich. Princeton: Princeton University Press, 2013.

Radhakrishnan, Sarvepalli, and Charles A. Moore. *A Source Book in Indian Philosophy*. Princeton: Princeton University Press, 2014.

"Rodney King." *Wikiquote*. Accessed July 17, 2018. https://en.wikiquote.org/wiki/Rodney_King.

Roosevelt, Franklin D. "Statement on Signing the Social Security Act." Accessed July 18, 2018. http://www.presidency.ucsb.edu/ws/?pid=14916.

Rorty, Richard. *Contingency, Irony, and Solidarity*. Cambridge: Cambridge University Press, 1989.

Schmitt, Carl. *Political Theology: Four Chapters on the Concept of Sovereignty*. Chicago: University of Chicago Press, 1985.

Schmitt, Carl. *The Concept of the Political*. Chicago: University of Chicago Press, 1996.

Schurmann, Reiner. *Broken Hegemonies*. Indiana: Indiana University Press, 2003.

Shelley, Percy Bysshe. *The Works of Percy Bysshe Shelley in Verse and Prose, Now First Brought Together with Many Pieces Not Before Published*. Oxford: Reeves and Turner, 1880.

Smith, Adam. *The Wealth of Nations*. Edited by Edwin Cannan. 6th Printing edition. New York: Modern Library, 1994.

"Statement by Secretary Henry M. Paulson, Jr. on Treasury and Federal Housing Finance Agency Action to Protect Financial Markets and Taxpayers." Accessed July 18, 2018. https://www.treasury.gov/press-center/press-releases/Pages/hp1129.aspx.

Thompson, Edward P. "The Moral Economy of the English Crowd in the Eighteenth Century." *Past and Present* 50 (1971): 76–136.

Thucydides, "History of the Pelopponesian War." 431 BCE. Accessed July 20, 2018. http://www.wright.edu/~christopher.oldstone-moore/Thucydides.htm.

Tocqueville, Alexis de. *Democracy in America*. New York: Harper Perennial, 1966.

United Nations. "Preamble to the Charter of the United Nations." June 16, 2015. Geneva: United Nations. Accessed November 19, 2019. http://www.un.org/en/sections/un-charter/preamble/index.html.

Waltz, Kenneth N. *Man, the State and War*. New York: Columbia University Press, 1959.

Waltz, Kenneth N. *Theory of International Politics*. Illinois: Waveland Press, 2010.

"Watch Barack Obama's 2004 Keynote Speech to Democratic National Convention | The Independent." Accessed July 17, 2018. https://www.independent.co.uk/news/world/am

ericas/barack–obama–key–note–speech–democratic–national–conference–dnc–dreams–of–m
y–father–boston–us–a7520291.html.

Webster, Daniel. "The Seventh of March Speech." March 7, 1850. Dartmouth College
Archives. Accessed July 17, 2018. https://www.dartmouth.edu/~dwebster/speeches/
seventh–march.html.

Wittfogel, Karl A. *Oriental Despotism: A Comparative Study of Total Power*. New Haven: Yale
University Press, 1957.

6

IMAGINING LIBERTY

Consent, Property, Merit

The Consent narrative

The contrast between the securitarian and libertarian imaginations would be hard
to overstate. Representing the borderland between what we call the political right
and the political left, security is the primal value of those who support the state, the
strongman and stability and is supported by scenes of suffering and violence, death,
deprivation and destruction. Liberty valorizes the individual, human rights, and
respect for persons. No less motivated and defined in reaction to abusive power
than the securitarian, the libertarian locates the abuse in the awesome powers of the
state itself. Commitment to liberty is animated in opposition to torture, arbitrary
power, and the greed of kings and despots. In contrast to security, liberty can
appear to be an unrealistic ideal, but it speaks to the reality of power and the need
to check it just as clearly.

There is ample opportunity to become confused about the libertarian imagination,
muddling its popularity among people who now think of themselves as conservative
with its radical critique of conservative power. When speaking about the libertarian
root narratives, we always have to keep in mind that small "l" libertarians should not
be confused with the political party—the large "L" Libertarians, even though we are
so familiar with the Libertarian political party precisely because it places such unadulterated stress on the libertarian narrative. While Libertarians in a contemporary
context are seen as a branch of the political right, small "l" libertarians are the original leftists, in fact defining what it means to be a political liberal—a classical liberal.
Libertarians criticize and fear the power of kings, of churches, and of tradition itself.
The rational individual is their hero. Spurred to action by the fear of government
power, they celebrate the freedom of the individual as a repudiation of that power.
The worst thing that can happen to a libertarian is that his freedom of choice is taken
away, his natural rights. The idealism of the libertarian derives from her fascination

with these rights, constantly threatened by the paternalistic impulses of the securitarian state. This rights emphasis is so discursively powerful that it is good to keep in mind that whenever rights talk is present in conflict data, there is a good chance that one of the three libertarian root narratives is in play, perhaps unconsciously. The triumph of the libertarian imagination in our own times is such that each of the other three root narratives are only effective when they can align their moral projects with the discourse of rights, introducing heterodoxy and ideological confusion in our debates about universal human rights, collective duties and human rights are always placed in an awkward juxtaposition.

The best pithy epigraph for the libertarian or liberal mindset would be that American saying, "the best government is that which governs least."[1] Liberals define their moral politics against the excesses of government power, even as they accept that some measure of security is always necessary. The great champions of the libertarian imagination can wrap their ideals in radical statements that would appear absurd in securitarian discourse. Think of the philosopher John Stuart Mill who wrote, "the only purpose for which power can be rightfully exercised over any member of a civilized community, against his will, is to prevent harm to others."[2] Or the saying inspired by Voltaire, "I disapprove of what you say, but I will defend to the death your right to say it."[3] And surely the most famous of is Benjamin Franklin's, "Those who would give up essential Liberty, to purchase a little temporary Safety, deserve neither Liberty nor Safety."[4] In each case, the touchstone is the sanctity of individual conscience, consent, and choice over rival principles.

Consider the famous Franklin aphorism. He makes it clear that the values of security and liberty rest in a kind of tension (what I would describe as the experience of ideological orthogonality), and the power of this contrast tends to divide history into a simple, linear, and binary story. In this story, every ideal that can be placed against the mindset of the securitarian is a liberal ideal. In this view, liberty, equality, and dignity refer to the same thing. Republic and a democracy are synonyms. We tend to take the critique of the securitarian state as a package and ignore the subtle distinctions that point out problems with different forms of social power within the political community. Root Narrative Theory helps us to see what is wrong with that.

Republican ideas are those that stress the rights of the Individual as contrasted with the State. Democratic stories tend to focus less on the individual and more on the People, conceived as an objective entity. Libertarian principles produce a different form of moral politics and a different self-concept than do securitarian ones. Dignity in liberty stories is not a function of group membership or the history of prior oppression, it is a feature of being a rational human being, as the philosopher Immanuel Kant described it, the idea of the rational being that obeys no law except that which at the same time it gives itself.[5]

The great early champion of these ideas in both their republican and democratic inflections (and one of the first to blur them) was Thomas Jefferson, and he remains one of the best examples of the Libertarian value system, despite the complexities of his personal life and ironic relations to the institution of slavery. The Jefferson who was lionized in nineteenth century America was Jefferson the libertarian icon more than the man. His texts helped to established the salience of the Consent narrative in the United States as much as any other author in history, and there is no better place to turn for illustration than the Declaration of Independence of the United States. Try to read these lines as if you have never heard them:

> We hold these truths to be self-evident, that all men are created equal, that they are endowed by their Creator with certain unalienable Rights, that among these are Life, Liberty and the pursuit of Happiness.—That to secure these rights, Governments are instituted among Men, deriving their just powers from the consent of the governed,—That whenever any Form of Government becomes destructive of these ends, it is the Right of the People to alter or to abolish it, and to institute new Government, laying its foundation on such principles and organizing its powers in such form, as to them shall seem most likely to effect their Safety and Happiness.[6]

This is a perfect illustration of the essential features of the Consent narrative. It is so familiar that it comes off as little more than cant, but it is so well remembered because it is such a compelling master narrative. If these lines were written today by some unknown political theorist, several aspects of the passage would serve as clear indicators of consent. First is the focus on unalienable rights. As stated above, rights talk is always a sign that the Consent narrative may be in play in any given passage, although its presence is never enough to make a clear identification. It is extremely common to see authors refer to rights that have less to do with individual freedom with respect to government coercion and more to do with duties and obligations and entitlements of various kinds, especially in cases in which the author invokes social and economic rights. These usually draw on other linguistic resources and root narrative models. More distinctive here is the specification of the antagonism driving the conflict, a government that "becomes destructive." It is institutional dysfunction that Jefferson identifies as the problem, and his proposal for separation from the British government is projected into this scene of abuse. Jefferson's consent story is quite different from that which President Ronald Reagan would offer in his inaugural address of 1981—"government is not the solution to our problem; government is the problem"[7]—but it draws on the same root narrative, the Lockean formulation of the Consent narrative that justifies revolution when the principle of "the consent of governed" is violated. It is Jefferson's moral logic. In this, both Jefferson and Reagan participate in a common rhetorical tradition, itself defined by the structure of relations among the paradigmatic forms of social power, and they are not alone.

Lest we become dismissive of the Consent narrative for its associations with the right wing of American political culture, we should remember how the plastic relations between issues and narrative can lead to surprising relations among thinkers. As with the securitarian narratives, consent, with its fear of government abuses, can be extended to wide varieties of political objectives. Consider this passage from the radical proponent of non-violent social action, Gene Sharp.

> The oft quoted phrase "Freedom is not free" is true. No outside force is coming to give oppressed people the freedom they so much want. People will have to learn how to take that freedom themselves. Easy it cannot be.[8]
>
> *(p. 123)*

Although we might be tempted to associate Sharp here more with Yoda than with Jefferson based on his choice of word order, few people would associate the work and objectives of Gene Sharp and Ronald Reagan. And yet their arguments are part of a larger family of political stories that defines itself against a certain kind of opponent: dictatorial and abusive government power or the means of administration. Most empirical accounts draw on an eclectic pattern of root narrative usage, and Reagan's and Sharp's arguments, overall, would present themselves quite differently, but they did both work heavily in the rhetorical domain of consent.

Among the most accessible histories of the development of the Consent narrative in the West is Lynn Hunt's *Inventing Human Rights*. [9] Hunt's story traces the development of the concept of human rights as a kind of emotional performance, peaking in intensity in the latter part of the eighteenth-century. Her story speaks of the importance of novels, empathy and self-evidence, and the gist of her account is consistent with the *summum malum* test of Root Narrative Theory, "we are certain that a human right is at issue when we feel horrified by its violation" (p. 26). Hunt's analysis is particularly important for illustrating the logic of this root narrative as we often encounter it today, in opposition to cruel punishments enacted by the state, that is in opposition to torture. She explains how it was that Voltaire picked up from the Italian, Cesare Beccaria, an aversion to the abuses of state power represented by corporal punishment and torture in its various forms.

> Beccaria helped valorize the new language of sentiment. For him, the death penalty could only be "pernicious to society from the example of barbarity that it affords," and when objecting to "torments and useless cruelty" in punishment, he derided them as "the instrument of furious fanaticism."
>
> *(p. 81)*

Hunt's discussion invariably brings to mind the gruesome opening pages of Michel Foucault's *Discipline and Punish* in which the account of the torture of the attempted regicide Damiens is described in minute detail.[10] Torture was simply a feature of state power in the era.

For Hunt, the very self-evidence of rights, and the sanctity attributed to the individual person, should be understood against the background of revulsion against a form of social power understood to be abusive. She writes:

> Torture ended because the traditional framework of pain and personhood fell apart, to be replaced, bit by bit, by a new framework, in which individuals owned their bodies, had rights to their separateness and to bodily inviolability, and recognized in other people the same passions, sentiments, and sympathies as in themselves.
>
> *(p. 112)*

Another example of the versatility of the Consent narrative comes from the American Civil Rights movement. Consider Gunnar Myrdal's great classic on American race relations, *The American Dilemma*, published in 1944 (explaining why he used the word Negro instead of another term).

> Negroes are arrested and sentenced for all sorts of actual or alleged breaks of the caste rules, sometimes even for incidents where it is clear that their only offense was to resist a white person's unlawful aggression. As this practice is against the formal rules of due process, and as, further, the social customs sanctioned in this way are themselves often directly contrary to the law, there is a strange atmosphere of consistent illegality around the activity of the officers of the peace and the whole judicial system in the South.[11]
>
> *(p. 536)*

There is little question that this passage is dominated by the moral premises of the dignitarian root narrative ("social customs" are presented as "contrary to law"), but the elements of the ethics of consent are here as well. The use of the phrase "unlawful aggression" speaks to the centrality of "the rule of law" for Myrdal's argument. He argues that the racist actions of the police do not fit with "the formal rules of due process." Due process is as consistent a policy to derive from the Consent narrative as one can imagine. It is about a check on the administrator's power by virtue of transparent legal process. Finally, his reference to "a strange atmosphere of consistent illegality" that impugns "the whole judicial system" is rhetorical leverage for Myrdal as he inveighs against the unjustifiable practices of the police that is designed to appeal to the Lockean liberal American reader. This tension and contrast between one form of moral appeal, one that acts to check the abusive powers of a superordinate caste, and another, which is directed against the institutional powers of the government is central to Myrdal's project to expose the "inconsistency which lurks in the basement of man's soul" (p. 61). The ethic of consent and its centrality to what he called "the American Creed" is the ground on which Myrdal hoped to shame white Americans from their supremacy. By borrowing energy from the Consent narrative, he hoped to inspire a dignitarian movement that would prove consistent with the irrational Lockeanism of public opinion in the United States. This is advanced conflict resolution practice.

The Lockean liberal values that would prove so useful the dignitarian agenda of thinkers like Myrdal and Dr. Martin Luther King were not developed as a critique of a caste system. They were developed as a critique of the destructive power of protective state, even if they could be used as arguments in support of the liberal rights of certain targeted categories. Liberals, more than anything else, wanted to be protected from the protector, recognizing that the other side of policing is military conquest. Max Weber, who among other things taught us how to distrust bureaucracy as the institution of political coercion, describes this process in his essay "Politics as a Vocation," itself a sophisticated example of a consent story.

> Everywhere the development of the modern state is initiated through the action of the prince. He paves the way for the expropriation of the autonomous and "private" bearers of executive power who stand beside him, of those who in their own right possess the means of administration, warfare, and financial organization, as well as politically usable goods of all sorts. The whole process is a complete parallel to the development of the capitalist enterprise through gradual expropriation of the independent producers. In the end, the modern state controls the total means of political organization, which actually come together under a single head.[12]

The demands of self-defense make it possible to use the dreadful power of military conquest to concentrate political power in structures that enable widespread coercion of the citizen as much as the alien. Opposition to this coercive power, "the concentration of the means of administration" in Weber's phrase, is the essence of the Consent narrative and the defining root narrative of the libertarian imagination. This is an important point; the solution to the problem of predatory intercommunal violence and divisive partisan criminality, the Hobbesian state, is the very source of the dysfunction and abuse for the Lockean liberal. One person's function is another's dysfunction.

Benjamin Constant was a prominent French writer from the early nineteenth century, active in the period after the French Revolution. His perspective on the abusive power of military forces once they have secured the field demonstrates the threat posed by the unifying power of a military undisciplined by civil constraints like due process and the rule of law, made toxic in its pivot from conquest to governance precisely because of the securitarian worldview of its members.

To make sense of Constant, we have to remember that he was developing his political ideas in the period after the French Revolution, the rise and fall of Napoleon, and the restoration of the French monarchy. As he described it, "at the time when it [*Political Writings*] was written, the continent was a vast prison." It is tempting to excerpt every section of Constant's *Political Writings* as illustration of the ethic of consent and its relationship to abusive institutional power, but two will suffice, the first drawn from his argument about military culture and its effect on the citizenry and the second from his discussion about how conquest leads to the pursuit of uniformity in all things.[13]

> To them [the army] the unarmed class appears vulgar and ignoble, laws are superfluous subtleties, the forms of social life just so many insupportable delays.

What they value above all, in social transactions as in military exploits, is the speed of manoeuvre. Unanimity seems to them as necessary as it is for troops to wear the same uniform. Opposition, for them, is disorder; reasoning insubordination, the courts councils of war, the judges soldiers under orders, the accused enemies and the trials battles.

(p. 61)

Many of the signal elements of the Consent narrative are on display here. There is a defense of law, subtlety, the independent pace of social life, deliberation (critical to due process), diversity of opinion and style, courts, reason and the sanctity of the potential for disagreement. This second except drives the point home.

The conquerors of our days, whether peoples or princes, wish their empire to present an appearance of uniformity, upon which the proud eye of power may travel without meeting any unevenness that could offend or limit its view… It is a pity that one cannot destroy all the towns to rebuild them according to the same plan, and level all the mountains to make the ground even everywhere. I am surprised that all the inhabitants have not been ordered to wear the same costume, so that the master may no longer encounter irregular colours and shocking variety.

(p. 73)

Again, we can easily recognize the critical indicators of the Consent narrative in this excerpt. Here the main EVIL is the specter of uniformity. The passage explains itself through parody, the kind brought on by an experience of The Terror of the 1790s and Napoleon's court. Looking ahead to the revolutions of the twentieth-century, Constant's mocking predictions look more like prescience.

Root narratives are not only useful for the wise and the just, they provide everyone, the privileged and the vicious included, with source material for justification of whatever policy they may happen to advocate. A good example is the novelist Ayn Rand, who pioneered a philosophy she called objectivism, which has been an inspiration to generations of young white men in the West, rivalled perhaps only by a simplistic reading of Nietzsche's philosophy. Whatever the merits of Rand's elitist approach to creative individualism, her success depended heavily on the appeal of the Consent narrative in American political culture.

In Rand's novel, *Atlas Shrugged*, the individual is thoroughly celebrated.[14] The commercial world that Constant thought so superior to the military's usurpation, restlessness, and uniformity is Rand's heroic setting. Not all business people are heroes, but only business people seem to matter at all. There are great ones who embrace diligence and virtue and bad ones who do not. The mass of the people are consumers of values, much like the more recent rhetoric of "job creators" versus other people implies. In Rand's iconography, most of the people fail to engage life as it is and therefore merely follow and gripe, but a few great men and women take on their actual responsibilities, like her protagonist John Galt, creating a world full of value and opportunity. Rand, despite the care she takes to avoid caricature, can't help at a powerful turning point in her novel but to reveal the true villains of the story, people like the "professor of sociology" who in his zeal for the collective fails to recognize the motive force of history: the individual.

> The man in Bedroom A, Car No. 1, was a professor of sociology who taught that individual ability is of no consequence, that individual effort is futile, that an individual conscience is a useless luxury, that there is no individual mind or character or achievement, that everything is achieved collectively, and that it's masses that count, not men.

In the novel, this professor and many others with equally pernicious views (when viewed from the vantage of the Consent narrative) were sent to their deaths as a result of their failure to embrace the responsibility for life that had been thrust upon them. They failed to live according to the individualist's dispensation and suffered appropriately for it. Whatever you think of Rand, you can explain the consistency of her worldview with Root Narrative Theory.

If Ayn Rand's worldview presents the Consent narrative as something of a caricature, radical libertarian views similar to hers have taken on a more profound cast. A telling example is the transformative work of popular economics, Friedrich Hayek's *Road to Serfdom*, published in 1944.[15] In the following example, he both articulates the critical values of liberalism and attacks what he regards as the collectivist vandalism that confronts it.

> It is true that the virtues which are less esteemed and practiced now—independence, self-reliance, and the willingness to bear risks, the readiness to back one's own conviction against a majority, and the willingness to voluntary cooperation with one's neighbors—are essentially those on which the working of an individualist society rests. Collectivism has nothing to put in their place, and in so far as it already has destroyed them it has left a void filled by nothing but the demand for obedience and the compulsion of the individual to what is collectively decided to be good.
>
> *(p. 217)*

Hayek's work is profound in that it not only provides a moral warrant for liberalism, but also a technical explanation that demonstrates to his satisfaction that economic planning as an alternative to market self-regulation is doomed to stagnation and failure. Hayek argues that even if Marx is right that we could produce a more equal society if we ran the whole of the economy as one giant industrial enterprise, the project would fail because we can't predict what is needed and in what quantities at any given time. Only markets can do that. This is a practical consideration, but also a moral one. Much as Adam Smith before him, Hayek draws a practical insight about economic organization into a full-blown form of moral politics.

> The effect of the people's agreeing that there must be central planning, without agreeing on the ends, will be rather as if a group of people were to commit themselves to take a journey together without agreeing where they want to go; with the result that they may all have to make a journey which most of them do not want at all.
>
> *(p. 104)*

Much like the moral of Rand's novel, Hayek contrasts the values of collectivism with the virtues of the liberal worldview. This list of virtues each extols flows nicely into a kindred perspective, which supports the sanctity of property, but the critical aspects here are more spiritual than material. All that one finds in the collective is "a void" and a "demand for obedience." The individual is no longer in a position to decide what is good for him or herself wherever the self-regulating market is not allowed to run its course. In both Rand and Hayek we can see the aristocratic and republican cast of the Consent narrative and why many inspired by it are critical of democracy and popular process.

To repeat a central point of Root Narrative Theory, Hayek's masterful story not only tutors our moral intuition, it also tutors our rational capacities. We learn to stand on his shoulders both by the depth of his moral vision and by the technical virtuosity of his argument. This is the power of narrative projection, or interpellation; it associates a technical analysis with emotional "tags" in memory, producing a composite cognition with both rational and emotional substrates. [16] After a successful authorial performance, it becomes easier to see the problem in the way the virtuoso author narrated it because, afterward, the motivations of actors and the institutional logic of situations becomes intuitive to us on a conscious level. Our thoughts are aligned whether we are thinking fast or slow. We find it easier after successful narrative projection to describe, explain, and predict situations in the terms provided by the great author, in part because we feel and believe the integrating story. It all just begins to make sense. Our moral emotions are carried by symbols, and these are the residues of past narrative performances.

The full import of Hayek's projection becomes clear once he moves past the plane of our virtues to that of our worldviews. Economic planning not only robs us of our independence and self-reliance, but also our minds.

> It is not rational conviction but the acceptance of a creed which is required to justify a particular plan. And, indeed, socialists everywhere were the first to recognize that the task they had set themselves required the general acceptance of a common Weltanschauung, of a definite set of values. It was in these efforts to produce a mass movement supported by such a single world view that the socialists first created most of the instruments of indoctrination of which Nazis and Fascists have made such effective use.
>
> *(p. 142)*

In effect, his story is, if we rely on government agencies to provide public goods to consumers, we hand the people over to the Nazis. That sort of chilling story will keep you up at night and alert to socialist threats by day.

The awesome power of government and the chilling effects on individual development are not ideas restricted to the political right. Ayn Rand's novel is popular primarily among those on the right, but another novel with similar aversions, George Orwell's *1984*, is perhaps as popular on the political left. Collectivism was an intellectual weakness for Rand, but it was a spiritual threat to Orwell, as it had been for Hayek and also Hannah Arendt. The most powerful image of Orwell's book is the phrase "two and two are five." Here we see how totalitarian logic can be portrayed as an attempt to restructure our intuition at its most basic level and where the ethic of consent draws its energy.[17]

> He picked up the children's history book and looked at the portrait of Big Brother which formed its frontispiece. The hypnotic eyes gazed into his own. It was as though some huge force were pressing down upon you—something that penetrated inside your skull, battering against your brain, frightening you out of your beliefs, persuading you, almost, to deny the evidence of your senses. In the end the Party would announce that two and two made five, and you would have to believe it.

Do you feel the chill of this passage? What you feel is the power of the Consent narrative. The logic of liberty. The evil of tyranny. Whatever the present uses of the story, consent is not a right-wing value. Many progressives and contemporary thinkers on the left are quick to dismiss the neoliberal peace and the Washington Consensus, as weaponized versions of free markets and limited government around the world, but few are willing to deny the potential horrors of the peculiar mixture of "ideology and terror" or the dire capacities of the "means of total domination" that characterize totalitarian state power as Arendt described in her classic study of the subject (p. 593).[18] These serve as clear evidence that the moral politics of the Consent narrative remains as powerful on the left as it is on the right, even as the ideological pallet of progressive politics has diversified.

The Property narrative

The Property narrative, as part of the family of libertarian narratives, is primarily oriented to pushing back against coercion, but not against the government per se, as with the ethic of consent, but against the people themselves, the great majority who have reason to covet the private wealth accumulated by successful individuals and families. Where Consent is best thought of as freedom from the government, Property is a kind of freedom from the People—other people. Unlike consent or any of the three securitarian narratives, property is an ethic that is rarely championed on the progressive side of the political divide, far more commonly finding support from conservatives and elites. Nevertheless, the moral logic of the ethic is consistent and powerful, fully capable of fueling sprawling and enduring socio-political movements. Indeed, it is not unfair to say that the Property narrative may be every bit as important for the development of liberalism in modern political thought as was the Consent narrative itself. There is little doubt that it is at the core of most commitments to capitalism as a liberal institution and symbol of freedom.

What defines the Property narrative? Property emerges from the space between coercion and exploitation—the space where Locke as hero meets Marx as villain. Property is defined by the moral logic employed by those who would defend the gains produced by private industry when they are threatened by expropriation, especially at the hands of an envious mass. It speaks not only to the material aspects of economic wealth, but also to the values of individual toil, thrift, and diligence that are so critical to the stories we tell about individual virtue and the principle of just deserts. We can tweak the primitive libertarian story to represent it, *Majorities use biased folkways to create political coercion of the Individual.*

The ethic produces moral fervor of an unparalleled scale in modern, liberal societies, but its effects are clear in more cynical visions of political life as well. Most people are familiar with the most striking lines of Machiavelli's prince—"but since love and fear can hardly exist together, if we must choose between them, it is far safer to be feared than loved"—but it is less well remembered that there was a third passion that played into his formulation: avoiding hate.

> Nevertheless, a Prince should inspire fear in such a fashion that if he do not win love he may escape hate. For a man may very well be feared and yet not hated, and this will be the case so long as he does not meddle with the property or with the women of his citizens and subjects. And if constrained to put any to death, he should do so only when there is manifest cause or reasonable justification. But, above all, he must abstain from the property of others. For men will sooner forget the death of their father than the loss of their patrimony.[19]
>
> *(Book XVII)*

It would be hard to imagine a sentiment less consistent with a liberal and universal view of personhood than this one that bundles half of the citizens of a political community into the category of property, but it does signal how important property is, even for the most cynical politicos among us, and is strong encouragement to take the issue of the political sanctity of property seriously. To confiscate property in the world of Machiavellian power politics is worse than putting one's subjects to death, but if Machiavelli only foreshadows the power of commitment to property, others build what could be properly thought of as a morally defensible property-based worldview. At a minimum, we can admit that property is at the core of a value-system salient among those few who have (or want) a lot of it, and theirs is a moral politics, not just a realm of permanent interests.

As with any of the root narratives, a folk wisdom has grown up around the Property narrative and its moral and empirical claims. It manifests in folk sayings like, "There ain't no such thing as a free lunch." It is alive in august theories about the development of contracts and modern social relations as in Henry Sumner Maine's *Ancient Law*:

> Nor is it difficult to see what is the tie between man and man which replaces by degrees those forms of reciprocity in rights and duties which have their origin in the family. It is contract.[20]

To get an unforgettable gut sense of the Property narrative, look at the children's story, *The Little Red Hen* by Florence White Williams, in which a little hen does all the work to make a loaf of bread while everyone else is too lazy to help her make it.

> Then, probably because she had acquired the habit, the Red Hen called: "Who will eat the Bread?" All the animals in the barnyard were watching hungrily and smacking their lips in anticipation, and the Pig said, "I will," the Cat said, "I will," the Rat said, "I will." But the Little Red Hen said, "No, you won't. I will." And she did.[21]

Many have developed moral arguments in defense of the individual's rights to property, but no one better than the Scottish political economist, Adam Smith, and Smith is an even better defender of property than he is of economic stability. In Smith we get one of the first extended discussions of how this ethic speaks to a moral worldview beyond the scope of mere selfishness. In all its manifestations, Smith's genius was to engage a theory of self-love as the basis of moral society.

> But man has almost constant occasion for the help of his brethren, and it is in vain for him to expect it from their benevolence only. He will be more likely to prevail if he can interest their self-love in his favour, and shew them that it is for their own advantage to do for him what he requires of them. Whoever offers to another a bargain of any kind, proposes to do this. Give me that which I want, and you shall have this which you want, is the meaning of every such offer; and it is in this manner that we obtain from one another the far greater part of those good offices which we stand in need of. It is not from the benevolence of the butcher, the brewer, or the baker that we expect our dinner, but from their regard to their own interest. We address ourselves, not to their humanity, but to their self-love, and never talk to them of our own necessities, but of their advantages. Nobody but a beggar chooses to depend chiefly upon the benevolence of his fellow-citizens.[22]
>
> *(p. 19)*

For those who have thought seriously about Smith, this passage is almost a cliché, but the critical identifying elements of the Property narrative is here: the moral integrity of the principle of self-interest and the appeal to the freely given agreement of the other. This is the essence of contract as a moral system, which also just happens to lead to the best possible outcomes for the whole of society.

Smith's narrative is so powerful because it provides an account though which to organize industrial enterprise that both highlights the abusive power of government and the challenge of social disorganization in a single stroke. Those who discount property-based liberalism as mere ideology in support of special interests and inherited privilege fail to reckon with the narrative force of the worldview in the context of absolutist tendencies in government and the idealistic appeal of a world in which those who tend their own garden, in Voltaire's phrase, contribute to what Smith called "the greatest public Prosperity." Classical liberalism and the Property narrative is wedded to this transformative vision of life outside the directive power of coercive authority, which as a story template can be every bit as compelling as the anti-capitalist and anti-racist critiques that would emerge in its aftermath. This imagery of the invisible hand, impossible to fully separate from the image of the deity, is not crucial to an account fitted to the Property narrative, but it is among the most powerful accomplishments of the European Enlightenment. It is the root of radical disagreement in dozens of cases of international conflict to say nothing of its effect on contentious politics in the United States.

The best example of the embattled classical liberal in the face of the development of socialistic alternatives to laissez-faire economic policy was Ludwig von Mises, a theoretical economist of Austrian descent who was instrumental in promoting what became known as the Austrian school of economics. Von Mises is best remembered as a champion of capitalism, which he certainly was, but he is most notable not for his technical defenses of the system but for the moral warrant he provides to capitalism's future defenders.

Where capitalism's critics see greed, exploitation, privilege and social immobility, von Mises saw in capitalism—that is the practical manifestation of the Property narrative—freedom, peace, equality, ethics, democracy, and tolerance. He could write, "The program of liberalism, therefore, if condensed into a single word, would have to read: property." His arguments in favor of property had everything to do with overcoming the dysfunctions of networks of abusive power, but the power he feared was the power of backwardness, bias, and tradition—the people acting as a collective against the interests of the entrepreneurial individual. Von Mises saw himself as a defender of the rights of the successful individual against the envious masses. Mises defended rights against democracy itself.

My methodological recommendation for identifying root narrative material is to look for root narratives in the kind of escalated language that draws our attention to EVIL: emotional, vivid and consuming images, intensity of conflict, and literary style, and von Mises could supply all of that. In his 1927 book *Liberalism*, he wrote:

> We call the social apparatus of compulsion and coercion that induces people to abide by the rules of life in society, the state; the rules according to which the state proceeds, law; and the organs charged with the responsibility of administering the apparatus of compulsion, government.[23]

The keywords here are "compulsion," and "coercion." His use of the term "apparatus of compulsion" provides the literary flair for an audience to conjure images of dysfunctional abuse. All forms of liberalism begin with the imagery of the abusive power embodied in such an apparatus, but they inflect their accounts by the social force that is most likely to gain control of it, turning the latent potential for atrocity into manifest examples of it. Government is the mechanism of abusive power, but, in von Mises, its directors are the people who are flawed in the aggregate as they are separately. In a later passage of *Liberalism*, von Mises writes:

> The champions of democracy in the eighteenth century argued that only monarch and their ministers are morally depraved, injudicious, and evil. The people, however, are altogether good, pure, and noble, and have, besides, the intellectual gifts needed in order always to know and to do what is right. This is, of course, all nonsense, no less so than the flattery of the courtiers who ascribed all good and noble qualities to their princes. The people are the sum of all individual citizens and if some individuals are not intelligent and noble, then neither are all together.... It was quickly discovered that the democracies committed at least as many errors as the monarchies and aristocracies had.

Von Mises saw in this critique of the potential abuses of the power of the "apparatus of compulsion" the danger of democracy. In this he echoes previous critics of democracy like Plato and Alexis de Tocqueville. His concerns point out a flaw in our thinking about democracy in the Anglo-American tradition. Liberal Democracy is not best rendered as the rule of the people for the people's sake as a people, but rather as equality of every individual before the law. Not the political vehicle of an exploited people, but the formal rights of protection from a biased state apparatus. Democracy in the liberal mold is more in line with what the ancient Athenians called *Isonomia* (equality of law) than *Demokratia* (rule by the people), "for while *Demokratia* does no more than describe a fact, *Isonomia* expresses an idea, indeed a whole set of ideas, by which the partisans of democracy justified the rule of the people," as the philosopher Gregory Vlastos described the distinction.[24] *Demokratia* is an idea much closer to populism than our sanctified notions of democracy. Where the people's rule can easily lead to a conception of a people's republic (a dangerous concept for the liberal thinker), equality of the law is a restraining concept that stresses the value of each individual in relation to the ruling institutions and a right to due process.

For von Mises, as for many proponents of the Property narrative, the refuge of the People is little but surrender of moral principles and individual decision making. Once this People is unleashed to deploy the weapons of law in its self-interest, von Mises saw the decline of initiative and the confiscation of well-won achievements—very consistent with the little red hen story.

The threat that democracy and "the social question" posed to those who raised it in the progressive era was based on interpretations like these. The moral logic of this category of thought explains why there are strong critics of democratic decision making on the right, but also why these critics of democracy are such ardent proponents of human rights, specifically individual rights to protection from expansionist state power. In this sense the opposition of democracy and human rights forms a center of gravity around which two rival, if often complementary, moral systems revolve. "Democracy" is the battle standard of the people as the People, as individual "rights" are for the individualist. The Property narrative favored the latter over the former. For the Property narrative, the threat of the power of the People, acting together outweighs the threat posed by successful individuals acting in their own self-interest. In the Property narrative, the individual is supreme and the fruits of his labor should follow the principle of "just deserts" and "equal opportunity," not equality of outcome (although the Property narrative is certainly not the only one to stress equality of opportunity).

These libertarian economic views, though bitterly criticized in the period of socialist upheavals of Europe, were well received, and in truth, anticipated in the United States. The logic of the liberal project was central to the developing self-concept of what Seymour Martin Lipset called "the first new nation."[25] Tocqueville saw both the advantages and dysfunctions of democratic populism in play in the United States, even at an early date; the obvious promise of a democratic nation was tempered by the problem generated by the rise of "the people" and its oppressive control over the apparatus of governance.

> In the proudest nations of the Old World works were published which faithfully portrayed the vices and absurdities of contemporaries; La Bruyère lived in Louis XIV's palace while he wrote his chapter on the great, and Molière criticized the court in plays acted before the courtiers. But the power which dominates in the United States does not understand being mocked like that. The least reproach offends it, and the slightest sting of truth turns it fierce; and one must praise everything, from the turn of its phrases to its most robust virtues. No writer, no matter how famous, can escape from this obligation to sprinkle incense over his fellow citizens. Hence the majority lives in a state of perpetual self-adoration; only strangers or experience may be able to bring certain truths to the Americans' attention.[26]

Although no defense of property, in itself, this passage fits well within the broader logic of the Property narrative, in that it points out the oppressive capacity and intolerance of the mob, along with threats to the expression of individual conscience imposed by an omnipotent majority.

Whatever this threat of majoritarian thinking, the way it developed in the United States was in line with the moral logic of the system of private property. Although many have criticized Louis Hartz for his thesis in his *The Liberal Tradition in America* as oversimplified, nevertheless Hartz captures something I am tempted to say essential about the trajectory of American political culture—at least the white dominated aspect of it—in his description of "irrational Lockeanism," defined by its "liberal fears and capitalist dreams" (p. 140).

The record of American political thought is a veritable jig-saw puzzle of theoretical confusion. But throughout it all the liberal temper of American theory is vividly apparent. Locke dominates American political thought, as no thinker anywhere dominates the political thought of a nation. He is a massive national cliché.[27]

(p. 140)

The American experiment of the nineteenth century, therefore, produced an ironic situation in which the people would rule in the most democratic form yet imagined, but in a way that would minimize its disruptive potential for the rights of property—a particular formulation of the concept of the rule of law that endures to this day. In retrospect, it should be little surprise that the system would operate as a popular government that erred in favor of the defense of property, because it was designed to do just that. In his "Federalist Number 10," James Madison couched his arguments for unity and collective defense under the U.S. Constitution in a larger argument about the rights of the proprietor under democratic government, a libertarian perspective every bit as central to his plan as the securitarian concerns.

> The diversity in the faculties of men, from which the rights of property originate, is not less an insuperable obstacle to a uniformity of interests. The protection of these faculties is the first object of government. From the protection of different and unequal faculties of acquiring property, the possession of different degrees and kinds of property immediately results; and from the influence of these on the sentiments and views of the respective proprietors, ensues a division of the society into different interests and parties. The latent causes of faction are thus sown in the nature of man.[28]

Even before the rise of radical Jacobism and the Babeuf "Conspiracy of Equals" in France, Madison provides one of the most compelling and celebrated examples of class analysis in Western history but framed in such a way that securitarian and libertarian values both come to the fore, surely one of the most masterful and enduring examples of reframing in history.

> But the most common and durable source of factions has been the various and unequal distribution of property. Those who hold and those who are without property have ever formed distinct interests in society. Those who are creditors, and those who are debtors, fall under a like discrimination. A landed interest, a manufacturing interest, a mercantile interest, a moneyed interest, with many lesser interests, grow up of necessity in civilized nations, and divide them into different classes, actuated by different sentiments and views. The regulation of these various and interfering interests forms the principal task of modern legislation, and involves the spirit of party and faction in the necessary and ordinary operations of the government.

Whether you are moved by this line of reasoning or not, this property story would come to have enduring effects on the development of legal practice in the United States and after the restructuring effects of World War II on global institutions on the rest of the world. Without the guiding code of the Property narrative, all of these developments either remain opaque to us or come off as a kind of global capitalist conspiracy, planned as they were and by elites, but these developments had everything to do with the moral force of arguments rehearsed and presented over many decades in this register.

As the emerging Washington Consensus was poised to take hold of the world in the 1940s, Friedrich Hayek used his popular book *The Road to Serfdom* to provide some of the most celebrated and consequential formulations of Property narrative, much as he had for Consent.

> It is the Rule of Law, in the sense of the rule of formal law, the absence of legal privileges of particular people designated by authority, which safeguards that equality before the law which is the opposite of arbitrary government. A necessary, and only apparently paradoxical, result of this is that formal equality before the law is in conflict, and in fact incompatible, with any activity of the government deliberately aiming at material or substantive equality of different people, and that any policy aiming directly at a substantive ideal of distributive justice must lead to the destruction of the Rule of Law. To produce the same result for different people, it is necessary to treat them differently. To give different people the same objective opportunities is not to give them the same subjective chance. It cannot be denied that the Rule of Law produces economic inequality— all that can be claimed for it is that this inequality is not designed to affect particular people in a particular way.[29]
>
> *(p. 117)*

In developing his perspective, Hayek could rely on prior figures who had made compelling arguments using the moral logic of the Property narrative, figures like Benjamin Constant, who could easily imagine the depredations of a newly democratic state.

> To go from one village to another, the straightest line is unquestionably the shortest. The inhabitants of the two villages would spare themselves time and effort if they followed this route. But if you can trace this line only by demolishing houses and devastating fields; if this after having traced it, you need police measures to prevent the passers-by from returning to their old paths; if you need guards to arrest the trespassers, prisons to receive them, gaolers to detain them, will this not cost more time and more effort.[30]
>
> *(p. 153)*

It was easy for the collective to imagine paths to the common good that overwhelmed the needs of the individuals, families and neighborhoods that made up society. The challenge to the rule of law emerges when leaders start "seeing like a state" as the anarchistic-leaning social scientist James C. Scott put it, what he described as "the imperialism of the high-modernist, planned social order" (p. 6).[31] In this sentiment, Scott, too, was an advocate for the Property narrative, albeit an ironic one.

These themes are rampant in American political discourse, especially among the leading politicians that became part of the conservative intellectual movement. Equality of opportunity was a central and often defining feature of resulting property stories, but especially when it was matched with a clear sense of the threat of "police measures" to level the results of the competition.

Critical to the development of this movement was the 1964 political campaign of Barry Goldwater, when Ronald Reagan entered politics and the African American vote shifted in a decisive and permanent way from the party of Lincoln to the party of the Lyndon Johnson's Great Society. As many politicians do, Goldwater had released a book ahead of that campaign to make the case for his presidency. It was called *The Conscience of a Conservative*, and it is a source of several apt illustrations of the Property narrative.[32] Here is one of my favorites:

> The system of restraints on the face of it, was directed not only against individual tyrants, but also against a tyranny of the masses. The framers were well aware of the danger posed by self-seeking demagogues — that they might persuade a majority of the people to confer on government vast powers in return for deceptive promises of economic gain.
>
> *(p. 18)*

Another good example of this is the former football player and then Congressman Jack Kemp, who was instrumental in imagining and implementing the big Reagan tax cut of 1981, a policy that is perfectly consistent with the Property narrative.

> The American Dream, was never that everyone would be leveled to the same result. The American Dream was that each individual would have the same opportunity to rise as high or as far as effort and initiative and God-given talent could carry him, or her, if you were born to be a master carpenter, or a mezzo-soprano—or even a pro-football player—here in America you could make it.[33]

Both Goldwater and Kemp attacked the bête noir of "equality of outcome." This reframe of the Reciprocity narrative was critical to the development of conservative ideology in the period and it owed much of its momentum to property stories. In this case, as in all the others, it is also essential to recall how versatile these narratives are. Any policy, any issue, any solution, any action (from affirmative action, economic statistics, to public libraries to anything else you can imagine) can be situated, reframed, and projected into the language of any of the root narratives.

Among the most striking illustrations of this semantic stretch of the Property narrative is the work of the development economist Hernando de Soto, one of the few examples of entrepreneurially minded thinkers—like Muhammad Yunus—who have imagined new ways to use markets to solve the problems of global poverty.

> I do not think Bill Gates or any entrepreneur in the West could be successful without property rights systems based on a strong, well-integrated social contract. I humbly suggest that before any brahmin who lives in a bell jar tries to convince us that succeeding at capitalism requires certain cultural traits, we should first try to see what happens when developing and former communist countries establish property rights systems that can create capital for everyone.[34]
>
> *(p. 224)*

Where some authors place their accent on the carrot, others chose the stick. Not only could property produce a more moral and prosperous world, but its absence could lead to numbing atrocities. No one was more important in developing the performative appeal of the Property narrative in the United States and, therefore, the world than the Nobel Prize winning economist, Milton Friedman. His book written with his wife, Rose Friedman is an extended paean to the ethic.

> A society that puts equality—in the sense of equality of outcome—ahead of freedom will end up with neither equality nor freedom. The use of force to achieve equality will destroy freedom, and the force, introduced for good purposes, will end up in the hands of people who use it to promote their own interests.[35]
>
> *(p. 148)*

As a final example of the tension with which the ethic or property confronts us in contrast with its Greimasian contrast, the Reciprocity narrative (which emphasizes the economic duties we own to one another in society), I offer the unforgettable statement of the prime minister of Great Britain Margaret Thatcher, who could take the imagery of this view to its logical conclusion.

> They are casting their problems at society. And, you know, there's no such thing as society. There are individual men and women and there are families. And no government can do anything except through people, and people must look after themselves first. It is our duty to look after ourselves and then, also, to look after our neighbours.[36]

In Thatcher, the normative and the descriptive aspects of the Property narrative have come together in a profound denial of the very concept of society, and therefore the old Social Question, which for her was a kind of mirage. The individual, the family and the neighborhood were real things—the "little platoons" to which Edmund Burke argued we truly belong—but society and "the People" that comprised it was itself something unreal, like a cloud that takes on classifiable forms but has no clear and defining boundary of its own. Thatcher's moral imagination was so complete that it had erased a vexing category of human experience. She owed that to the Property narrative.

The Merit narrative

The perspective developed in this section, illustrating the uses of the Merit narrative, will not be unfamiliar to my readers, but it may be disagreeable. It is fair to say that this section is among the most difficult for me to write, in part because there are so few scholars around me who frame their work in its vocabulary and points of emphasis, but more broadly because those who have developed this category of argument often find themselves on the wrong side of what I take to be morally compelling political movements for racial justice, gender equality, and sexual freedom. True, the liberal logic of this mode is appealing in its celebration of individual freedoms, but when applied to the big status categories, as it most commonly is in the West, the ethic comes across as little more than an apology for injustice: a defense of existing privilege. Were it not for the structural logic of Root Narrative Theory that implies that viable alternative root narratives can be constructed by mixing and matching of antagonist and protagonist functions of the primary root narrative categories, I might have been tempted to skip over this category entirely, missing the power of the logic for my own biases. But as with each of the twelve root narrative categories, the perspective has its own internal consistency and when arguments are pitched there, they can become extremely compelling and morally satisfying to advocates.

The primitive sentence that specifies the Merit narrative reads as follows: *Foreigners use armed violence to create political coercion of the Individual.* This is an awkward sentence that doesn't sound colloquial. We need to use cognate concepts to give it currency, *Minorities use intimidation to create unfair contracts for Successful People.* In this formulation, we can easily see how the Merit narrative has been put to recent use in ways that make its logical process appear brutal and cruelly abstract in many cases, no doubt because we are living through the era in which its specifying contrary, the Inclusion narrative, is among our most cherished approaches to human liberation. A guiding principle of Root Narrative Theory is that we are all prisoners of our own root narrative profiles. Based on my own profile, any moral logic that is defined in opposition to the inclusion of those who have been excluded by virtue of their race, gender, religion, nationality or sexual orientation is likely to generate substantial opposition. Without the structural logic of antagonist/protagonist function pairs, I would have been inclined to write about arguments in the merit category as mere extensions of either the Consent narrative (anti-government coercion) or Property narrative (anti-popular coercion) variations, which in many cases they are, but I think it does indeed stand alone as a root narrative.

Hard as it was to accede to the structural logic of this ethic, it was also hard to find a single word to describe it. After many experiments, I settled on "merit" because it is a term that is consistently used by those whose political values correspond to the ethic, and because it is an apt word for the perspective, however offensive it may be to those who feel it is ill applied to their condition.

The Merit narrative assumes that individuals can find themselves confronted by the threat of coercion by members of an outgroup. This could be in the form of quality of life conflicts in gentrifying neighborhoods, the imposition of some kind of remediation of group differences in employment or education, or demands for recognition and respect in cultural arenas like the Oscars or in popular music. Rather than giving in to what is perceived as coercion from allegedly undeserving challengers—actions that deny free choice and freely given respect—proponents of the Merit narrative argue that they have the right to withhold their respect, to associate with whom they choose, and to struggle against behaviors they find offensive, irrespective of the history of status oppression that gave rise to the problems in the first place. This is infamously preserved in the U.S. Supreme Court decision known as Regents of the University of California v. Bakke.

> While the goal of achieving a diverse student body is sufficiently compelling to justify consideration of race in admissions decisions under some circumstances, petitioner's special admissions program, which forecloses consideration to persons like respondent, is unnecessary to the achievement of this compelling goal, and therefore invalid under the Equal Protection Clause.[37]

Merit was the worldview of the neoconservative movement of the late 1960s and early 1970s, in which individual achievement was put forward as a more compelling goal than redressing status inequality. In fact, neoconservatives saw any attempt to override fair contracts based on individual merit as itself a form of violence—a coercive act that would never solve the real problem. The public intellectual, Irving Kristol, who coined the term neoconservative, framed the neoconservative as "a liberal who has been mugged by reality." The story ran that neoconservatives wanted to work for racial justice and overcoming status barriers, but they had themselves been attacked when they tried to point out what they took to be the truth of the problem. And their truth was bounded by the story structure of the Merit narrative, a species of the libertarian imagination, defined primarily by the *summum malum* of the protagonist function of its primal story, the *political coercion of the Individual.*

Where the Consent narrative located the source of coercion in the violent powers of the government, and the Property narrative located that source in the force of numbers of a jealous majority, the Merit narrative locates the abusive power in the disruptive capacities of the aggrieved minority. The Merit narrative is a philosophy developed in contrast to inclusion efforts on the assumption that the proposed solutions are causing trouble worse than the problems they set out to combat. This type of individualistic argument has become popular in the wake of the Civil Rights Movement's powerful master narrative, but it is nothing new; it is a perspective that goes back to the early days of classical liberalism, notably to the French Revolution where Stanislas Marie Adélaïde, comte de Clermont-Tonnerre proposed an unforgettable merit story in a famous speech:

> But, they say to me, the Jews have their own judges and laws. I respond that is your fault and you should not allow it. We must refuse everything to the Jews as a nation and accord everything to the Jews as individuals.[38]

Whatever, the appeal or lack thereof of the Merit narrative, there is a special consistency in play in its arguments that has been quite popular with libertarian audiences, especially in the United States, which cannot be reduced to the logic at work in either consent or property stories. A merit story specifically states that legacies of discrimination cannot be overcome by violating the individual rights of those who were not targets of this discrimination. This non-reducibility is what makes the category useful as a part of Root Narrative Theory. The story structure independently undergirds arguments that we see circulating in the public sphere, providing them with both empirical and moral warrants for their use. Because so many of the forms of its appearance have been contentious and unpopular in contemporary intellectual circles (usually because they are coded as racist), I will begin the explication with the most generous examples of the story that we can find, many of these taking hold in the wake of Kant's philosophy and the German Enlightenment. The best figure to capture the spirit of this German approach to liberty is the linguist, philosopher, and educational reformer, Wilhelm von Humboldt. Humboldt (the older brother of the famous naturalist Alexander von Humboldt) was a friend of Goethe and Schiller and contemporary of Immanuel Kant, who borrowed from the great philosopher a deep metaphysical attachment to the primacy of reason, no doubt anchoring his unflappable individualism in Kant's categorical imperative and conception of the dignity of the rational soul.

Humboldt's varied career speaks to the opportunities available to an aristocrat in that age to develop an unparalleled sense of individual identity. This privilege provided him with the energy and spirit to defend his thoroughgoing individualism, because he was able to remove himself from that sense of dependence that enervates the ethic. Because he developed his ideas in the opening stages of the Enlightenment, just as the promise of individual dignity was becoming practically viable, his example avoids all of the vitiating associations we tend to bring to the concept of merit as used in this story structure, especially as it relates to contemporary matters of diversity and inclusion.

Humboldt is most famous to the world of political philosophy for his book *The Sphere and Duties of Government* also known by the name *The Limits of State Action*, which was written in 1792 but not published, for various reasons, until the middle of the nineteenth century.[39] Humboldt is so helpful as an illustration of the Merit narrative because of his broad appeal across the ideological spectrum; few condemn him as a bigot. He was celebrated by the grandfather of libertarianism in the

United States, Friedrich Hayek, as "Germany's greatest philosopher of freedom,"[40] but also by the leftist, Noam Chomsky, in similar terms. In a celebrated lecture Chomsky delivered at what was called the Poetry Center in New York City in February of 1970, he quoted the following lines from von Humboldt:

> Whatever does not spring from a man's free choice, or is only the result of instruction and guidance, does not enter into his very being but remains alien to his true nature. He does not perform it with truly human energies, but merely with mechanical exactness. And if a man acts in a mechanical way, reacting to external demands or instruction, rather than in ways determined by his own interests and energies and power, we may admire what he does, but we despise what he is.[41]

Humboldt's dedication to the free choice of the individual, uncoerced by the "mechanical exactness" imposed by the power of the state, speaks to the entrancing power of the argument for the free and rational individual. I often think of Humboldt and the rhetorical space he was trying to open in terms of the apocryphal "Incident in Teplitz," in which Beethoven, in a visit with Goethe in Teplitz, refused to bow to an oncoming delegation of royals, thereby demonstrating his value as an individual of merit, rather than the mere issue and representation of a landed estate.[42] Indeed, Hayek attributes to Humboldt and his contemporaries the spark that lit the English imagination for liberty, writing in 1944, "when eighty years ago John Stuart Mill was writing his great essay *On Liberty*, he drew his inspiration, more than from any other men, from two Germans—Goethe and Wilhelm von Humboldt"[43] (p. 61).

Humboldt's individualism, in its freshness and authenticity, appears in countless examples across the historical record. In his discussion of the abusive power of the police, Humboldt wrote, "I do not esteem it good that the state should compel any one to do anything to gratify the wish or further the interest of another," which to him "seems like passing sentence on the feelings and individuality of another" (p. 129), which because of its call for constraint on the right of the collective to impose its mandates on the individual marks it as a perspective consistent with the Merit narrative. It was not that Humboldt thought it appropriate to forgive immorality and intolerance, but he shared a view with John Stuart Mill, developed decades later, that the good, true, and beautiful would survive free competition in what Mill would call a "marketplace of ideas." As we might put it today, cream rises.

> Even a possible exposure to more positively hurtful influences,—as where the beholding this or that action, or the listening to a particular argument, was calculated to impair the virtue, or mislead the reason and sound sense of others,—would not be sufficient to justify restrictions on freedom. Whoever spoke or acted thus did not therein infringe directly on the right of any other; and it was free to those who were exposed to the influence of such words and

actions to counteract the evil impression on themselves with the strength of will and the principles of reason. Hence, then, however great the evils that may follow from overt immorality and seductive errors of reasoning, there still remains this excellent consequence, that in the former case the strength and resistive force of character, in the latter the spirit of toleration and diversity of view, are brought to the test, and reap benefit in the process.

(Humboldt, p. 122)

Humboldt's strident defense of individual reason and the power of the good to triumph in the end is one of the key markers of this distinctive source of moral authority. Many would follow on this model, applying Humboldt's merit story in opposition to various otherwise admirable schemes to use the coercive power of the state to promote the ends of morality.

As it happens, the Merit narrative is one most clearly deployed today in cases where the state has decided to combat racial and gender discrimination, a sacralized position itself, often supported by the logic of the Inclusion narrative. We might be tempted to dismiss all merit stories as a species of racist dog-whistle that its advocates hope no one else will hear, but the attempt to pollute the Merit narrative using the logic of the dignitarian imagination, has only served to obscure the logical power of merit stories for those who are convinced by them. This is a perfect example of how radical disagreement, disagreement at the level of root narrative commitments, only leads to further escalation and disagreement. Both sides know that the other is either wrong, immoral, or both.

If we go back to a time before neoconservativism, when those liberals had not yet been mugged by reality, we can see how merit stories built such momentum in Lockean liberal America. Poverty had become a driving issue in American politics since the publication of Michael Harrington's book, *The Other America*, in 1962,[44] and the majorities of the Democratic Party of that decade decided that they would do something to address it. It was hard to avoid the fact that poverty was not uniformly distributed in society and African Americans, in particular, suffered from it at higher rates than others. Whenever an issue becomes pressing in public conversation, the root narratives are deployed to make moral and technical sense of it. This happened in the 1960s.

Among the stories circulating at the time, was what was called "the culture of poverty" argument, and this is among the most powerful merit stories ever developed. Much like the Samuel Huntington's "clash of civilizations," this story combined close empirical analysis with the logical structure of a root narrative in a moment of political expediency, a combination hard to overcome. Later, opponents will attack such stories as myths.

This framing of the argument is attributed to the anthropologist Oscar Lewis, who had published ideas from an ethnography of Mexican families in a famous book in 1959, three years prior to Harrington's. The story picked up momentum after Harrington's book, but became a blockbuster when it was given widespread distribution, by President Lyndon Johnson's Assistant Secretary of Labor, Daniel Patrick Moynihan in his own infamous report, "The Negro Family."[45]

In both Lewis's and Moynihan's version of the story, it was necessary to attempt to overcome the cultural conditions in which many people were raised so that they would have some chance of being competitive in modern society. We can recognize the culture of poverty thesis as a version of the merit story in the sense that it suggests that members of these cultures or sub-cultures will not be able to compete and thrive in a system of fair contracts, and any pressure to solve the problem by giving them advantages that do not address their cultural deficits will be counterproductive. We also see in this argument how the liberal claims to have been mugged by reality. The whole goal of the culture of poverty argument is to find a way to overcome racial disparities in educational and occupational attainment. Future neoconservatives who became quite wedded to the Merit narrative were "mugged" by those who they perceived took advantage of their dignitarian concerns. Here is a famous passage from the executive summary of the Moynihan report.

> First, the racist virus in the American bloodstream still afflicts us: Negroes will encounter serious personal prejudice for at least another generation. Second, three centuries of sometimes unimaginable mistreatment have taken their toll on the Negro people. The harsh fact is that as a group, at the present time, in terms of ability to win out in the competitions of American life, they are not equal to most of those groups with which they will be competing.

There is no reason why this story necessarily leads to individualistic apathy in the face of widespread suffering. In some respects, the culture of poverty thesis is much more a dignitarian story than a libertarian, but in the closing sentence of this passage we see the next shoe that would drop for the meritocrats. Amid the dignitarian concerns, there is a conditional demand in this analysis fashioned with the logic of the Merit narrative. Unless members of the disadvantaged minority agree to cooperate in efforts to redress the cultural deficit created by "centuries of sometimes unimaginable mistreatment," then they will be condemned to fail "in the competitions of American life." No doubt, Moynihan never imagined that he would be attacked so vehemently for his story, as he was, or that harsh libertarian versions of it would become the basis of an important part of the conservative intellectual movement in the United States, but it is easy to see why later scholars would accuse Moynihan of blaming the victim (a phrase coined for him).

When we examine a version of Oscar Lewis's culture of poverty story, we can also see why, given his ultimately unflattering portrait, it might have been easy to direct blame onto these victims of culture. This excerpt is from an article he published on the culture poverty idea in *Scientific American* in 1966.

> Provincial and local in outlook, with little sense of history, these people know only their own neighborhood and their own way of life. Usually they do not have the knowledge, the vision or the ideology to see the similarities between their troubles and those of their counterparts elsewhere in the world. They are not class-conscious, although they are sensitive indeed to symbols of status.[46]

Both Oscar Lewis and Daniel Patrick Moynihan were committed to using the powers of government to resolve the problems of poverty, but not all those in the thrall of the Merit narrative were so inclined, especially if it meant betraying libertarian principles. We can see vivid examples of this reaction in the work of economists like Milton Friedman, who elaborated the story with explicit technical arguments that have since been used to oppose anti-discrimination laws. A good illustration is Friedman's classic, *Capitalism and Freedom*, published in 1962, just a year before the dramatic March on Washington for Jobs and Freedom led by Martin Luther King.

> On the contrary, I believe strongly that the color of a man's skin or the religion of his parents is, by itself, no reason to treat him differently; that a man should be judged by what he is and what he does and not by these external characteristics. I deplore what seem to me the prejudice and narrowness of outlook of those whose tastes differ from mine in this respect and I think the less of them for it. But in a society based on free discussion, the appropriate recourse is for me to seek to persuade them that their tastes are bad and that they should change their views and their behavior, not to use coercive power to enforce my tastes and my attitudes on others.[47]
>
> *(pp. 94–95)*

Friedman reacts to the pressures to expand government intervention into the market in ways that would open opportunities for minority groups. His reasoning for opposing the coming anti-discrimination legislation is grounded firmly in his libertarian commitment to the logic of the Merit narrative.

> Fair employment practice commissions that have the task of preventing "discrimination" in employment by reason of race, color, or religion have been established in a number of states. Such legislation clearly involves interference with the freedom of individuals to enter into voluntary contracts with one another. It subjects any such contract to approval or disapproval by the state. Thus it is directly an interference with freedom of the kind that we would object to in most other contexts. Moreover, as is true with most other interferences with freedom, the individuals subjected to the law may well not be those whose actions even the proponents of the law wish to control.[48]
>
> *(p. 95)*

Over fifty years after the enactment of anti-discrimination laws in the United States, Friedman's views are now seen as somewhat heterodox, but the fact that he is one of the most celebrated economists in history suggests that even heterodox views find their audience when they are cast into the grooves of the deep structures of moral politics.

Although these merit stories have found a significant base for political support, they are highly controversial as well. If Moynihan was guilty of demanding that the culture of oppressed groups be included in the conversation about what we will do to overcome the legacy of hundreds of years of ethnic oppression, Friedman proposed that we do nothing at all. Someday, what his colleague Gary Becker called "the taste for discrimination" would be selected out of the culture by market forces. The cream would rise.

Other versions of the story were more pessimistic. Where Lewis and Moynihan blamed the culture for racial disparities in social stratification, others went straight for biology, and there is no greater champion of the Merit narrative in the American conversation than Charles Murray who is infamous for his 1994 co-authored book, *The Bell Curve*, in which he proposed statistical arguments in support of the thesis that African Americans were intellectually inferior to whites and Asians.[49] Infamous already for his criticisms of the dignitarian polices of the 1960s from his 1984 book, *Losing Ground*, Murray would only dig deeper into the ideological currents of the Merit narrative over the course of his career.[50] It would be hard to argue from its overt arguments that *Losing Ground* was written by a racist, but it is clear that the book was written by an opponent of race-conscious social policy. He even cynically accused those who advocated for active government intervention of a form of *sub rosa* prejudice for their views that he assumes can only be formulated from a position of racial disrespect—not from an alternative root narrative.

> The result was that the intelligentsia and policymakers, coincident with the revolution in social policy, began treating the black poor in ways that they would never consider treating people they respected.... A central theme of this book has been that the consequences were disastrous for poor people of all races, but for poor blacks especially, and most emphatically for poor blacks in all-black communities—precisely that population that was the object of the most unremitting sympathy.
>
> *(Murray, pp. 222–223)*

The "curious logicality" of Murray's root narrative convinces him that his righteousness is well placed. If you are spreading well-meaning lies, you are doing no one any favors. Murray believes that racial disparities exist because the groups differ in their innate capabilities, and his views have widespread support outside of establishment channels. As the conservative social critic Lawrence Mead put it in his book *Beyond Entitlement*: "Government could ensure blacks fairer chances to get ahead, but it could not give them in any simple way the capacities to make use of these opportunities."[51]

The Merit narrative now appears commonly in open form, undisguised in its opposition to the moral claims of oppressed status groups and nowhere more than in the debate about political correctness, a term originally used ironically as an in-joke among members of the new left of the 1970s and 1980s. President Donald Trump now uses it as a way to justify hardline positions on terrorists and immigrants.

I think the big problem this country has is being politically correct. I've been challenged by so many people and I don't, frankly, have time for total political correctness. And to be honest with you, this country doesn't have time, either.[52]

Another powerful illustration of the narrative is Allan Bloom's *The Closing of the American Mind*, which is meaningful to me because it was written about me, well not literally about me, but about the mindset of students like me who were coming into Bloom's classes at the University of Chicago in the 1980s as compared to those from previous generations. What most made us different from those earlier cohorts was that we did not seem to be as animated by merit stories about great white thinkers as had previous students. Instead, we were more excited to learn from previously marginalized voices: black people, women, gay writers, non-Westerners, etc. In short, we were dignitarians. This impulse was forcefully resisted by writers like Bloom, who resorted to a Burkean ethos, celebrating the wisdom of the ages and the tendency for cream to rise in the domain of thought. Bloom's book is often interesting and full of challenging references to lessons available to us from the best thinkers of the past: it is worth a read, but his use of the logic of the Merit narrative in relation to policies of affirmative action in higher education becomes more startling as the years pass.

Affirmative action now institutionalizes the worst aspects of separatism. The fact is that the average black student's achievements do not equal those of the average white student in the good universities, and everybody knows it. It is also a fact that the university degree of a black student is also tainted, and employers look on it with suspicion, or become guilty accomplices in the toleration of incompetence. The worst part of all this is that the black students, most of whom avidly support this system, hate its consequences. A disposition composed of equal parts of shame and resentment has settled on many black students who are beneficiaries of preferential treatment. They do not like the notion that whites are in the position to do them favors. They believe that everyone doubts their merit, their capacity for equal achievement. Their successes become questionable in their own eyes. Those who are good students fear that they are equated with those who are not, that their hard-won credentials are not credible. They are the victims of a stereotype, but one that has been chosen by black leadership.

(Bloom, p. 97)

What marks this passage as an example of the Merit narrative? It comes from his use of the language of competence and achievement in its relation to asymmetrical cultural difference. This is the source of the heat in this paragraph and orients the statement in moral space. It is a plea for equal treatment and a lesson in what Bloom takes to be the practical consequences of misplaced good intentions. It certainly is jarring and much more awkward to read thirty years after its publication, but it is an idea that has become quite common in practical politics, even when phrased with less strident clarity. Perhaps readers will be tempted to code this as racism pure and simple (what here would fall under the Nation narrative), but I think that would be a mistake. Although Bloom is clearly enamored of the value of his own, Western, tradition, the logic and moral force of his argument in this passage is not driven by that logic. Here he refers to individual competence and the principle of merit (in other places in the book he dismisses merit in favor of ancient principles of commitment, but that is another story). If we code this passage as mere racism, we miss the libertarian basis of the radical disagreement and will have little insight into the nature of the radical disagreement it represents.

What applies to Bloom applies in many other cases in which dignitarian claims are countered with appeals to liberty. Not all merit stories about intellectual achievement are so cruel. One of my favorite examples is drawn from a powerful argument of one of my favorite philosophers, the Canadian, Charles Taylor. In an essay titled "The Politics of Recognition" that has become a touchstone for the interpretation of claims for respect from minority groups in philosophical conversation, Taylor writes about merit and cultural life that echoes those old individualisms of von Humboldt and Kant, invoking the sanctity of individual reason.

> It makes sense to demand as a matter of right that we approach the study of certain cultures with a presumption of their value.... But it can't make sense to demand as a matter of right that come up with a final concluding judgment that their value is great, or equal to others'. That is, if judgment of value is to register something independent of our wills and desires, it cannot be dictated by a principle of ethics. On examination, either we will find something of great value in culture C, or we will not. But it makes no more sense to demand that we do so than it does to demand that we find the earth round or flat, the temperature of the air hot or cold.[53]

(p. 69)

One can imagine Charles Taylor here as the character in Orwell's *1984* proclaiming that two and two cannot be made to equal five. This is a statement of classical liberalism framed with the ethic of the Merit narrative. It is not that Taylor is unaware of the subtlety of the arguments in favor of multicultural appreciation, but here he pushes back in the vocabulary of another final vocabulary, the powerful and compelling story of individual merit, individual taste, and individual judgement that defines any good merit story.

Notes

1 Volokh, "Who First Said, 'The Best Government is That Which Governs Least'? Not Thoreau."
2 Mill, *On Liberty*.
3 Hall, *The Friends of Voltaire*.
4 Franklin, "Pennsylvania Assembly: Reply to the Governor."
5 Kant, *Groundwork for the Metaphysics of Morals*.

6 Jefferson, *Declaration of Independence*.
7 Reagan, "Inaugural Address."
8 Sharp, *From Dictatorship to Democracy*.
9 Hunt, *Inventing Human Rights*.
10 If you don't know what I am talking about, glance over the first few pages of: Foucault, *Discipline and Punish*.
11 Myrdal, *An American Dilemma*.
12 Gerth and Mills, *From Max Weber*.
13 Constant, *Political Writings*.
14 Rand, *Atlas Shrugged*.
15 Hayek, *The Road to Serfdom*.
16 Marcus et al., *Affective Intelligence and Political Judgment*.
17 Orwell, *1984*.
18 Arendt, *The Origins of Totalitarianism*.
19 Machiavelli, *The Prince*.
20 Maine, "Ancient Law."
21 White Williams, *The Little Red Hen*.
22 Smith, *The Wealth of Nations*.
23 Von Mises, *Liberalism*.
24 Vlastos, "Isonomia."
25 Lipset, *The First New Nation*.
26 Tocqueville, *Democracy in America*.
27 Hartz, *The Liberal Tradition in America*.
28 Madison, "The Federalist No. 10."
29 Hayek, *The Road to Serfdom*.
30 Constant, *Political Writings*.
31 Scott, *Seeing like a State*.
32 Goldwater, *The Conscience of a Conservative*.
33 Kemp, "Speech."
34 de Soto, *The Mystery of Capital*.
35 Friedman and Friedman, *Free to Choose*.
36 The Guardian, "Margaret Thatcher: A Life in Quotes."
37 Regents of University of California v. Bakke.
38 Clermont-Tonnerre, "Speech on Religious Minorities and Questionable Professions."
39 Humboldt, *The Sphere and Duties of Government*.
40 Hayek, *The Road to Serfdom*.
41 Chomsky, "Wilhelm von Humboldt and Classical Liberalism."
42 Gramophone, "A Meeting of Genius: Beethoven and Goethe, July 1812."
43 Hayek, *The Road to Serfdom*.
44 Harrington, *The Other America*.
45 Moynihan, "The Negro Family."
46 Lewis, "The Culture of Poverty."
47 Friedman, *Capitalism and Freedom*.
48 Friedman, *Capitalism and Freedom*.
49 Herrnstein and Murray, *The Bell Curve*.
50 Murray, *Losing Ground*.
51 Mead, *Beyond Entitlement*.
52 The New York Times, "Donald Trump on Political Correctness."
53 Taylor and Gutmann, *Multiculturalism*.

Bibliography

Arendt, Hannah. *The Origins of Totalitarianism*. Vol. 244. Boston, MA: Houghton Mifflin Harcourt, 1973.

Bloom, Allan, *The Closing of the American Mind: How Higher Education Has Failed Democracy and Impoverished the Souls of Today's Students*. New York: Simon and Schuster, 1987.

Chomsky, Noam. "Wilhelm von Humboldt and Classical Liberalism." *Chomsky's Philosophy*. Accessed July 18, 2018. https://www.youtube.com/watch?v=JmbLXl–mlL4.

Clermont-Tonnerre, "Speech on Religious Minorities and Questionable Professions." December 23, 1789. Accessed July 20, 2018. http://chnm.gmu.edu/revolution/d/284.

Constant, Benjamin. *Political Writings*. Cambridge: Cambridge University Press, 2012.

De Soto, Hernando *The Mystery of Capital: Why Capitalism Triumphs in the West and Fails Everywhere Else*. New York: Basic Books, 2000.

Foucault, Michel. *Discipline and Punish: The Birth of the Prison*. New York: Vintage, 1995.

Franklin, Benjamin. "Pennsylvania Assembly: Reply to the Governor." November 11, 1755, published in *Votes and Proceedings of the House of Representatives, 1755–1756* (Philadelphia, 1756), pp. 19–21.

Friedman, Milton. *Capitalism and Freedom: Fortieth Anniversary Edition*. Chicago: University of Chicago Press, 2002.

Friedman, Milton, and Rose Friedman. *Free to Choose: A Personal Statement*. San Diego: Mariner Books, 1990.

Gerth, Hans H., and C. Wright Mills. *From Max Weber: Essays in Sociology*. New York: Oxford University Press, 1946.

Goldwater, Barry. *The Conscience of a Conservative*. Mansfield Centre, CT: Martino Fine Books, 2011.

Gramophone. "A Meeting of Genius: Beethoven and Goethe, July 1812." *Gramophone Magazine*, n.d. Accessed August 18, 2019. https://www.gramophone.co.uk/features/focus/a-meeting-of-genius-beethoven-and-goethe-july-1812.

The Guardian. "Margaret Thatcher: A Life in Quotes." *The Guardian*, Sec. Politics, April 8, 2013. Accessed July 18, 2018. https://www.theguardian.com/politics/2013/apr/08/margaret-thatcher-quotes.

Hall, Evelyn Beatrice. *The Friends of Voltaire*. London: Smith Elder & Company, 1906.

Harrington, Michael. *The Other America*. New York: Simon and Schuster, 1997.

Hartz, Louis. *The Liberal Tradition in America*. New York: Harvest, 1955.

Hayek, F. A. *The Road to Serfdom: Text and Documents—The Definitive Edition*. Edited by Bruce Caldwell. Chicago: University of Chicago Press, 2007.

Herrnstein, Richard J., and Charles Murray. *The Bell Curve: Intelligence and Class Structure in American Life*. New York: The Free Press, 1994.

Humboldt, Wilhelm Von. *The Sphere and Duties of Government*. Mansfield Centre, CT: Martino Fine Books, 2014.

Hunt, Lynn Avery. *Inventing Human Rights: A History*. New York: W.W. Norton & Company, 2007.

Jefferson, Thomas. *Declaration of Independence*. National Archives' transcript, 1776. Accessed November 7, 2019https://www.archives.gov/founding-docs/declaration-transcript.

Kant, Immanuel. *Groundwork for the Metaphysics of Morals*. New Haven: Yale University Press, 2002.

Kemp, Jack. "Speech", Tuesday, July 15, 1980. *LawDocsBox*. Accessed July 18, 2018. https://lawsdocbox.com/Politics/74188430-Jack-kemp-speech-tuesday-july-15-1980-ladies-and-gentlemen.html.

Lewis, Oscar. "The Culture of Poverty." *Scientific American* 215, no. 4 (1966): 19–25.

Lipset, Seymour Martin. *The First New Nation*. New York: Basic Books, 1963.

Machiavelli, Niccolò. *The Prince*. Translated by N.H. Thompson. Reprint edition. New York: Dover Publications, 1992.

Madison, James. "The Federalist No. 10", *The Federalist Papers*, November 23, 1787. Accessed July 17, 2018. http://web.csulb.edu/~jlawler/Course%20DW/Federalist_10.htm.

Maine, Henry Sumner. "*Ancient Law: Its Connection with the Early History of Society and Its Relation to Modern Ideas. 1861.*" New York: Dorset, 1986.

Marcus, George E., W. Russell Neuman, and Michael Mackuen. *Affective Intelligence and Political Judgment*. Chicago: University of Chicago Press, 2000.

Mead, Lawrence M. *Beyond Entitlement*. New York: Simon and Schuster, 2008.

Mill, John Stuart. *On Liberty*. Edited by Elizabeth Rapaport. Cambridge, MA: Hackett Publishing Company, 1978.

Moynihan, Daniel Patrick. "The Negro Family: The Case for National Action.", Washington, DC: U.S. Department of Labor, March, 1965. Accessed August 18, 2019. https://www.dol.gov/general/aboutdol/history/webid-moynihan.

Murray, Charles. *Losing Ground: American Social Policy 1950–1980*. New York: Basic Books, 1984.

Myrdal, Gunnar. *An American Dilemma: The Negro Problem and Modern Democracy*. New York: Harper Publishing, 1944.

The New York Times. "Donald Trump on Political Correctness." *The New York Times*. Accessed August 18, 2019. https://www.nytimes.com/live/republican-debate-election-2016-cleveland/trump-on-political-correctness/.

Orwell, George. *1984*. New York: Signet Classics, 1950.

Rand, Ayn. *Atlas Shrugged*. New York: Signet, 1996.

Reagan, Ronald. "Inaugural Address." January 20, 1981. Accessed November 17, 2019. https://www.reaganfoundation.org/ronald-reagan/reagan-quotes-speeches/inaugural-address-2.

Regents of University of California v. Bakke, 438 U.S. 265 (1978)

Scott, James C. *Seeing like a State: How Certain Schemes to Improve the Human Condition Have Failed*. New Haven: Yale University Press, 1999.

Sharp, Gene. *From Dictatorship to Democracy: A Conceptual Framework for Liberation*. New York: The New Press, 2012.

Smith, Adam. *The Wealth of Nations*. Edited by Edwin Cannan. 6th Printing edition. New York: Modern Library, 1994.

Taylor, Charles, and Amy Gutmann. *Multiculturalism*. Princeton: Princeton University Press, 1994.

Tocqueville, Alexis de. *Democracy in America*. New York: Harper Perennial, 1966.

Vlastos, Gregory. "Isonomia." *The American Journal of Philology* 74, no. 4 (1953): 337–366.

Volokh, Eugene. "Who First Said, 'The Best Government is That Which Governs Least'? Not Thoreau." *Washington Post*, September 6, 2017. Accessed July 20, 2018. https://www.washingtonpost.com/news/volokh-conspiracy/wp/2017/09/06/who-first-said-the-best-government-is-that-which-governs-least-not-thoreau.

Von Mises, Ludwig. *Liberalism*. Indianapolis: Liberty Fund, 2005.

White Williams, Florence. *The Little Red Hen*. Scotts Valley, CA: CreateSpace Independent Publishing Platform, 1924.

7

IMAGINING EQUALITY

Reciprocity, Nation, Accountability

The Reciprocity narrative

Let me begin this chapter with a bold claim: the Reciprocity narrative is currently both the most important and the most underperforming category of the twelve root narratives. What makes it so important are the conditions that it is best suited to counter-narrate, which are becoming so general and acute. If economic inequality is the problem, then the Reciprocity narrative is the most natural language for the solution. What makes it underperforming, is that it is used less often than one would expect given the intensity of economic inequality, a phenomenon that I have elsewhere labeled "the eclipse of equality." In my view, the Reciprocity narrative is a good example of how root narrative categories themselves can rise and fall in salience depending on the direction of moral politics in a population. Even though economic inequality is peaking to levels not seen for decades, the fact that the Reciprocity narrative has fallen out of use means that we are using other root narratives to tell the story about the issue, because the issue and the pain it causes does not go away. If the root narrative best suited to make sense of a form of use is dilapidated or if its use has become merely formulaic, other narratives will do its work for it. People try to relieve the pressure of injustice by trying to solve another problem, using a different moral vocabulary. For example, politicians might direct the narrative towards cutting taxes to address pressures on livelihoods coming from corporate policies, just as they might try to dispel racism by promoting economic growth. Neither of these approaches is likely to address the core experience of abusive power that is driving the conflict, even if it provides a satisfying "way of seeing" for the aggrieved parties. Critical as this issue of care and feeding of the appropriate root narratives may be, there is no way outside of the root narrative structure to demonstrate what is really going on and why it matters, and so this paragraph really reveals more about my own root narrative profile than anything else. Nevertheless, it seems clear to me from the evidence and my experience that the old-fashioned class politics represented by the Reciprocity narrative is less popular than it once was, even if the problems it was developed to redress are powerful as ever.

What is the Reciprocity narrative and why should we care? As I have already said, the Reciprocity narrative is the category of critical analysis that points the finger at inequality of economic power, seeing the power of the rich and powerful as abusive and in need of checks and balances. The Reciprocity narrative relies on a belief in the tendency for societies to become internally stratified and for this system of social stratification to play out in favor of the privileged. The folk saying to capture the idea might be, "the rich get richer, and the poor get poorer." The primitive sentence that captures the narrative reads, *Elites use bargaining power to create unfair competition for the People.* Because the root narrative has become a bit threadbare, we need a little help in remembering how to feel the power of the story structure.

"Elite" refers to a group of people who are privileged in the system of social stratification defined in universal terms. After the experience of the new social movements of the twentieth century, we are all dignitarians and we tend to think about stratification in particular terms, as a result of culture or identity-based dis-crimination. These abuses are worthy of their own root narrative, which follow a different logic than the Reciprocity narrative. The abusive power in a reciprocity story is the bargaining power of the elite, not the social customs of the majority. In a reciprocity story, "Elite" is generic and bears no ascriptive characteristics. It doesn't have cultural content apart from the notion of one type of person having economic power over another person.

The kind of generic power the elite person has is bargaining power. Bargaining power is the power to demand something and get it in an otherwise free exchange, an exchange that works out for you but not for the other person. Bargaining power doesn't imply that you have access to violent force, it only requires that you have clout or pull that the other person doesn't have. Because you have patience and the other person does not, you have a kind of power over the other person. This is the power of the rich over the poor. The poor are desperate and the rich are patient. The rich can borrow at low interest rates, while the poor have to use check-cashing services. The rich have collateral to cover their risks while the poor have debts to pay. The rich can weather a bad deal until things begin to look better, while the poor will starve if they miss the next opportunity. You get the picture. These are examples of story elements that are typical for the Reciprocity narrative. Bargaining power might be supported by the violence of the state or the hatred of the caste structure, but it does not require these supplements.

The protagonist function for the story structure, the victim/hero role is played by an entity called the People. This is a notoriously vague word and it is used by many different kinds of people in often contradictory ways. The protagonist in reciprocity stories is the People as a majority, bound by a political community with history and borders, who are not themselves part of an internal Elite. The concept of the People presumes a stratification system that differentiates "the many" from "the few." Because there has never been a society that did not resort to some sort of stratification system of this kind, the concept is robust and most people can understand the idea if they only briefly consider it.[1] The divide has been referenced in all cultures and through the history of political theory. Here is one of my favorite examples from Machiavelli's *Discourses on Livy*.

> Nor do they consider that in every republic there are two different tendencies, that of the people and that of the upper class, and that all of the laws which are passed in favor of liberty are born from the rift between the two, as can easily be seen from what happened in Rome.[2]
>
> *(p. 29)*

This point of the People being the non-Elite really cannot be overstressed for the analyst wanting to use Root Narrative Theory, because libertarian and dignitarian and even securitarian stories so often use the word Elite and People in their own ways. For a libertarian, the People is merely the collection of the individuals and families in a given territory; we saw that with Margaret Thatcher. For a dignitarian, the People are whatever oppressed group is in need of defense. For the securitarian, the People are the abstract subjects of the state, which the leader represents and embodies.

These three forms are fair uses of the term "the people," but they miss the critical insight of the Reciprocity narrative and egalitarianism more broadly. In this kind of story, the People refers to anyone who is lacking in resources and subject to unfair deals because of this state of relative deprivation. This is why the injustice the people suffer from is "unfair competition." In the primitive story, no one is putting a gun to the head of the poor when bad deals are made. In a reciprocity story, people are free and choices are being made, but in ways that cheat the poor and disadvantaged. Society may be moving along as it should without war, tyranny, or racism, but the People continue to lose out, largely because they do not own property, which is portrayed as the subject of driving ambition and exploitation. Jean-Jacques Rousseau tells a powerful reciprocity story in his *Second Discourse* published in 1755.

> Finally, consuming ambition, the fervor to raise one's relative fortunes less out of true need than in order to place oneself above others, inspires in all men a base inclination to harm each other.... All these evils are the first effect of property, and the inseparable effects of nascent inequality.[3]

I have claimed that the Reciprocity narrative is underperforming, that it is being used less often as a source of critical insight in political dysfunction than one would expect, and yet if it has been somehow neutralized as a seedbed for political programming, it is remarkably common in the popular conversation. This is a kind of paradox, people often refer to the moral logic of the class story, but they see it as romantic and impractical. Economic inequality has become almost like the weather. It is just something that happens as a result of natural forces. We might complain about it but getting upset serves no purpose.

The explanation for this naturalization of unjust bargaining power is the subject for another book, probably having much to do with the failure of socialist societies and the vilification of Marxism; what matters here is that we get a clear sense of what the Reciprocity narrative implies and how it presents in empirical data. Accordingly, I will use a wide array of examples that are chosen to make the narrative visible, based on the assumption that we have become accustomed to seeing right through it. This strategy is reflected even in the name I have chosen for the ethic, "reciprocity," borrowed from Karl Polanyi to emphasize what he saw as the most natural way for traditional societies to manage economic affairs.[4] Over the course of history and spans of culture, human beings seem to demand that economic affairs are organized so that they benefit both sides of the property divide in equal measure. In order to make the case for the ubiquity of the concept, even in the most thoroughly capitalist of capitalist societies, I will use examples primarily drawn from the U.S. case.

Perhaps because economic inequality has always been a source of tension in American history, obvious examples of the ethic in action can be found in every aspect of American political culture, even places where they seem most supportive of the ideals of classical liberalism. We can see it in the writings of Thomas Jefferson as in this example from a letter written in 1816 to Charles Yancey.

> We are now taught to believe that legerdemain tricks upon paper can produce as solid wealth as hard labor in the earth. It is vain for common sense to urge that nothing can produce nothing; that it is an idle dream to believe in a philosopher's stone which is to turn everything into gold, and to redeem man from the original sentence of his Maker, "in the sweat of his brow shall he eat his bread."[5]

Here, the elements of the critique of the power of wealth are clear: "tricks upon paper" are contrasted with "hard labor," and the celebration of the worker and "the sweat of his brow," implying the superiority of what Marx would have called use-value over exchange-value. No one would accuse Jefferson of having statist sympathies or confuse his image of Jeffersonian democracy with Marxist socialism, but his commitment to the Reciprocity narrative was as complete as was the Jacobin Robespierre's in France.

If Jefferson was one version of an American class warrior, he was positively tame in comparison to Andrew Jackson. Jackson can be cited for his broader populist appeals, but he has provided some of the most resonant class rhetoric in the American repertoire, as this example from his confrontation with representatives of the national bank demonstrates.

> I have had men watching you for a long time, and am convinced that you have used the funds of the bank to speculate in the breadstuffs of the country.

When you won, you divided the profits amongst you, and when you lost, you charged it to the bank. You tell me that if I take the deposits from the bank and annul its charter I shall ruin ten thousand families. That may be true, gentlemen, but that is your sin! Should I let you go on, you will ruin fifty thousand families, and that would be my sin! You are a den of vipers and thieves. I have determined to rout you out, and by the Eternal, (bringing his fist down on the table) I will rout you out![6]

These populist examples would prove influential throughout the nineteenth century, and insofar as they relied upon arguments drawn from the Reciprocity narrative, the Jefferson and Jackson wing of the Democratic Party is well described as a class faction—certainly not a socialist party on the Marxist model—but at its origins, a class party nonetheless.

This tendency only became more apparent as industrial conditions and the development of private enterprise revealed the newly emerging powers of combination and trusts in industry. Where family businesses once dominated, by the late nineteenth century, corporations were enjoying powers that were never before imagined by business, and the whole of the developed world was considering socialist counternarratives. In the United States, this took the form of what might be called Bryanism, after Williams Jennings Bryan, known as the Great Commoner, who rose to power amid the rebellion of the populist movement to lead successive charges for the presidency with the Democratic Party of the early twentieth century. He is best remembered today for his dramatic speech given at Madison Square Garden in his first failed presidential bid with the Democratic Party in 1896, the "cross of gold speech." It is important to recognize the core elements of the class narrative in the speech even though it praises business and free exchange of goods.

But we stand here representing people who are the equals before the law of the largest cities in the state of Massachusetts. When you come before us and tell us that we shall disturb your business interests, we reply that you have disturbed our business interests by your action. We say to you that you have made too limited in its application the definition of a businessman. The man who is employed for wages is as much a businessman as his employer. The attorney in a country town is as much a businessman as the corporation counsel in a great metropolis. The merchant at the crossroads store is as much a businessman as the merchant of New York. The farmer who goes forth in the morning and toils all day, begins in the spring and toils all summer, and by the application of brain and muscle to the natural resources of this country creates wealth, is as much a businessman as the man who goes upon the Board of Trade and bets upon the price of grain. The miners who go 1,000 feet into the earth or climb 2,000 feet upon the cliffs and bring forth from their hiding places the precious metals to be poured in the channels of trade are as much businessmen as the few financial magnates who in a backroom corner the money of the world.[7]

This celebration of the common people as businessmen—read bourgeoisie—could not on its face stand in more contrast to the background of European socialism, but the villains and the nature of their abuse of power in the story were largely the same: unfair economic advantages granted to "the employer," "the great metropolis," "the merchant of New York," "the Board of Trade," "the financial magnates," etc. When looking for narrative content in a conflict text, the presence of EVIL (emotional, vivid, intense, and literary language) is always the best indicator, and there were few orators who could identify evil in the market system like Bryan could, even as he fended off European ideas and the specter of Karl Marx.[8]

In a speech ten years later in the same venue, he renewed many of his critiques of trusts, tariffs and unfair taxes, but he was clear in his break with the s-word.

> Socialism presents a consistent theory, but a theory which, in my judg-
> ment, does not take human nature into account. Its strength is in its attack
> upon evils, the existence of which is confessed; its weakness is that it
> would substitute a new disease—if not a worse one—for the disease from
> which we suffer.[9]

This American form of class politics lacks nothing of the fervor that always animates spiraling escalation, but it casts off most of the programmatic agenda of socialism that was so disruptive of the twentieth century around the world, largely because the libertarian tradition in the United States was so strong. With a few exceptions, American political leaders would evade the socialist label, even if many lesser figures relied on the identity to promote programs for social change in the United States that until the 1970s carried powerful egalitarian currents into economic policy making. Under the crushing pressure of economic inequality, the socialist label may be making a comeback in American politics, but we should be careful to look for the Reciprocity narrative in those places where that association remains toxic, lest we miss its presence in conflict data.

A good example of how the ethic of reciprocity developed in the emerging neoliberal context of the United States of the middle part of the twentieth century is in the work of the putative founder of neoliberalism, Paul Samuelson, an economist famous for his multi-edition textbook and his theories that bridged the classical-Keynesian divide: he is the putative father of neoliberalism. Among his theories was the concept of a "public good," which I see as a clever adaptation of the ethic of responsibility to the technical nomenclature of a social science committed to premises of competitive individualism. In other words, this is how a free marketer would imagine the Reciprocity narrative within an otherwise libertarian frame. A public good, for Samuelson, was something produced under conditions that came to be called non-rivalrous and non-exclusionary, which means, respectively, that the good is not used up when someone else uses it and it cannot be kept away in an effective way from others. This is what makes the good public rather than private like food or clothing. The following excerpt is from the article in which he defines the core features of a public good.

It is in the selfish interest of each person to give false signals, to pretend to have less interest in a given collective consumption activity than he really has, etc. I must emphasize this: taxing according to a benefit theory of taxation can not at all solve the computational problem in the decentralized manner possible for the first category of "private" goods to which the ordinary market pricing applies and which do not have the "external effects" basic to the very notion of collective consumption goods.[10]

The basic story told in this shamanistic, technical mode is formulated in the terms of a reciprocity story. True to the claim that every account of social phenomena is subject to the constraints of Root Narrative Theory, even the mathematical abstractions of the neoclassical synthesis draw upon the symbolism of reciprocity like "selfish interest," "false signals," and market failure. The point is that some people will cheat others and benefit from their privilege at the expense of the people at large. Little doubt that the presence of EVIL in this passage is minimal, but the concept of the public and its goods is dramatic and far reaching, for Samuelson established a mathematical basis for government provision of goods for "the People" on the basis of the worldview of the Consent narrative, a position as far from Marxism as we can imagine.

The student of Root Narrative Theory has to become cunning in pursuit of the narrative content of arguments. Good authors know how to bury the lede. In Samuelson as well as in Bryan, Jackson, and Jefferson, the EVIL that animated their arguments was private interests working against the well-being of the people. The public good was the concept that convinced many individualists that the old social questions (those class sensitive egalitarian critics) might have solutions after all.

This was not the only attempt to impress the language of publicness in support of the Reciprocity narrative. The public, as the German philosopher, Jürgen Habermas, famously argued, is a term coeval with the development of bourgeois society, one that bridges the gap between the egalitarian and libertarian imaginations. "The public" is a term that fits well with the Bryanite wing of the Democratic Party, a philosophy predicated on the abusive powers potential in the market with no clear call to elevate the underdog at the expense of the overdog. We are all in this together. The public often presents as a business-friendly form of the class critique.

Habermas is an interesting figure in the history of social criticism, of root narration, because he emerged from a critical Marxism developed in conversation with classical liberalism and human rights theory, in some ways not unlike a figure like the orthodox Marxist, Karl Kautsky, who inveighed against the Leninist interpretation of the "dictatorship of the proletariat." Habermas is morally complex; his ideas rely on many root narrative forms, not only one. Although Habermas's later thinking would stress the importance of communication in relation to ethics, his breakthrough text, *The Structural Transformation of the Public Sphere*, developed the concept of the public as a way to salvage the Reciprocity narrative in the era of McCarthyism. The very concept of "the public sphere" is therefore a particular kind of reaction to Marxism, as every egalitarian philosophy since the Communist Manifesto has been.[11]

Taking two points of Habermas's argument as a line through the text as a whole, we can see the major contour of his argument and how he appropriates the logic of the Reciprocity narrative to transformative yet liberal ends.

> The bourgeois public sphere may be conceived above all as the sphere of private people come together as a public; they soon claimed the public sphere regulated from above against the public authorities themselves, to engage them in a debate over the general rules governing relations in the basically privatized but publicly relevant sphere of commodity exchange and social labor.
>
> *(p. 27)*

Habermas uses the concept of the public in much the same way that Samuelson did, as a place where private ends are conjoined in pursuit of public interests, but over the course of nineteenth-century economic development, as he says "from the time of the great depression that began in 1873" (p. 143) the bourgeois public sphere (a libertarian public sphere) went through the structural transformation that introduced the elements of class structure and economic inequality (egalitarian plot elements and institutional features) into it in a definitive way.

> When the laws of the market governing the sphere of commodity exchange and of social labor also pervaded the sphere reserved for private people as a public, rational-critical debate had a tendency to be replaced by consumption, and the web of public communication unraveled into acts of individuated reception, however uniform in mode. Through this development the privacy that had its referent in the public as audience was turned into a travesty. The literary patterns that once had been stamped out of its material circulate today as the explicit production secrets of a patented culture industry.
>
> *(p. 161)*

If there was any doubt of Habermas's Marxian origins, they are dispelled in this statement, in which his mentor Theodore Adorno's imagery of the "culture industry" emerges.[12] Irrespective of Habermas's claims, we see evidence here of the grammar of the Reciprocity narrative, one that links the concept of the public to class politics. The public is the space in which the people can be imagined as an entity without status differentiation, with no monopoly of interpretation in place, and with a universalistic sense of inclusion on the Kantian principles of reason and humanity. This imagery of the unified and undifferentiated people is how the libertarian tends to see the world even after the great hierarchical developments of modern corporate organization have played out.[13] Habermas can envision the ideal of libertarian aspirations, but he sees the concept as corrupted by economic interests and commercialism and in need of further transformation. The corrupting force, the EVIL in the passage, is "the sphere of commodity exchange and of social labor." Put in root narrative terms, bargaining power is used to cheat the People.

If Paul Samuelson and Jürgen Habermas present two very different kinds of reciprocity stories, there are endless examples from mainstream political discussion that provide clear and instructive illustrations for the conflict analyst. Each of the following examples yields a different angle on the reciprocity narratives from the U.S. case on the theory that if we can find reciprocity stories in U.S. history, we can find them anywhere.

Among the most confrontational of purveyors of reciprocity stories among Democratic presidential candidates, was Harry Truman, who expressed the argument that his party stood for the many where his opponents stood for the few with memorable flair.

> Now it is time for us to get together and beat the common enemy. And that is up to you. We have been working together for victory in a great cause. Victory has become a habit in our party. It has been elected four times in succession, and I am convinced it will be elected a fifth time in November. The reason is that the people know that the Democratic Party is the people's party, and the Republican party is the party of special interest, and it always has been and always will be.[14]

Truman was under no illusions about who his base was. His was the "people's party," and his upset of the Republican, Thomas Dewey, in 1948 was arguably the biggest in American history until Trump bested Hillary Clinton in 2016. If the common enemies for Truman were the special interests, for the labor leader, Walter Reuther, reciprocity was signaled by the usurpation of human rights by corporate management.

> Management has no divine rights. Management has only functions, which it performs well or poorly. The only prerogatives which management has lost turned out to be usurpations of power and privilege to which no group of men have exclusive right in a democratic nation.[15]

Reuther's statement was also made in 1948, which turned out to be a kind of high point for the Reciprocity narrative in American politics. Over the next several decades, as the Great Depression and the New Deal faded from direct experience, management would strive to recover its lost prerogatives that the brief rise of the labor movement had constrained. Organized labor in America may have been as strong at this moment as it would ever be, but you can sense its precarious ideological footing with Reuther's allusion to the anti-monarchical image: management, like the king, had no divine right to rule.

The union management relationship is a natural place for the Reciprocity narrative to present, but the story structure also had a powerful history in criticism in consumer movements. After all, it is easy to see the consumer, like the worker, as an atomized and abstract group of players in the economy pitted against, out-flanked, and out-bargained by organized capital. A great example is Ralph Nader's scathing critique of the auto industry from the consumer's side of the supply chain, *Unsafe at Any Speed*, published in 1965.

> A great problem of contemporary life is how to control the power of economic interests which ignore the harmful effects of their applied science and technology. The automobile tragedy is one of the most serious of these man-made assaults on the human body. The history of that tragedy reveals many obstacles which must be overcome in the taming of any mechanical or biological hazard which is a by-product of industry or commerce. Our society's obligation to protect the "body rights" of its citizens with vigorous resolve and ample resources requires the precise, authoritative articulation and front-rank support which is being devoted to civil rights.[16]

In Nader's story, not only were the selfish actions of the corporation a threat to the livelihood of the people, they were a threat to the bodily security of its citizens as well. Harkening back to the language of Samuelson and Habermas, the groups that would flow from Naderism always reserved pride of place for the word "public" in their efforts, even as they pilloried the economic elite. The word "public" emerged in Naderism as a class concept for libertarian societies. We can see the this in the reciprocity stories that Naderite organizations like The Public Citizen tell about themselves.

> Public Citizen is a nonprofit consumer advocacy organization that champions the public interest in the halls of power. We defend democracy, resist corporate power and work to ensure that government works for the people – not for big corporations. Founded in 1971, we now have 500,000 members and supporters throughout the country.[17]

President Bill Clinton is often remembered, like Prime Minister Tony Blair of Britain, for turning the Democratic Party from its populist roots to a more centrist and market-friendly progressivism. Clinton was a different kind of post-Reagan Democrat, but his message remained true to the basic structures of the Reciprocity narrative. We can see this in the opening lines of his 1992 acceptance speech.

> One sentence in the Platform we built says it all. The most important family policy, urban policy, labor policy, minority policy, and foreign policy America can have is an expanding entrepreneurial economy of high-wage, high-skilled jobs. And so, in the name of all those who do the work and pay the taxes, raise the kids, and play by the rules, in the name of the hardworking Americans who make up our forgotten middle class, I proudly accept your nomination for President of the United States. I am a product of that middle class, and when I am President, you will be forgotten no more.[18]

There was certainly something new here, or was it something old? The core of this New Democrat's message was similar to the New Frontier rhetoric of John F.

Kennedy that represented such a break with the class populism of the first part of the twentieth century. You have the sense in this excerpt that "a rising tide lifts all boats." And yet, Clinton's appeal to an "entrepreneurial economy" in which "all those who do the work and pay the taxes" feels a lot more like William Jennings Bryan than it does Ronald Reagan. In the days of the Great Commoner, the middle class was comprised primarily of farmers. Bryan's populism was a kind of middle class theory. If you like, Clinton became the populist leader for the transition to post-industrialism in the 1990s. His "forgotten middle class" is undoubtedly a nod to Franklin Roosevelt's class rhetoric, but it builds on the indigenous American populism that inveighed against a corporate ideology "too limited in its application the definition of a businessman." In this as in many other examples, Clinton simply updated class populism to new circumstances, at least in his rhetoric.

Every great surge of the Democratic Party had some element of this brand of ideological egalitarianism behind it, but just as consistently had no reference to either Marx or Socialism. Although Al Gore's "people vs. the powerful" campaign in 2000 is often lambasted by those who fear a return to "class warfare" rhetoric, his commitment to egalitarian rhetoric was relatively weak, especially as compared to the flash-in-the-pan candidate, John Edwards, who made his break in 2004 with his "Two Americas" speech.

> I have spent my life fighting for the kind of people I grew up with. For two decades, I stood with kids and families against big HMOs and big insurance companies. When I got to the Senate, I fought those same fights against the Washington lobbyists and for causes like the Patients' Bill of Rights. I stand here tonight ready to work with you and John [Kerry] to make America stronger. And we have much work to do, because the truth is, we still live in a country where there are two different Americas, one, for all of those people who have lived the American dream and don't have to worry, and another for most Americans, everybody else who struggle to make ends meet every single day. It doesn't have to be that way.[19]

The narrative sources of this speech are clear enough. Edwards was a contemporary incarnation of a nineteenth century populist. He was moved by the spirit of the Reciprocity narrative. And he was destroyed. It may come as no surprise that popular as Edwards's reciprocity story was to the base of the Democratic Party, it was widely decried as a kind snake oil by party elites and insiders. Leadership is always resistant to the return of an eclipsed root narrative category—Harry Truman used to attack neoliberalism as "horse and buggy economics" and now those nineteenth-century ideas are seen as cutting edge—but Edwards had hit the rhetorical nerve for the age of economic inequality. His own demise was postponed long enough for him to leave a mark on the policy environment. It was his persistent use of reciprocity stories in the primaries that finally pressured Barack Obama to adopt a universal health care policy in the 2008 presidential contest

(Edwards was the first to propose a plan for universal healthcare in a 2007 debate), a policy that would come to be known as Obamacare and would serve as the most salient part of Obama's policy agenda.[20] Even though the Reciprocity narrative would define his legacy, Obama's commitment to the muse of reciprocity was revealed to be not so deep. He was willing to give up on the so-called "public option," whose class-based linguistic and root narrative origins we can better see now.

Even as party leaders and elected officials seemed to be increasingly moved by the dignitarian imagination, the language of reciprocity continued to push its way onto the agenda, and was a constant feature of Democratic Party discourse from its early years straight through its most recent achievements.[21] For reasons about which we could speculate, Democrats never fully embraced the story structure, always framing their critiques in business-friendly terms, almost never engaging the full force of the tradition, almost never referring to their project as socialism (although the term "social justice" did survive as a way to refer to dignitarian concerns). There is one exception, that of the Bernie Sanders campaign of 2016.

For a long time, Sanders looked as if he might go the way of John Edwards and be mocked out of the conversation for his commitments to egalitarian social policy, but he never was, and his campaign mounted a surprising challenge to the seemingly unstoppable force of Hillary Clinton, whose appeal had much more to do with inclusion stories about the hope for the female president. Sanders's victory speech in the New Hampshire primary is straight-up reciprocity story—something that was not supposed to happen.

> Tonight, we served notice to the political and economic establishment of this country that the American people will not continue to accept a corrupt campaign finance system that is undermining American democracy, and we will not accept a rigged economy in which ordinary Americans work longer hours for lower wages, while almost all new income and wealth goes to the top 1 percent.[22]

This reference to the 1 percent was not just a throwaway line but owed its origin to the most surprising example of the ethic to appear in recent years, the best seller by the economist Thomas Piketty, *Capital in the Twenty First Century*, in which he demonstrated that the incomes of those in the top 1% percent of the income distribution had exploded since the Reagan era.[23]

> The overall importance of capital today, as noted, is not very different from what it was in the eighteenth century. Only its form has changed: capital was once mainly land but is now industrial, financial, and real estate. We also know that the concentration of wealth remains high, although it is noticeably less extreme than it was a century ago. The poorest half of the population still owns nothing, but there is now a patrimonial middle class that owns between

a middle and a third of total wealth, and the wealthiest ten percent now own only two-thirds of what there is to own rather than nine-tenths.

(p. 377)

Although mixed economy progressives had avoided the specter of Karl Marx and of European socialism for over a century, when it came time to discuss the issue of surging income and wealth inequality, a phenomenon once denied but now increasingly conceded, both socialism and Marx came back. Nothing and nobody else would do.

The nation story

One of the unanticipated benefits of the logic of Root Narrative Theory— unanticipated at least to me—is that is lends analytical precision to the concept of populism. Almost every study of populism begins in a kind of fog, with vague references to class politics, economic inequality, government corruption, atavistic attitudes, anti-immigrant and anti-Semitic orientations, etc.; with the analysis of the deep structures of abusive power in Root Narrative Theory, we can generate a clear sense of the source of moral authority in play in the three major strands of egalitarian thinking, two of which tend to populism and only one to socialism. In this sense, Root Narrative Theory helps to push egalitarian thinking past Marxism and toward both a deeper appreciation of its implica- tions and toward a grounded critique of democratic (or perhaps demotic) thought itself.

The practical need to understand populist thinking is clear enough. In the wake of the Great Recession of 2008–2010 many versions of political activity that have been described as populist emerged and consolidated around Europe, in particular, but really all over the world. The most interesting feature of this populism is that it tends to strike analysts as elusive, sometimes taken as little more than a mood or a condition of mass delusion. It is the great mystery movement of our time, demanding something like Freud's Victorian question, what does woman want? In this case, the question becomes, what do the People want? They are the new Other. In a recent essay, the philosopher Jacques Ranciere writes about this phenomenon in the following terms.

> A day does not go by when one does not hear denounced in Europe the risk of populism. For all that, it is not easy to grasp exactly what this word means...it is a certain attitude of rejection in relationship to prevailing gov- ernment practices. [24]

The fascination with populism, especially in Europe is born of fear. People remember the fascist movements of the 1930s and hope never to see them return. This is why when Donald Trump opened his presidential campaign with ethno- nationalist rhetoric, fear of the resurgence of populism erupted.

When do we beat Mexico at the border? They're laughing at us, at our stupidity. And now they are beating us economically. They are not our friend, believe me. But they're killing us economically. The U.S. has become a dumping ground for everybody else's problems. It's coming from more than Mexico. It's coming from all over South and Latin America, and it's coming probably – probably – from the Middle East. But we don't know. Because we have no protection and we have no competence, we don't know what's happening. And it's got to stop and it's got to stop fast.[25]

With this unforgettable opening statement, Trump began his campaign to capture the energy generated by the frustration of the white working classes, resulting in the most improbable upset in American presidential history. Rather than writing off his rhetoric as mere pathology, Root Narrative Theory provides us with the tools to analyze this statement as moral politics. It helps us to cut to the root of radical disagreement. Trump is invoking the power of the Nation narrative, one of the three egalitarian root narratives, and the one most likely to produce jingoistic resentment of foreigners.

To reconfigure a root narrative, we keep the protagonist function of the major category but replace the antagonist function. The primitive sentence of the Nation narrative goes as follows, *"Foreigners use armed violence to create unfair competition for the People."* We can rephrase the primitive sentence with cognate concepts to make it clearer: Foreigners use pressure tactics to create unfair competition for American workers. This narrative shares the protagonist function with socialism but differs in the antagonist function that is drawn from the securitarian narrative. It is the People, the American workers, who are being cheated but by foreigners, not by big business. Do you see the subtle difference here? In a securitarian story, foreigners are out to kill us. In a story like this one, the foreigners are out to cheat us. There is a big difference but a lot in common between the two. It matters because the Nation narrative is better suited for making arguments about the economy as an issue and for providing explanations about rising inequality than the Defense narrative is. After all, it doesn't make much sense that you can't afford to retire because China is fortifying islands in the South China Sea, but it might make sense instead to say you can't afford to retire because China is manipulating its currency and stealing jobs from our country. Steve Bannon knew the story, "Because immigration is about not just sovereignty. It's about jobs."[26]

The sort of populist argument that Trump appeals to is nothing new in American history, but it has never been elevated to the prominence it now enjoys. In earlier eras, thoughtful leaders had always managed to thwart the rise of this sort of demagogue before he came to ultimate power. In 1942 the Vice President of the United States, recognizing how easy it was to turn the populist energies of support for the common man in perverse directions gave a speech that would inspire Aaron Copeland to compose his *Fanfare for the Common Man*. The vice president was Henry Wallace, and the speech has come to be known as the "Century of the Common Man" speech. Try not to spot the EVIL in this excerpt.

The demagogue is the curse of the modern world, and of all the demagogues, the worst are those financed by well-meaning wealthy men who sincerely believe that their wealth is likely to be safer if they can hire men with political "it" to change the sign posts and lure the people back into slavery. Unfortunately for the wealthy men who finance movements of this sort, as well as for the people themselves, the successful demagogue is a powerful genie who, when once let out of his bottle, refuses to obey anyone's command. As long as his spell holds, he defies God Himself, and Satan is turned loose on the world.

(Wallace, p. 371)

It is easy to exaggerate the threat that nationalist populism represents. After all, the United States has been such a stable democracy, and it has such thorough checks on centralizing power. As Joe Biden has argued, "I believe history will look back on four years of this president and all he embraces as an aberrant moment in time."[27] But the egalitarian imagination in its turns to nationalist and leveling populism has had tragic consequences in the twentieth century. The turn from socialist to nationalist variations of populist agitation in Europe has been surrounded with enduring horror. Only a hint at the problem is enough to settle the matter of why Trump's demonization of an ethnic group and attacks on the free press carries terrifying connotations. Forgive me for briefly excerpting Adolf Hitler:

Certainly in days to come the Jews will raise a tremendous cry throughout their newspapers once a hand is laid on their favorite nest, once the move is made to put an end to this scandalous press and once this instrument which is public opinion is brought under state control and no longer left in the hands of aliens and enemies of the people. I am certain that this will be easier for us than it was for our fathers. The scream of the twelve-inch shrapnel is more penetrating than the hiss from a thousand Jewish newspaper vipers. Therefore let them go on with their hissing.[28]

It is not hard to see why, writing in the context of global war with the principles of Hitler's national socialism, Friedrich Hayek would have recognized the tendency within the egalitarian moral grammar of socialism to pivot from anti-capitalism to anti-minoritarianism—elevating the interests of one people over and above all others. Hayek speculated on the rise of Nazism in his *The Road to Serfdom* and noted that the egalitarian features of the Nazi ideology were simply obscured by its anti-internationalism.

A careful observer must always have been aware that the opposition of the Nazis to the established socialist parties, which gained them the sympathy of the entrepreneur, was only to a very small extent directed against their economic policy. What the Nazis mainly objected to was their internationalism and all the aspects of their cultural programme which were still influenced by liberal ideas.[29]

Hayek located the essence of Nazism at the point where it elevated the concept of the People over the rights of individuals, an idea it shared with socialism. He argued that the two parted company in the way they defined the exploiter: for the socialist, the capitalist; for the Nazi, the foreigner. This connection at the level of the protagonist vitiated both Nazism and socialism for Hayek. For him the very notion of the People as a political category paved the road to serfdom.

This image of the People as political protagonist is the kernel of the egalitarian imagination, the source of both its sublimity and horror. It is a source of sublimity when matched with the ethic of unity, touching on the mystic chords of memory that Lincoln spoke of. It is a source of horror when directed against a scapegoat people, whether Jewish, Muslim, or Latino. When the people begin to ruminate on those who cheat them, it is easy to spread the blame in many directions.

Anyone familiar with Hayek's work may have wondered why his anti-socialism was so uncompromising, his insight about the political role of the concept of the People is the most likely candidate answer. Hayek saw what, according to the logic of Root Narrative Theory, is a feature of populist thinking, not a bug. Outrage against the cheaters is a very fungible thing, and to make this point precise, I should say that this implies that there is something in the democratic mindset itself, the theory of the People's rule and their glory, and not only in what we call populism, that leads directly to nationalist exclusion and the threat of a tyranny of the majority, as Tocqueville argued. This explains why the republican principle of classical liberalism with its emphasis on limited government and human rights has always been so important as a check on collectivist ambitions.

People's Republics have a tendency toward this style of everyman populism and a line of thinking that propagates nation stories is commonly disturbing. The People are at their worst when they worry about other people cheating them— trying to replace them. Where Hitler said of his use of propaganda, "all propaganda must be popular and its intellectual level must be adjusted to the most limited intelligence among those it is addressed to," Hayek countered, "it is, as it were, the lowest common denominator which unites the largest number of people."[30] The moral pollution of this little man mode of thought became a central motif of the twentieth century, nowhere better captured than by John Paul Sartre:

> The anti-Semite has no illusions about what he is. He considers himself an average man, modestly average, basically mediocre. There is no example of an anti-Semite's claiming individual superiority over the Jews. But you must not think that he is ashamed of his mediocrity; he takes pleasure in it; I will even assert that he has chosen it. This man fears every kind of solitariness, that of the genius as much as that of the murderer; he is the man of the crowd. However small his stature, he takes every precaution to make it smaller, lest he stand out from the herd and find himself face to face with himself.[31]

Of course, Hayek's insight into the downsides of the rule by People (demos in Greek) was nothing new. There were plenty of biting criticisms of democracy and egalitarian thinking in its birthplace, ancient Greece. Thucydides was less than flattering in his characterizations of the mob, and Plato was as worried about the tyrannical tendencies of democracy as critics of his like Karl Popper were about his political elitism. As Plato wrote, "the people have always some champion whom they set over them and nurse into greatness.... This and no other is the root from which a tyrant springs; when he first appears, he is a protector" (Plato, 565c).

As with all of the material of Root Narrative Theory, the celebration of the little man or ordinary person is universally known around the world. All people have some conception of the common people. Known in China as the *lao baixing*, or the old 100 names, in Spanish as *el pueblo*, or *norod* in Russian, to name just a few examples, the common people around the world are often imagined in the same way: as hardworking, abstemious in their habits, simple in their tastes, honest in their dealings, humble in their faith, and dutiful to their nation. They are the people you know and who know you; remember the slogan for the American television program *Cheers*, "a place where everybody knows your name." The common people are often portrayed as rural and less well educated than the elites of the cities and schools, and they tend to embrace less nuanced or cosmopolitan forms of cultural representation.

In all of this, "the People" as a category demonstrate a tendency to exclude, even as there is little recognition that this exclusion is in any way exclusionary. It is almost synonymous with goodness. After all, criminals and miscreants are excluded by their own actions. They choose to place themselves outside the mores of the moral community, and anyone who likewise chooses to criticize those mores is easy to dismiss as a deviant.

Given the ubiquity of the concept of the People, it is little surprise that the division was present in the early days of the French Revolution. The cultural type was celebrated in a newspaper of the Jacobins known as Père Duchesne, or "old Duchesne," and served as a symbol of the ordinary working man—a kind of Archie Bunker of his day. This character was described in the newspaper in the following terms.

> In the evening, when he enters his hovel, his wife rushes to greet him, his small children hug him, his dog bounds up and licks him. He recounts the news that he heard at the section. He's as happy as a clam when telling about a victory over the Prussians, the Austrians, or the English. He tells how a traitorous general, a follower of Brissot, was guillotined. While telling his children about these scoundrels, he makes them promise to always be good citizens and to love the Republic above all else.[32]

The familiar and unassuming cultural profile of Père Duchesne marks him as a man of the People: the simple tastes, the scorn he directs to those who break with the cultural code, and the ferocity of his political vision towards those who would harm the well-being of the people. It is little surprise that this imagery was central to the Terror, imagery at the core of the cultural populism that defines itself against the Other, and once the Other is defined, as happened in the Terror, it is easy to stigmatize anyone as an "enemy of the people," even those in otherwise egalitarian social movements. A classic place to locate the contemporary use of this language and the maxim of its perspective is with Vladimir Lenin.

> The rich and the rogues are two sides of the same coin, they are the two principal categories of parasites which capitalism fostered; they are the principal enemies of socialism. These enemies must be placed under the special surveillance of the entire people; they must be ruthlessly punished for the slightest violation of the laws and regulations of socialist society. Any display of weakness, hesitation or sentimentality in this respect would be an immense crime against socialism.[33]

Lenin's statement is typical of many left-wing variations on the theme of the Nation narrative. The principle idea is the threat to the People that comes from those Others who are somehow outside of the political community less for their ownership of property and more for their personal, social or national characteristics. These are the real "enemies of socialism." As articulated by Maximilien Robespierre, "The revolutionary government owes to the good citizen all the protection of the nation; it owes nothing to the Enemies of the People but death."

It would be hard to argue that the "rogues" that Lenin decried were rogues by choice, but the Nation narrative transforms these elements, who become, once constituted, those who stand outside the People and cheat and victimize them. In the popular political mind, it is easy to paint the foreigner as an unfair competitor, even to the point of exploitation—stealing our jobs, engaging in usury, cheating us in trade negotiations, etc.—as much as the wealthy and the government could ever do. Again, detestable as it often is, this form of populism is not so much a bug as a feature of the egalitarian imagination. It has to be constantly considered as a potential perversion of the basic idea of economic fairness.

These exclusionary ideas were never part of the major forms of European socialism, even if they were typical of the proto-socialist democratic movements orbiting the French Revolution. Nevertheless, the memories of the extremes of the various forms of egalitarianism in the Revolution (anti-rich, anti-foreigner, anti-government) posed an ever-present threat to the prospect of socialism, which in almost all cases was thought of as a kind of "industrial democracy" as the English socialists Sydney and Beatrice Webb described it. The grisly and polluted aspects of the history of demotic egalitarianism made it a kind of litmus test for socialists and communists to commit themselves to cosmopolitanism throughout the nineteenth century and beyond, a version of which appeared in the *Communist Manifesto* itself:

> National differences and antagonisms between peoples are daily more and more vanishing, owing to the development of the bourgeoisie, to freedom of commerce, to the world-market, to uniformity in the mode of production and in the conditions of life corresponding thereto. The supremacy of the

proletariat will cause them to vanish still faster. United action, of the leading civilized countries at least, is one of the first conditions for the emancipation of the proletariat.[34]

Marxist leaders tended to read the supremacy of the proletariat in non-ethnic terms, but the people whom they mobilized were not always so careful to distinguish between the "supremacy of the proletariat" and the supremacy of their ethnic group. After all, what was the difference? This is why socialists from the very start were so careful. Their movement grew out of the great populist excesses of the French Revolution and the Terror, and the movement's leaders had no intention to repeat them. In a letter from 1794, the architect of the Terror, Maximilien Robespierre flirted with this kind of leveling nationalism that proved so dangerous.

> Thus everything that tends to excite love of country, to purify morals, to elevate souls, to direct the passions of the human heart toward the public interest, ought to be adopted or established by you.... We must smother the internal and external enemies of the Republic or perish, in this situation, the first maxim of your policy ought to be to lead the people by reason and the people's enemies by terror.[35]

In this way socialists labored under the shadow of the Jacobins and learned to distrust their own egalitarian ethos. The cosmopolitan mantra was not adopted because the commitment to human rights (a libertarian idea) or social inclusion (a dignitarian idea) were such a natural fit with the egalitarian imagination, but for quite the opposite reason. Egalitarian thinking had a tendency in it to exclude. This produced a typical Marxist orientation to ethnic conflict, which is captured in these lines by Karl Kautsky's analytic interpretation of the Marxist Erfurt Program of 1890.

> Every May Day shows in the most impressive manner that it is the masses of industrial workers in all the great centers of population of all civilized lands that feel in themselves the consciousness of the international solidarity of the proletariat, that protest against war and declare that national divisions are no longer divisions between peoples, but between exploiters.[36]

Marxism and its ideological offshoots rebelled against the exclusionary tendency of egalitarian thought, but the tendency was always ready to present itself in leveling movements, a haunting feature of those versions of populism that become somehow most authentic. Consider the dramatic final speech of the Eva Duarte Peron, Evita. The speech was delivered on October 17, which in Argentina, at that time, was tellingly known as Loyalty Day.

> Let the enemies of the people, of Perón and the Fatherland come. I have never been afraid of them because I have always believed in the people. I have always believed in my beloved *descamisados* because I have never forgotten that

without them October 17 would have been a date of pain and bitterness, for this date was supposed to be one of ignominy and treason, but the courage of this people turned it into a day of glory and happiness. Finally, *compañeros*, I thank you for all your prayers for my health; I thank you with all my heart. I hope that God hears the humble of my Fatherland so that I can quickly return to the struggle and be able to keep on fighting with Perón for you and with you for Perón until death.[37]

The tendency to exclude those who refuse to join the People in their commitment to the higher calling of the group, whether religious or secular-political, has long roots and is tied to the notion of inheritance, financial well-being, and the glory of the people and the nation. There is a fear of replacement in the concept. We can see this in the anti-Semitic writings of the early Christian Fathers of the Catholic Church. One example that foreshadows later uses is Justin Martyr, an early example of what is now called secessionism, the idea that Christianity replaced the covenant of the Jews, who wrote the following in his *Second Apology* (*Dialogue with Trypho*):

> And Trypho remarked, "What is this you say? that none of us shall inherit anything on the holy mountain of God?" And I replied, "I do not say so; but those who have persecuted and do persecute Christ, if they do not repent, shall not inherit anything on the holy mountain. But the Gentiles, who have believed on Him, and have repented of the sins which they have committed, they shall receive the inheritance along with the patriarchs and the prophets, and the just men who are descended from Jacob, even although they neither keep the Sabbath, nor are circumcised, nor observe the feasts."[38]

Indeed, anti-Semitism is one of the most common forms of exclusionary populism that turns the Nation narrative into something much darker than patriotic egalitarianism. We can see this in the recent white supremacist rally in Charlottesville, Virginia where a chant rang out, "Jews will not replace us," and also in the legacy of southern populism in once celebrated figures like Thomas E. Watson, who ran for Vice President with William Jennings Bryan, served the state of Georgia in the House and Senate, served as a newspaper publisher for populist papers with names like *The People's Party Paper* and *The Jeffersonian*, and played the leading role in securing postal delivery to rural areas without incurring special charges. Beyond all of those services rendered to the People, Watson is perhaps best remembered for his role in the infamous case of Leo Frank, a Jewish factory director who was lynched on suspicion of having murdered a young Christian girl. Watson's language was often couched in the language of reciprocity, but notably also in that of the Nation narrative. Unlike the conflicted socialists, Watson, the populist, was a consistent egalitarian.

> Did [Jefferson] dream that in 100 years or less, his party would be prostituted to the vilest purposes of monopoly; that red-eyed Jewish millionaires would be

chiefs of that Party, and that the liberty and prosperity of the country would be… constantly and corruptly sacrificed to Plutocratic greed in the name of Jeffersonian Democracy?[39]

This passage is clearly a blend of themes of both the Reciprocity and Nation narratives, but the anti-Semitic element dominates the passage, suggesting how easy it is to target outgroups in the egalitarian project. And this kind of anti-Semitism promulgated in the name of the People is not restricted to Christian communities, it is also common in the Muslim world. There are likely as many examples to draw from this domain as there are from the Christian populist sources. One glaring example that would fit the Nation narrative are the speeches of the former president of Iran, Mahmoud Ahmadinejad.

It has now been some 400 years that a horrendous Zionist clan has been ruling the major world affairs, and behind the scenes of the major power circles, in political, media, monetary, and banking organizations in the world, they have been the decision makers, to an extent that a big power with a huge economy and over 300 million population, the presidential election hopefuls must go kiss the feet of the Zionists to ensure their victory in the elections.[40]

Like Watson before him, Ahmadinejad blends the ethic of reciprocity artfully, if viciously, with that of nation, drawing energy from both in a creative blend of vitriol. No doubt economic problems in Iran are often explained away with just this sort of justification. Ahmadinejad's audience was as susceptible to the cocktail as was Watson's. Both use the imagery of the cheating Other as a foil: a nation, not a defense story.

Given our modern concerns, this conflation of anti-capitalist critique and anti-Semitic rant is jarring, but the imagery of the exploiting Other can be any sort of outsider, and the populist ire can be used by parties of the left and right with equal ease. This is why it is so important to consider the implications of the Nation narrative to those places that call themselves "people's republics." We can see the kernels of this line of thinking in the following statement of the Communist Party of Kampuchea, a Cambodian group, in 1978. Here the exploiting Others are the Vietnamese, who are portrayed as working against the "clean" and "ordinary" people, the Cambodian version of Pére Duschene.

The Vietnamese thus crawled into our country by what they term "legal" means, especially in Takeo and Svay Rieng. But when power came into the hands of the party, everyone saw that we could hold aloft the banner of independence. They realized communists were clean, that we live as ordinary people live, while in the old days, when people lived in a capitalist way, the society disintegrated. As soon as people understood, they followed the communist way and we could easily mobilize forces.[41]

These are dark stories, but no people has a monopoly of this form of populist thinking, nor is the Nation narrative always used for divisive and nefarious purposes. Nevertheless, the specter of the abusive demos (or even better in Greek *ochlos* for rabble) is always haunting the egalitarian. This is most pressing when the concept of democracy is pressed to its limit.

A perfect closing example of this is the United States Senator, Stephen A. Douglas, who stood against Abraham Lincoln in the run up to the American Civil War. In the following excerpt, taken from the first debate between Lincoln and Douglas in 1858, we see how the notion of the popular sovereignty can lead to shocking conclusions, justifying slavery and supremacy in the name of democratic decision making.

> We must leave each and every other State to decide for itself the same question. In relation to the policy to be pursued toward the free negroes, we have said that they shall not vote; whilst Maine, on the other hand, has said that they shall vote. Maine is a sovereign State and has the power to regulate the qualifications of voters within her limits. I would never consent to confer the right of voting and of citizenship upon a negro, but still I am not going to quarrel with Maine for differing from me in opinion.... Now, my friends, if we will only act conscientiously and rigidly upon this great principle of popular sovereignty, which guaranties to each State and Territory the right to do as it pleases on all things, local and domestic, instead of Congress interfering, we will continue at peace one with another.[42]

There are several things that are astonishing about this passage, but surely the most is how Douglas invokes the principle of democracy and popular choice to justify the exclusion of African Americans from their political rights. He exempts black people from the ranks of the People, treating them as a kind of absolute Other, derogated through the principle of the popular will. His position was that it was acceptable for one group of citizens to enslave members of another group through democratic process. Douglas was a radical for the popular ideal.

This portrait of the Nation narrative has been substantially more pejorative than others. The healthy use of the egalitarian imagination may be essential for a flourishing society, and conflict researchers will certainly be able to find extremely prosocial uses of the Nation narrative. Although, every group has the need to take what Aristotle called "proper pride" in itself, with the Nation narrative, perhaps more than with any of the others, we are at risk if we forget its shadow—the dark side of democracy. Remember that Stephen Douglas defeated Lincoln in that election of 1858, and even if Douglas's perspective on "popular sovereignty" would be remembered as among the most reviled in American history, its legacy remains with us to this day, pointing to the obvious need to counter majoritarian pressures in any just society.

The Accountability narrative

The Reciprocity narrative is a familiar category of thought. It is the category of the socialist imaginary, in which authors inveigh against the rich getting richer, the domination of the many by the few, and the tendency for the rules of the game to shift over time in favor of those who play it better than others. This is the essence of class analysis and class politics. We see it in the development of socialist movements in Europe, in Marxian thought in all its variations, and we see it in all the progressive economic movements around the world that attempt to limit economic inequality in its various forms. As a conceptual category, reciprocity is relatively relatable, but as we consider the other two egalitarian root narratives, the terrain becomes more uneven, because we move away from what we think of as class politics and enter the domain of populism, and populism has always been a confused concept. The Accountability narrative is a second form of populism that takes a different tack than the Nation narrative described above.

Since it was lofted in the later part of the nineteenth century in the American South and West, the word populism is an ideological balloon that has never really landed. In excavating the concept, I find it helpful to resort to etymology. Although there are precursors in other langauges, the first recorded instance we have of the word in the Oxford English Dictionary comes from 1891 as the third-party phenomenon known as the Populist Party was gathering momentum for a big electoral push in 1892. The preamble to the party's platform begins with discourse fully consistent with the Reciprocity narrative described above:

> The people are demoralized; most of the States have been compelled to isolate the voters at the polling places to prevent universal intimidation and bribery. The newspapers are largely subsidized or muzzled, public opinion silenced, business prostrated, homes covered with mortgages, labor impoverished, and the land concentrating in the hands of capitalists. The urban workmen are denied the right to organize for self-protection, imported pauperized labor beats down their wages, a hireling standing army, unrecognized by our laws, is established to shoot them down, and they are rapidly degenerating into European conditions.[43]

On the whole this language sounds like it could have just as easily been lifted from the *Communist Manifesto* as from the Omaha Platform, however, its origins had little to do with European socialism. As we saw in the discussion about reciprocity above, American class politics—which is as much as to say populism—was more agrarian than industrial, more entrepreneurial than proletarian, and more individualistic than collective. American class theorists seldom gave up on the idea of a business society—a bourgeois society—even though they were every bit as dedicated to attacking the abuses of economic power as their European cousins. We will see that this story of economic abuse can accommodate the big government as the villain just as well as it can big business.

To make sense of the Accountability narrative, we should remember the moral logic undergirding Root Narrative Theory. The basic premise is simple: moral politics is defined in opposition to the abuse of power. We can differentiate standpoints of political morality by virtue of the form of power to which they are opposed. In the egalitarian imagination, the characteristic and defining form of power is economic: the clout and bargaining power enjoyed by rich people over the poor. What kind of power is this? It is not the power to kill (at least not directly) like predation is. It is not the power to coerce through bureaucratic rules, although as we will see in this section that is always a potential byproduct of inequality. It is also not the power for one group of people to dominate another on the basis of social status—language, religion, customs, folkways, etc., although, again, it usually has implications for the status order. Instead, economic power is the power to cheat, to gain unfair advantage in a competition for material resources. The three roots of the egalitarian imagination all refer to some form of being cheated by someone or some system that is privileged in an economic competition. It is the sense of something material being taken by unfair means.

Any given root narrative category is defined by its protagonist function, by the victim/hero and what he suffers. Substituting the appropriate antagonist function, we can see that the primitive sentence for the Accountability narrative is, *Government uses force of law to create unfair competition for the People*, or in the vernacular, *Government uses corruption to produce ruinous taxation of the People*. In the Reciprocity narrative, the cheaters are the rich. In the Accountability narrative, the cheater is the government itself. It is a subtle shift, but a crucial one, because the reciprotarian dedicates his life to using any and all institutions to level the playing field between the rich and the poor. The Accountability narrative pushes thought in a different direction; here the state itself is the enemy and agent of economic exploitation. Therefore, the logic of political morality demands pushback on the state itself and its cheating and corrupt pseudo-representatives.

Drilling a little deeper into etymology, we can see why the story of government cheating is so intuitive. In English (only privileged here because I am writing in English and using it as the platform from which to assign terms to the Root Narrative Theory), the word cheat comes from "escheat," which was the word for a property that had no legal heir and therefore fell into government hands. The first use of the word in the Oxford English Dictionary is from 1377. This is really interesting, because the period from around 1400 until 1592, when the word was first used to mean "any product of conquest or robbery," was one in which the English state had been behaving badly with respect to the People—think Henry VIII—in particular with respect to confiscating properties for its own enrichment. It is not hard to imagine how the concept of the escheat could transition to conquest and then to our modern general usage from there. This pattern of state "cheating" is clearly nothing special to England or to the period of European state formation but seems to be one of the major forms of abusive power.

Consider the justifications behind the Protestant Reformation, and Martin Luther's *Ninety-Five Theses* posted in 1517, themselves easy to cast in the language of the Accountability narrative. To get a sense of what Martin Luther was angry about, think about the meaning of the word "indulgence," which was the practice of paying the church a kind of tax to redeem one's sins. It was a fantastic fund raiser, and if you have ever marveled at St. Peter's Basilica in Rome (which broke ground in 1506), you see how much revenue the indulgence was capable of generating and why it would have been so tempting for a German monk to articulate the ways that the People (the *volk* in German) were being cheated by the mega-state of the Catholic Church in the early 1500s. Luther refers to indulgences 45 times in the *Ninety-Five Theses*. This is clearly a document about accountability, about the people being cheated by their official leaders for the leaders' own interests. The standard word we would use for this critique in English is "corruption." Therefore, the ethic of accountability is defined in opposition to government corruption, especially as it refers to venality or material gain of those in office. Accountability as used here might simply be thought of as anti-corruption. And this anti-corruption was as important to the leaders of American populism as they developed their ill-defined movement as it had been for Martin Luther at the dawn of the Reformation.

The mechanism for self-aggrandizement for papal officials in the Renaissance had one form. It had another in the corporation building phase of American capitalism. Turning back to the U.S. Populist Party platform of 1892, we can see how the narrative of government corruption had shifted from government officials benefitting themselves directly to those same officials benefitting themselves by promoting their business partners and associates—to crony capitalism. In the lines of the preamble of the Populist Party Platform, just after those quoted above we see this turn to the government as the locus of People-cheating.

> The fruits of the toil of millions are badly stolen to build up colossal fortunes for a few, unprecedented in the history of mankind; and the possessors of these, in turn, despise the Republic and endanger liberty. From the same prolific womb of governmental injustice we breed the two great classes—tramps and millionaires. The national power to create money is appropriated to enrich bond-holders; a vast public debt payable in legal-tender currency has been funded into gold-bearing bonds, thereby adding millions to the burdens of the people.[44]

You can see how quickly the populist mind can pivot from a critique of the rich to a critique of government. It is a very short walk, especially in a democratic system in which the rulers are held to close account by the election system, itself potentially dominated by the wealthy.

This anti-government populism has a long history in the United States, drawing upon the libertarian tendencies of the political culture. It is hard not to think again of Andrew Jackson when tracing the origins and story structures behind American populism. The logic of the Accountability narrative is clearly indicated in that Veto Message Regarding the Bank of the United States from July 10, 1832.

In the full enjoyment of the gifts of Heaven and the fruits of superior industry, economy, and virtue, every man is equally entitled to protection by law; but when the laws undertake to add to these natural and just advantages artificial distinctions, to grant titles, gratuities, and exclusive privileges, to make the rich richer and the potent more powerful, the humble members of society—the farmers, mechanics, and laborers—who have neither the time nor the means of securing like favors to themselves, have a right to complain of the injustice of their government. There are no necessary evils in government. Its evils exist only in its abuses. If it would confine itself to equal protection, and, as Heaven does its rains, shower its favors alike on the high and the low, the rich and the poor, it would be an unqualified blessing.

In its Jacksonian form, anti-corruption populism—the Accountability narrative—is often thought of as benighted or regressive. Jackson was himself an obvious white supremacist who is better remembered for ethnic cleansing and the "trail of tears" than for his egalitarian instincts, but in the nineteenth century things were generally the opposite. Jackson was the same sort of nineteenth century populist hero as was Thomas Jefferson. The energy for his celebration came as much from the Accountability narrative as from any other form of moral politics.

This line of anti-corruption populism is alive today as well. We can see it in this dissent in the Supreme Court decision written by Justice John Paul Stevens from the infamous Citizen's United case, which dealt with spending limits in federal elections. It tracks the Jacksonian populist logic quite closely.

In the context of election to public office, the distinction between corporate and human speakers is significant. Although they make enormous contributions to our society, corporations are not actually members of it. They cannot vote or run for office. Because they may be managed and controlled by non-residents, their interests may conflict in fundamental respects with the interests of eligible voters. The financial resources, legal structure, and instrumental orientation of corporations raise legitimate concerns about their role in the electoral process. Our lawmakers have a compelling constitutional basis, if not also a democratic duty, to take measures designed to guard against the potentially deleterious effects of corporate spending in local and national races.[45]

The characteristics that identify the passage as an accountability story are: the critique of corporate power; the focus on the performative consequences of unequal resources; and the conflicting interests of the corporation as an institution with the rights of the people. These all point to the corruption of government operations. The source of the corruption is wealth, but the antagonism arises from the use of wealth to pervert good governance. The government as the law itself is therefore the direct agent of abuse against which the dissent argues. This interpretation of the law is portrayed as the corrupting influence that cheats the "eligible voter."

The critique of the venal propensity of the government is often turned to what we would now call progressive ends, as the examples above attest, but the Jacksonian tendency is just as often turned against the People as it is used by them. This is because the government is the very vehicle that the People have available to them to stand up to the powers of the few. As John Kenneth Galbraith put it, government is the best vehicle to act as a "countervailing power" to the forces impeding equal economic opportunity. When you undermine it, you limit the ability of people to stand up to the wealthy.[46]

Socialism is the natural manifestation of this countervailing power when taken to the limit, but the dysfunctional potential of organizational corruption even became clear in socialist governments in the early part of the twentieth century, playing out as what the sociologist Robert Michels called the "iron law of oligarchy." This oligarchical tendency inherent in bureaucratic structure itself could undermine the egalitarian mission of both the socialist organizations and the government apparatus they relied upon.

> It is organization which gives birth to the dominion of the elected over the electors, of the mandataries over the mandators, of the delegates over the delegators. Who says organization, says oligarchy.[47]

Michels's theory is an accountability story. It points to the abusive power of the means of administration, but one that accuses the administrators of exploitation or cheating, a perspective that blends seamlessly into later critiques of the "new class" by communist critics of Communism like Milovan Djilas and his view of pernicious power exercised through control over organizational resources under communism. Whatever their politics, those schooled in the Accountability narrative are not surprised when bureaucratic organizations reward their friends and partners.

> The roots of the new class were implanted in a special party, of the Bolshevik type. Lenin was right in his view that his party was an exception in the history of human society, although he did not suspect that it would be the beginning of a new class.[48]
>
> *(p. 39)*

There is a strong affinity in this argument for the Consent narrative in that the goal is to limit the coercive power of the state, but the argument is different. Because it focuses on the economic abuses of the officials rather than their desire for control, "the new class" is an egalitarian concept, not a libertarian one, but because the two narratives share an antagonist, the government, the concept resonates with thinkers of both types, and can build common ground across the divide. This is how strange bedfellows in politics are made.

This is why the conservative movement in the United States has been so committed to promoting (performing in the sense used here) the message that Ronald

Regan made famous in his inaugural address of 1981, "government is not the solution to our problem, government is the problem." Although the goal of the argument was to animate the Consent narrative, his imagery did double duty. Reagan targeted not only the government but also those who occupied it, "government by an elite group," allowing a pivot from a libertarian critique to an egalitarian one that drew some of those egalitarians along to his side. His was a direct rebuttal to the advocates of the Reciprocity narrative—all those populist Truman Democrats—framed in a rival language within the egalitarian imagination. Little wonder he created a phenomenon called the "Reagan Democrat."

This was an important and world altering achievement. In a desperate attempt to counter the socialist tendencies of his time, the Republican president Theodore Roosevelt had helped to establish one of the most enduring catchphrases of the egalitarian imagination, the notion of "special interests." HIs speech from 1910, known as the New Nationalism speech is an apt illustration.

> Now, this means that our government, national and state, must be freed from the sinister influence or control of special interests. Exactly as the special interests of cotton and slavery threatened our political integrity before the Civil War, so now the great special business interests too often control and corrupt the men and methods of government for their own profit. We must drive the special interests out of politics.[49]

Reagan engaged Roosevelt on this very terrain, using egalitarian rhetoric (that is populism) to split the old New Deal coalition that had been fragmented over the course of conflict about Vietnam, civil rights, and cultural change. Through a process of sympathetic magic born of his cultural affinity with the median voter (who Scammon and Wattenberg provocatively described as unyoung, unpoor, and unblack[50]), Reagan identified the People themselves with the corporations who had once been demonized by presidents like Roosevelt as "malefactors of great wealth."

> We hear much of special interest groups. Well, our concern must be for a special interest group that has been too long neglected. It knows no sectional boundaries or ethnic and racial divisions, and it crosses political party lines. It is made up of men and women who raise our food, patrol our streets, man our mines and factories, teach our children, keep our homes, and heal us when we're sick—professionals, industrialists, shopkeepers, clerks, cabbies, and truck drivers. They are, in short, "We the people," this breed called Americans.[51]

At the opening of the twentieth century, Teddy Roosevelt had warded off the forces of gathering socialism through anti-corruption measures. He saw corporations as an example of abuse of organizational resources for private ends. This view would be developed by Roosevelt's cousin, Franklin Roosevelt into a scheme for social protection that undergirded his New Deal. At century's end, Reagan used that same imagery to begin to dismantle that New Deal. In a sense, Reagan opted for the old deal of the populist Democrats like Jefferson and Jackson. His efforts upended the American political party system. By the end of the twentieth century, corporations were people, too.

The fact that Reagan made this performative turn is well known, but Root Narrative Theory helps to explain how he did it. It was a pivot within a primal counternarrative— between two root narratives that shared a common protagonist (the People) but differed in their interpretation of the antagonist. Yes, the people were being cheated, but not by private businesses but instead by a governing elite who used hard-earned tax dollars to pursue their own selfish agendas. Reagan was a kind of modern-day Martin Luther. He attacked the venality and corruption of the governing officers. After Reagan's achievement, the whole world was different. When America sneezes, the world catches a cold.

Ronald Reagan had been instrumental in this development from his first brush with national politics in the Goldwater campaign of 1964, but others had helped to develop the new master narrative as well. A good example was a political operative named William Rusher, a leading editor of the insurgent conservative magazine, *The National Review*, who had been instrumental in the development of the Goldwater campaign and of the burgeoning conservative movement as a whole. In 1975 he published a manifesto titled *The Making of the New Majority Party*,[52] which helped to establish the brand of right-wing populism that is so common in politics around the world today.

Remember that the premise of Root Narrative Theory is that we are looking for EVIL in the conflict documents we study, an acronym for emotional, vivid, intense, and literary characterizations of political phenomena. In Rusher's book, we find the playbook for vilification that will run from the mid-1970s through the Reagan era, to Steven Bannon, Breitbart news, and Donald Trump. The villain serving as the generative binary for the new proponents of the right-wing egalitarian imagination was what Rusher imagined as the makers and the takers, where the takers used government to cheat and defraud the makers—language targeted to the dead center of the language of accountability. Here is Rusher.

> But the battles of the Roosevelt years are over, as irrevocably as Antietam and Gettysburg. The basic economic division in this country is no longer (if it ever was) between the haves and the have-nots. Instead, a new economic division pits the producers—businessmen, manufacturers, hard-hats, blue-collar work-ers and farmers—against a new and powerful class of non-producers comprised of a liberal verbalist elite (the dominant media, the major foundations and research institutions, the educational establishment, the federal and state bureaucracies) and a semi-permanent welfare constituency, all coexisting happily in a state of mutually sustaining symbiosis.

Many of these themes had been present in Richard Nixon's campaigns, but Nixon was an intellectual magpie with no consistent ideology. Rusher, as a movement conservative, believed in the power of ideas, arguing that it was time to abandon the Republican Party to found a new conservative party he imagined as the Independence Party, which would blend the egalitarian and libertarian themes of American political culture to capture the new majority he believed was out there. As the neoconservative Irving Kristol described the broader movement, "[It was] a new kind of class war—the people as citizens versus the politicians and their clients in the public sector."[53]

As things happened, the Republican Party rebelled in 1976; Reagan mounted a primary challenge to Gerald Ford, the incumbent; Ford lost in the general election to Jimmy Carter; Reagan's revolutionaries managed to portray Carter as an example of the failed liberalism of the past; In 1980 Reagan successfully promoted his accountability egalitarianism to the white working classes and served two presidential terms that transformed the old New Deal Coalition beyond recognition: the rest is history. The producerist movement that Rusher imagined did not manage to create a new major party, but it did conquer the old Republican Party.

If we follow the vector of the logic of the accountability story that he helped to develop, we can say that the Republican Party survived in name, but not in spirit. Where Eisenhower and Nixon had accommodated themselves to the class logic of the New Deal and its ethos of economic reciprocity, the Republican Party under Reagan, Patrick Buchanan, Newt Gingrich, Sarah Palin, the Tea Party and finally Steve Bannon and Donald Trump, embraced Rusher's egalitarian conservatism, mixed with an exclusionary classical liberalism. The Party of Lincoln became something not well described by that label. Rusher had diagnosed the political problem in a way that would resonate with his "new majority" for decades.

> This process has reached the point where society's role is wholly reformed, and it is seen as the omnipresent nurse, servant and protector of the individual, who in turn is conceived as having no reciprocal obligations whatever. In return for the progressive diminution of his liberty (and even ultimately of his identity) he receives from the Guardian State an endlessly proliferating series of "rights." He has a "right" to an education, up to any limit that appeals to him (including a "right" to matriculate, regardless of his record). He has a "right" to a job—or, if he chooses not to work, a "right" to a guaranteed minimum income anyway, simply for being human. He has a "right" to free medical care, and to a dignified old age. Meanwhile he has a "right" to any life-style of his choosing, substantially without regard to its impact on the life-style of others or on the public mores of his community.
>
> *(p. 220)*

This image of a "guardian state" was the incarnation of the liberalism Rusher rejected, but the blame was to sit with the verbalist elite who dominated the government and used it for its own nefarious ends. This was the very seat of EVIL.

> We will reject the leadership of an elite which, operating through the bureaucracy, the educational establishment, the media, and the major foundations and research institutions, has persistently led this nation ever further from its moral and psychological moorings.
>
> *(p. 221)*

The fact that egalo-conservatives relied so heavily on the image of the elite-in-government, cements their credentials as egalitarians. The new majoritarianism was "the people vs. the powerful" in a different register. These themes continue to return from Rusher's articulation until now in various forms. They had found a stable place in the conversation in part because they had built an ideological home. Rusherism had occupied the root narratives in a novel way.

As if to highlight how germane Rusher's synthesis was for the conservative insurgency, in the wake of the 1994 landslide congressional election that made Newt Gingrich Speaker of the House, the Republicans offered what was called a "Contract with America" to spell out their new vision. Its programmatic agenda is still quite relevant for Republican congresses, but its major justification demonstrates how powerful this egalitarian anti-statism had become for the movement.

> This year's election offers the chance, after four decades of one-party control, to bring to the House a new majority that will transform the way Congress works. That historic change would be the end of government that is too big, too intrusive, and too easy with the public's money. It can be the beginning of a Congress that respects the values and shares the faith of the American family.[54]

Again, if Rusher had not founded a new party this new majority in Congress certainly felt like one. This was because it built on novel narrative foundations. And this libertarian-tinged version of Rusher's accountability story runs like a thread through the right-wing populism of our own era.

Although Sarah Palin was rather restrained when as the unknown vice-presidential candidate she delivered her speech to the Republican national convention in 2008, by the time she endorsed Donald Trump's candidacy in 2016, she was channeling William Rusher's version of movement conservatism, full-throttle. It is the producers versus the non-producers: the makers versus the takers:

> And he tells us Joe six packs, he said, "You know, I've worked very, very hard. And I've succeeded. Hugely I've succeeded," he says. And he says, "I want you to succeed too." And that is refreshing, because he [Trump], as he builds things, he builds big things, things that touch the sky, big infrastructure that puts other people to work. He has spent his life looking up and respecting the hard-hats and the steel-toed boots and the work ethic that you all have within you. He, being an optimist, passionate about equal-opportunity to work. The self-made success of his, you know that he doesn't get his power, his high, off of OPM, other people's money, like a lot of dopes in Washington

do. They're addicted to OPM, where they take other people's money, and then their high is getting to redistribute it, right? And then they get to be really popular people when they get to give out your hard money. Well, he doesn't do that. His power, his passion, is the fabric of America. And it's woven by work ethic and dreams and drive and faith in the Almighty, what a combination.[55]

Surely this Accountability narrative of Palin's has that "curious logicality" of -isms that Hannah Arendt wrote about. In a widely circulated discussion at the Vatican, Donald Trump's adviser, Steven Bannon, carried the themes of this producerist populism into the realm of general critique.

The tea party in the United States' biggest fight is with the Republican establishment, which is really a collection of crony capitalists that feel that they have a different set of rules of how they're going to comport themselves and how they're going to run things. And, quite frankly, it's the reason that the United States' financial situation is so dire, particularly our balance sheet. We have virtually a hundred trillion dollars of unfunded liabilities. That is all because you've had this kind of crony capitalism in Washington, DC. The rise of Breitbart is directly tied to being the voice of that center-right opposition. And, quite frankly, we're winning many, many victories.[56]

Root Narrative Theory provides us with a way to speak about populist rhetoric in more precise ways. The primal critique of the Accountability narrative is much the same as it is with the class theories undergirding most socialist analyses, but the target of concern has shifted. Where socialist ideologues work in the idioms of reciprocity, right-wing populists draw on conceptions of government corruption and accountability. As elites have recognized this potential line of fracture within the socialist camp, they have exploited it and pushed the alternative conception of egalitarian thinking, sometimes for concerns consistent with some vision of the left and sometimes of the right. The populism that results is usually somehow inconsistent with the redistributive ideal of socialism because it questions the most likely mechanism of that redistribution, the state itself.

Perhaps the best way to end this discussion of accountability is with the critic of state power who most directly stood up to Marx himself on this very issue, Mikhail Bukunin.

I hate Communism because it is the negation of liberty and because humanity is for me unthinkable without liberty. I am not a Communist, because Communism concentrates and swallows up in itself for the benefit of the State all the forces of society, because it inevitably leads to the concentration of property in the hands of the State, whereas I want the abolition of the State, the final eradication of the principle of authority and the patronage proper to the State, which under the pretext of moralizing and civilizing men has hitherto only enslaved, persecuted, exploited and corrupted them.[57]

At least Bakunin and Sarah Palin agreed on one thing, they distrusted "the concentration of property in the hands of the State" enough to lead them both to hate Communism. There are some problems that more democracy simply cannot fix. Popular sovereignty of equals before the law is itself no protection against the socializing conformity of the general will. This requires a new category of thought: the dignitarian imagination.

Notes

1 Grusky, *Social Stratification*.
2 Machiavelli, *Discourses on Livy*.
3 Rousseau, *The Social Contract and The First and Second Discourses*.
4 As in all cases of naming the root narratives and their constituent ethics, it has been a challenge to settle on one that does all the work I want it to do. There is the dictionary definition of the word to take into consideration. There are all of the commonsense connotations of the word to consider as well. There is the question of the emotional weight of the word and its ability to bring appropriate images to mind. Finally, there is the theoretical history of the word and how it tends to invoke certain kinds of authors, policies, and agendas as it is used. In other words, I face all the same problems that anyone else does in trying to develop a language through which to speak about conflict and politics, even as I attempt to create a meta-language for political description. The case of reciprocity has been among the hardest for me and as for now, I have grasped for Polanyi's lifeline to carry me through this part of the journey. Nothing will really do, but the denotation of the word fits better than any other I can find to point to the mutual obligations of buyer and seller, employer and employee, lender and borrower, insurer and insuree. Things become unreciprocal when one party has excessive bargaining power over the other and when this power is used to produce unfair advantage, especially over long periods of time.
5 Founders Archives, "Founders Online."
6 Cited in Morris, *Fit for the Presidency?*
7 Dickinson, Official Proceedings of the Democratic National Convention.
8 Bryan was not the only leader who struggled to render the reciprocity narrative legible to the American public, who had been so successfully inoculated against its implications for industrial society. Among my favorite examples is this line from the labor theorist, Jack Barbash, who described the work of John R. Commons as follows, "Some intellectual movements, it turns out, are as important for the opposition they stir up as they are in their own right. Commons and the Wisconsin School 'Americanized' the labor problem to save it from guilt by Marxist association." See Adams and Meltz, Industrial Relations Theory.
9 The Independent.
10 Samuelson, "The Pure Theory of Public Expenditure."
11 Habermas, *The Structural Transformation of the Public Sphere*.
12 Bronner and Kellner, *Critical Theory and Society*.
13 A powerful and sustained argument about how the industrial revolution displaced the progressive features of individualism and brought about the need for collective interpretations of equality is Elizabeth Anderson's *Private Government*.
14 Truman, Public Papers of the Presidents of the United States.
15 Lichtenstein, *Walter Reuther*.
16 Nader, *Unsafe at Any Speed*.
17 Public Citizen, "About Us."
18 Clinton, "Address Accepting the Presidential Nomination at the Democratic National Convention in New York."

19 It is a curious feature of reciprocity narratives that they are very hard to find on the web. One place where Edwards speech still survives is, Rhetorik, "John Edwards Rede Am Nationalen Demokratischen Kongress."
20 Halpin and Harbage, "The Origins and Demise of The Public Option."
21 Gerring, *Party Ideologies in America 1828–1996*.
22 Washington Post Staff, "The Transcript of Bernie Sanders's Victory Speech."
23 Piketty, *Capital in the 21st Century*.
24 Badiou et al., *What is a People?*
25 The Associated Press, "What Did Donald Trump Say about Immigrants?"
26 Zakaria, "Interview with Steve Bannon."
27 Yglesias, "Joe Biden's Surprisingly Controversial Claim that Trump is an Aberration, Explained."
28 Hitler, *Mein Kampf*.
29 Hayek, *The Road to Serfdom*.
30 Hayek, *The Road to Serfdom*.
31 Sartre and Walzer, *Anti-Semite and Jew*.
32 "Père Duchesne Idealizes the Sans–culottes."
33 Lenin, "How to Organise Competition?"
34 Marx, *Selected Writings*.
35 Boyer, University of Chicago Readings in Western Civilization.
36 Kautsky, *The Class Struggle*.
37 Perón, "Speech to the Descamisados."
38 Martyr, Second Apology (Dialogue with Trypho.)
39 Cited in Kazin, *The Populist Persuasion*.
40 Anti-Defamation League, "Iranian President Mahmoud Ahmadinejad in His Own Words."
41 Internet Archive, Selected Documents of the Khmer Rouge.
42 U.S. National Park Service. "First Debate: Ottawa, Illinois."
43 Hanover Historical Texts Project, "Populist Party Platform."
44 Hanover Historical Texts Project, "Populist Party Platform."
45 Citizens United v. Federal Election Comm'n 558 U.S. 310.
46 Galbraith, *American Capitalism*.
47 Michels, *Political Parties*.
48 Djilas, *The New Class*.
49 Slack, "President Teddy Roosevelt's New Nationalism Speech."
50 Scammon and Wattenberg, *The Real Majority*.
51 Reagan, "Inaugural Address."
52 Rusher, *The Making of the New Majority Party*.
53 Stahl, *Right Moves*.
54 United Press International, "Contract with America."
55 Saul, "Sarah Palin's Speech Endorsing Donald Trump in Full."
56 Feder, "This is How Steve Bannon Sees the Entire World."
57 Carr, *Michael Bakunin*.

Bibliography

Adams, Roy J., and Noah M. Meltz. *Industrial Relations Theory: Its Nature, Scope, and Pedagogy*. Lanham, MD: Scarecrow Press, 1993.

Anderson, Elizabeth. *Private Government: How Employers Rule Our Lives (and Why We Don't Talk about It)*. Princeton: Princeton University Press, 2019.

Anti-Defamation League. "Iranian President Mahmoud Ahmadinejad in His Own Words." *Anti-Defamation League*. Accessed July 19, 2018. https://www.adl.org/news/article/iranian-president-mahmoud-ahmadinejad-in-his-own-words.

The Associated Press. "What Did Donald Trump Say about Immigrants?" *The Boston Globe*, June 29, 2015. Accessed July 19, 2018. https://www.bostonglobe.com/arts/television/2015/06/29/what-did-donald-trump-say-about-immigrants/ForaqpQHjwgeKRdVUdYrdM/story.html.

Badiou, Alain, Judith Butler, Georges Didi-Huberman, Sadri Khiari, Jacques Rancière, and Pierre Bourdieu. *What is a People?* New York: Columbia University Press, 2016.

Boyer, John W. *University of Chicago Readings in Western Civilization, Volume 7: The Old Regime and the French Revolution*. Chicago: University of Chicago Press, 1987.

Bronner, Stephen Eric, and Douglas MacKay Kellner. *Critical Theory and Society*. New York: Routledge, 1989.

Carr, E. H. *Michael Bakunin*. New York: Vintage Books, 1961.

Citizens United v. Federal Election Comm'n 558 U.S. 310 (2010), p. 183.

Clinton, William J. "Address Accepting the Presidential Nomination at the Democratic National Convention in New York." Online by Gerhard Peters and John T. Woolley, The American Presidency Project. Accessed July 19, 2018. https://www.presidency.ucsb.edu/node/220260.

Dickinson, Edward B. *Official Proceedings of the Democratic National Convention: Held in Chicago, Ill., July 7th, 8th, 9th, 10th and 11th, 1896. Containing, Also, the Democratic National Committee, Etc. with an Appendix*. Logansport, IN: Wilson, Humphreys & Company, 1896.

Djilas, Milovan. *The New Class*. New York: Frederick A. Praeger, 1957.

Feder, J. Lester. "This is How Steve Bannon Sees the Entire World." *BuzzFeedNews*, November 15, 2016. Accessed July 19, 2018. https://www.buzzfeednews.com/article/lesterfeder/this-is-how-steve-bannon-sees-the-entire-world#.efqoQjgLb.

Founders Archives. "Founders Online: Thomas Jefferson to Charles Yancey, January 6, 1816." National Archives. Accessed July 19, 2018. http://founders.archives.gov/documents/Jefferson/03-09-02-0209.

Galbraith, John. *American Capitalism: The Concept of Countervailing Power*. London: Routledge, 2017.

Gerring, John. *Party Ideologies in America 1828–1996*. Cambridge: Cambridge University Press, 1998.

Grusky, David B. *Social Stratification: Class, Race and Gender in Sociological Perspective*. Edited by Marta Tienda and David B. Grusky. Social Inequality Series. Boulder: Stanford University Press, 1994.

Habermas, Jurgen. *The Structural Transformation of the Public Sphere: An Inquiry into a Category of Bourgeois Society*. Cambridge, MA: The M.I.T. Press, 1989.

Halpin, Helen A., and Peter Harbage. "The Origins and Demise of The Public Option." *Health Affairs* 29, no. 6 (June 1, 2010): 1117–1124. https://doi.org/10.1377/hlthaff.2010.0363.

Hanover Historical Texts Project. "Populist Party Platform." 1892. *Hanover Historical Texts Project*. Accessed July 19, 2018. https://history.hanover.edu/courses/excerpts/111pop.html.

Hayek, F. A. *The Road to Serfdom: Text and Documents—The Definitive Edition*. Edited by Bruce Caldwell. Chicago: University of Chicago Press, 2007.

Hitler, Adolf. *Mein Kampf*. Translated by Ralph Manheim. Boston: Houghton Mifflin Company, 1998.

The Independent. New York: Independent Publications Incorporated, 1906.

Internet Archive. *Selected Documents of the Khmer Rouge*, late 1970s. Internet Archive. Accessed November 21, 2019. http://archive.org/details/SelectedDocumentsOfTheKhmerRouge.

Kautsky, Karl. *The Class Struggle*. Sligo: HardPress Publishing, 2012.

Kazin, Michael. *The Populist Persuasion: An American History*. Ithaca, NY: Cornell University Press, 1998.

Lenin, Vladimir. "How to Organise Competition?" *Pravda*, no. 17, January 20, 1929. Online at Marxists.org. Accessed July 19, 2018. https://www.marxists.org/archive/lenin/works/1917/dec/25.htm.

Lichtenstein, Nelson. *Walter Reuther: The Most Dangerous Man in Detroit*. Champaign, IL: University of Illinois Press, 1997.

Machiavelli, Niccolò. *Discourses on Livy*. Chicago: University of Chicago Press, 2009.

Martyr, Justin. *Second Apology (Dialogue with Trypho.) Internet Medieval Source Book*. New York: Fordham University. Accessed July 19, 2018. https://sourcebooks.fordham.edu/basis/justin-apology2.asp.

Marx, Karl. *Selected Writings*. Edited by Lawrence H. Simon. Cambridge, MA: Hackett Publishing Company, 1994.

Michels, Robert. *Political Parties: A Sociological Study of Oligarchical Tendencies of Modern Democracy*. New York: The Free Press, 1962.

Morris, Seymour. *Fit for the Presidency?: Winners, Losers, What-Ifs, and Also-Rans*. Lincoln: University of Nebraska Press, 2017.

Nader, Ralph. *Unsafe at Any Speed*. New York: Grossman Publishers, 1965.

Perón, Maria Eva. "Speech to the Descamisados." October 17, 1951. *Archives of Women's Political Communication*, Iowa State University. Accessed August 19, 2019. https://awpc.cattcenter.iastate.edu/2017/10/11/final-speech-october-17-1951/.

Piketty, Thomas. *Capital in the 21st Century*. Cambridge, MA: Harvard University Press, 2014.

Plato. *The Republic*. Cambridge: Cambridge University Press, 2000.

Public Citizen. "About Us." *Public Citizen*. Accessed August 9, 2019. https://www.citizen.org/about/.

Reagan, Ronald. "Inaugural Address." Online by Gerhard Peters and John T. Woolley, The American Presidency Project. Accessed July 18, 2018. https://www.presidency.ucsb.edu/node/246336.

Rhetorik. "John Edwards Rede Am Nationalen Demokratischen Kongress." *Rhetorik website*. Accessed July 19, 2018. http://www.rhetorik.ch/Aktuell/kerry/edwards.html.

Rousseau, Jean-Jacques. *The Social Contract and The First and Second Discourses*. New Haven: Yale University Press, 2002.

Rusher, William A. *The Making of the New Majority Party*. New York: Sheed and Ward, 1975.

Samuelson, Paul A. "The Pure Theory of Public Expenditure." *The Review of Economics and Statistics* 36, no. 4 (1954): 387–389. https://doi.org/10.2307/1925895.

Sartre, Jean-Paul, and Michael Walzer. *Anti-Semite and Jew: An Exploration of the Etiology of Hate*. Translated by George J. Becker. New York: Schocken, 1995.

Saul, Heather. "Sarah Palin's Speech Endorsing Donald Trump in Full." *The Independent*, January 20, 2016. Accessed November 21, 2019. http://www.independent.co.uk/news/people/sarah-palins-speech-endorsing-donald-trump-in-full-a6822771.html.

Scammon, Richard M., and Ben J. Wattenberg. *The Real Majority*. New York: Coward, McCann & Geoghegan, Inc., 1971.

Slack, Megan. "President Teddy Roosevelt's New Nationalism Speech." December 6, 2011. The White House. Accessed November 21, 2019. https://obamawhitehouse.archives.gov/blog/2011/12/06/archives-president-teddy-roosevelts-new-nationalism-speech.

Stahl, Jason. *Right Moves: The Conservative Think Tank in American Political Culture since 1945*. Chapel Hill, NC: University of North Carolina Press, 2016.

Truman, Harry S. *Public Papers of the Presidents of the United States: Harry S. Truman, 1948, Volume 4*. Ann Arbor, MI: University of Michigan Press, 1963.

United Press International. "Contract with America." November 9, 1994. UPI Archives. Accessed July 19, 2018. https://www.upi.com/Archives/1994/11/09/Following-is-the-text-of-the-Contract-with-America/5995784357200/.

U.S. National Park Service. "First Debate: Ottawa, Illinois." August 21, 1858. *Lincoln Home National Historic Site* (U.S. National Park Service). Accessed July 19, 2018. https://www.nps.gov/liho/learn/historyculture/debate1.htm.

Wallace, Henry. "Century of the Common Man speech." 1942. Society for Historians of American Foreign Relations. Accessed November 19, 2019. https://shafr.org/teaching/draft-classroom-documents/century-of-the-common-man.

Washington Post Staff. "The Transcript of Bernie Sanders's Victory Speech." *Washington Post*, February 10, 2016. Accessed July 19, 2018. https://www.washingtonpost.com/news/post-politics/wp/2016/02/10/the-transcript-of-bernie-sanderss-victory-speech/?noredirect=on&utm_term=.01ca2cb68156.

Yglesias, Matthew. "Joe Biden's Surprisingly Controversial Claim that Trump is an Aberration, Explained." *Vox*, May 13, 2019. Accessed August 19, 2019. https://www.vox.com/2019/5/13/18535239/joe-biden-trump-aberrant-aberration.

Zakaria, Fareed. "Interview with Steve Bannon." CNN, June 3, 2018. Accessed July 20, 2018. http://transcripts.cnn.com/TRANSCRIPTS/1806/03/fzgps.01.html.

8

IMAGINING DIGNITY

Recognition, Liberation, Inclusion

The Recognition narrative

We finally come to a root narrative category that should be readily intuitive to most of us as essential for the analysis and resolution of protracted conflicts around the world. The dignitarian imagination is the cast of thought that allows us to criticize racism, sexism, anti-Semitism, ethnocentrism, homophobia and a host of other demeaning forms of bigotry. The dignitarian imagination is all about the title of one of Aretha Franklin's most famous songs, R-E-S-P-E-C-T,[1] respect as a political category, not merely something to be sought after and struggled over in private life. True to the assumptions of Root Narrative Theory, we learn the meaning of a political concept through a story about how a particular form of power has been abused. The primitive dignitarian story defines the majority of accepted culture and its ideals as a form of power that is often weaponized and put to use against minorities and outgroups: *Majorities use biased folkways to create cultural disrespect of the Other.* We can now easily see the abusive form of this cultural power and artfully deploy its terms of condemnation: white supremacy, patriarchy, religious dogma, ethnic chauvinism, heteronormativity, etc., each of which defines a dignitarian antagonist.

Political history, theory and practice in the modern period focused on other institutional obstacles to justice before the dignitarian imagination could fully flourish in its own right. First came the fixation on state formation and the problem of security, then the liberal revolutions against military power and political tyranny, followed by the rebellion against economic concentration. Although the dignitarian category of thought is as fundamental and ancient as are the other three root narrative categories, somehow, it was only when these other domains of power had been fully explored and broadly challenged that the theory of human dignity could be directly articulated.

The demand to protect the dignity or group status of a particular people is as old as Moses; "Then the LORD said unto Moses, Go in unto Pharaoh, and tell him, Thus saith the LORD God of the Hebrews, Let my people go, that they may serve me." And yet the political demands for diversity and inclusion only began to take hold in formal politics as late as Woodrow Wilson's famous 1918 "Fourteen Points" address to the U.S. Congress. It was not until 1906 that the concept of ethnocentrism was introduced to sociology by Willian Graham Sumner. The word racism, in its various forms, only developed over the course of the early decades of the twentieth century, and it was not until 1922 that Walter Lippman introduced our figurative use of the term stereotype, a metaphor he borrowed from the printing industry. Folkways as a subject of explicit political concern only developed with the advent of the science of the sociological imagination.

Given its conception in the origins of sociological and anthropological thought, it is tempting for some to identify the dignitarian imagination with the concept of social identity or to dismiss it as identity politics or cultural relativism, as if no animating principles were involved in its definition. Although this association of dignitarian thought and identity is appropriate in that identity in the sense of identification with a particular way of life refers precisely to the principle at stake in the moral politics of the root narrative, social identity formation is actually a much broader process. All forms of moral politics involve social identity formation. Each of the root narratives involves a process of identification, organized around a binary contrast imposed by the story structure. For example, securitarian stories pit "us against them," with "them" defined as dangerous foreigners, partisan elites, or unruly criminals. In each case an identity of us is deployed for political effect. The same is true of libertarian stories that contrast "the Individual vs. the State." Strong pressures for identity formation are at work here as well. It is also obvious that the various forms of socialism and populism rely on processes of identification, either with a social class or some conception of a People that is subject to unfair competitive pressures. Each of the root narratives produce powerful identities that draw their meaning from images of abusive power, but none of these identities are the same as the kind of identity that is the subject of the dignitarian imagination.

The logic of dignitarian thought follows its primitive story; it is about discrimination against a group of people simply because they are different. The victim/hero of dignitarian stories is a minority community like Latinos in the United States, or an outgroup like women in patriarchal society. The antagonist is always defined in terms of biased cultural identification, but can be differentiated into direct expressions of disrespect as in the Recognition narrative, abuses of institutional advantage for bigoted purposes as in the Inclusion narrative, or abuses of state power for cultural advantage as in the Liberation narrative. In each case the identity of the narrator is defined in a subtle but significantly different way.

Anyone who attempts to dismiss the importance of dignitarian root narratives is ignoring many of the most troubling dynamics of political struggle since the era of World War I. Radical disagreements in contemporary conflicts often rest on contrasting dignitarian foundations. And if the political implications of dignitarian thinking are easier for outsiders to recognize in what I call its Inclusion and Liberation forms because of their typical calls for concrete institutional reforms like desegregation and political independence, it is the recognition stories that carry the spirit of the ethic in its purest form, the demand for social status, and they are only dismissed at peril. Dignitarian thought as recognition targets the very concept of hate itself, a concept as powerful as it is abstract.

In 1964, the sociologist, E. Digby Baltzell, published *The Protestant Establishment: Aristocracy and Caste in America,*[2] a book that would be consequential, not in the normal sense of influence over a generation of students and colleagues who would read and emulate the work, which it was, but in the sense of offering us a new way of understanding ourselves. He coined a new and catchy term: WASP for White Anglo-Saxon Protestant, which helped to frame the story of American society as a caste system. Baltzell's book is a perfect place to begin a discussion about the Recognition narrative, because describing, as it does, the privilege that protestants from certain European origins reserved to themselves by the middle of the twentieth century, it reminds us that once upon a time, even white Catholics were considered an outgroup—at least in American political culture—and the struggle to overcome this outgroup status is a more general and enduring feature of political life than many in our liberal and forward-looking society would care to believe.

In that once upon a time, a Catholic like John Fitzgerald Kennedy was not considered a suitable candidate for the presidency. We can see the traces of this cultural caste system in the discursive artifacts of the era. For example, we find the following discussion of the role of religion on the website of the JFK library, detailing the discrimination and bigotry he faced as a Catholic candidate.

> Only one Catholic, Governor Alfred E. Smith of New York, had ever been the presidential nominee of one of the major parties. Smith's 1928 campaign was dogged by claims that he would build a tunnel connecting the White House and the Vatican and would amend the Constitution to make Catholicism the nation's established religion. He was overwhelmingly defeated—even losing much of the then Democratic Solid South. JFK established an informal network of advisers on the religious issue—including speechwriter Ted Sorensen, Dean Francis Bowes Sayre Jr. of the National Cathedral and several journalists. It was clear from the outset that Kennedy had to enter the state primaries to prove to skeptical party leaders that he was a viable national candidate.[3]

Anti-Catholic bigotry on the part of the elite protestant establishment (and of all those who identified with it) had undermined the candidacy of the only previous Catholic to win the nomination and JFK was the canary in the coalmine of cultural change of the post-World War II era: the Barack Obama of his time. This same Alfred Smith was known for a maxim that helps us to make sense of the primary obstacle to the moral politics of dignitarian stories, "the cure for the evils of democracy is more democracy." Smith made the statement amid a struggle in 1925 with the wealthy residents of Long Island (and Robert Moses) over access to public parks and he saw in democracy a check on the "sacred constitutional property rights" that his opponents defended.[4]

In this environment, where the class politics of the Reciprocity narrative was widely circulated and confidently performed, the cause of democracy was seen as a class issue. The defenders of property rights already had access to summer relief in the hot New York summers, while the People needed parks and public spaces made available to them for relief and refreshment. Even if majoritarian pressure could overwhelm wealthy opponents, it had little to offer Smith himself as protection from anti-Catholic bigotry in his election campaign in 1928. When majorities are the abusers, more democracy does nothing to help. At least in the short run, democratic process only serves to re-instantiate the cultural biases and privileges of the majority. This threat of tyranny in the consensual power of the majority is precisely the thing that Alexis de Tocqueville had warned the world of.

> So in the United States the majority has an immense power in fact and a power of opinion almost as great; and once the majority has formed on a question, there is, so to speak, no obstacle that can, I will not say stop, but even slow its course and leave time for the majority to hear the cries of those whom it crushes as it goes.[5]
>
> *(Volume Two, Chapter 7)*

This power of the majority to crush those who cry out was obvious to Tocqueville not only because he was a member of a minority, the aristocracy, that had not fared well under the majoritarian tendencies of the Revolution, but also because he could clearly anticipate the destructive effects of the racialized and majoritarian politics of the nineteenth century. Even when the laws were formally written to protect these outgroups, Tocqueville saw that the opinion of the majority itself was an abusive power that would not be capable of curing itself.

> When a man or a party suffers from an injustice in the United States, to whom do you want them to appeal? To public opinion? That is what forms the majority. To the legislative body? It represents the majority and blindly obeys it. To the executive power? It is named by the majority and serves it as a passive instrument. To the police? The police are nothing other than the majority under arms. To the jury? The jury is the majority vested with the right to deliver judgments. The judges themselves, in certain states, are elected by the majority. However iniquitous or unreasonable the measure that strikes you may be, you must therefore submit to it or flee.

And in the footnote to this passage, he reveals an anecdote from a conversation he had with a Quaker in Pennsylvania about what it is that kept African Americans from voting there when they had the formal right to. I have always felt that this passage was what sealed Tocqueville's thinking about the abusive powers of the majority—as majority—and provided him with his insight about the "tyranny of the majority."

> "So, among you, Blacks have the right to vote?"—"Undoubtedly."—"Then, how come at the polling place this morning, I did not see a single one in the crowd?"—"This is not the fault of the law," the American said to me; "Negroes, it is true, have the right to present themselves at elections, but they abstain voluntarily it seems."—"That is very modest of them."—"Oh! it isn't that they refuse to go, but they are afraid that they will be mistreated there."

As is clear from this example, the existence of formal legal rights is no guarantee of protection against informal harassment and discrimination, an insight into the politicization of everyday life and the force of opinion. And John Stuart Mill would provide an even more cutting description of this abusive force.

> Protection, therefore, against the tyranny of the magistrate is not enough: there needs protection also against the tyranny of the prevailing opinion and feeling; against the tendency of society to impose, by other means than civil penalties, its own ideas and practices as rules of conduct on those who dissent from them[6]

The forces of racism and sexism and all of the other forms of group-based exclusion are so familiar to us that we have almost lost our ability to see them clearly. Because we are all dignitarians now, these are phenomena that are simply known, but their source is a nebulous network of social power anchored in the very patterns of social life. These nebulous powers are the folkways, the cultural practices, canalizations of habit, and currents of opinion. Their abuse and weaponization against those outside constitute, in relief and contrast, the dignitarian imagination.

Both Tocqueville and Mill developed important insights that are consistent with dignitarian root narratives, but they really were libertarian thinkers. This is why I have chosen to associate the category of the dignitarian imagination with Frantz Fanon instead (and avoided other thinkers like Hegel or Herder whose ideas are relevant for the root narrative but speak to other issues as well). Unlike either Tocqueville or Mill, Fanon located the critique of majoritarian power in colonial abuses, not in violations of equal protection of law for individuals. His was a group concept in which the conquered fights back against the abuses of the conqueror. Fanonian politics was about fighting back against the power of hegemonic culture, about preserving one's own heritage, and of developing an independent sense of self-concept, removing the occupier from one's own psyche. As the Tunisian author Albert Memmi wrote in *The Colonizer and the Colonized*, "Who can completely rid himself of bigotry in a country where everyone is tainted by it, including its victims?"[7]

We can see the intellectual challenge to simply name the problem of political dignity—the problem of fighting back—in early attempts like Gunnar Myrdal's influential study of American race relations. The challenge was to first define the problem against the backdrop of the other, dominant root narratives whose political implications were more obvious. In the language of Root Narrative Theory, Myrdal's challenge was to shift the category of the moral imagination from the libertarian to the dignitarian.

> The "American Dilemma," referred to in the title of this book, is the ever-ranging conflict between, on the one hand, the valuations preserved on the general plane which we shall call the "American Creed," where the American thinks, talks, and acts under the influence of high national and Christian precepts, and, on the other hand, the valuations on specific planes of individual and group living, where personal and local interests; economic, social, and sexual jealousies; considerations of community prestige and conformity; group prejudice against particular persons or types of people; and all sorts of miscellaneous wants, impulses, and habits dominate his outlook.[8]

The dignitarian understands with deeper conviction what Tocqueville glimpsed in his interviews; the evils of democracy that cannot be cured by democracy alone. The solution is not merely one of increasing and promoting freedom, but of constraining the power of the majority to act on its preferences—and in many cases to actively change those preferences. The evil of misrecognition requires something other than formal, liberal, individual equality. It requires recognition, inclusion, and respect, for formerly dominated outgroups, which is to say it requires channels of resistance to prevailing opinion and feeling.

As was true of the previous root narratives, Root Narrative Theory provides us with a systematic way to differentiate the three sub-roots of the larger dignitarian root narrative. The Recognition narrative is what results when group dignity is threatened with majority opinion. The Inclusion narrative is what results when group dignity is contrasted with the rights of economically privileged individuals. The Liberation narrative is what results when group dignity is attacked as a threat to the security of the broader political community. Each is equally important in different settings and each reveals a distinctive moral logic that effective communicators will learn to recognize and engage.

How else would you explain disputes like that between Cornell West and Ta-Nehisi Coates on the reception of Coates's book *Between the World and Me*?[9] The dispute was brief in duration and emerged when Cornell West published a critique of Coates in the *Guardian* Newspaper in late 2017, which seems to have dumbfounded Coates. West wrote:

> The disagreement between Coates and me is clear: any analysis or vision of our world that omits the centrality of Wall Street power, US military policies, and the complex dynamics of class, gender, and sexuality in black America is too narrow and dangerously misleading. So it is with Ta-Nehisi Coates' worldview.[10]

The controversy was engaging enough that Coates deleted his Twitter account as a result of it and expressed clear concern that one of his idols from his youth was taking aim at him in this way when they should instead be unified in their opposition to racial oppression. A full month after the piece in the *Guardian*, Coates is quoted in reference to comments he made about his confusion about West's critique.

> Coates addressed the controversy at a panel Tuesday hosted by *The Atlantic*, saying he remains confused why the feud started in the first place, and that he can't seem to find a huge difference in the things West has spoken about and what Coates himself has written.[11]

The revealing line here is, "he can't seem to find a huge difference." This is the typical effect of ideological dumbfounding. The persistence of this dumbfounding effect in Coates's version of the story strikes me as evidence that we are dealing here with a clash of root narratives, one that West recognizes as such and Coates does not.

In Cornell West's stories, there is a wide array of different types of adversary, some libertarian, some egalitarian, and some dignitarian. He is eclectic in his invocation of alternative ideological roots. In his critique of Coates, West draws special attention to Wall Street and the U.S. Military, neither of which figure in Coates's perspective. Because West is such a nuanced thinker, his arguments are full of reference to a wide palette of critique, making for a complex profile of counternarratives in his speaking and writing. This is typical of West's work. We might think of him as a multi-rooted, dignitarian thinker, balanced in his ideological profile, even when directly targeting white supremacy. This gives him suppleness in assault and flexibility in his evaluations. He certainly can spot a reductionist argument when he sees one, whether it be Marxist or anti-racist.

On the other hand, Coates is far more focused. His anti-supremacist agenda speaks to a single sub-root of the dignitarian imagination in a far more consistent form than most other leading African American intellectuals writing today, especially in his *Between the World and Me*, a beautiful and thoughtful reflection on his own journey in dealing with racial oppression. The book reads like an updated version of Fanon's *Black Skin, White Masks*, systematically avoiding attacks on the effects of housing discrimination or the institutions of the racial caste system, focusing instead like a laser on the existential blight of supremacy itself, thought of as a cultural phenomenon—which he describes as being of "cosmic significance."

The beauty of Coates's book is the clarity with which he focuses the reader's attention on this fundamental logic, in uncompromising, painstaking and intimate terms, but it is important to insist that Coates does not avoid discussion about the institutions that supported racism like redlining and stop-and-frisk policing, rather he tends to render these events and institutions meaningful by projecting them into his own version of this dignitarian ethic. For Coates, like the early Fanon, almost any institution is a reflection of the divisive Dream of whiteness. All problems (at least those he shares in the book) are nails for this hammer. Any issue can be fit or interpellated into a recognition story.

If the book is beautiful and touching, conveying a vulnerability that is rare for authors as angered by injustice as he is, its greatness is limited insofar as it is also reductionistic, reframing all problems in the cultural terms of recognition. It is a book targeted at the derogating power of white supremacy as a cultural system, as social status, not one providing much insight into institutional systems of discrimination or the challenges of managing security in the context of deep-seated racial bias. Coates is concerned most with the culture of racism and the representation of racial deference rather than its institutional supports; this is what divides him from the world. Coates, in this argument at least, is an intellectual purist.

> I saw that what divided me from the world was not anything intrinsic to us but the actual injury done by people intent on naming us, intent on believing that what they have named us matters more than anything we could ever actually do.
>
> *(p. 120)*

It is the naming and the capacity to name that enrages him, a statement with a biblical ring. The racialized status system, its signifying capacity, is Coates's source of EVIL. Although this is easy to dismiss as identity politics, what is so radical about the book and the perspective is that it attacks the problem head on and without compromise. An inclusion story will turn the question of supremacy against formal organizations. Its logical solutions are institutional. A liberation story will turn the question of supremacy against biased laws and state systems. Its logical solutions are legal and political. Instead, recognition focuses the question of supremacy on the integrity and stability of the dominant culture itself. Its logical solutions are symbolic, which can make them more, not less, important. In the Recognition narrative, anti-supremacism questions the culture of the People, that is the people who are numerous enough, powerful enough, self-conscious enough, and well organized enough to express their will on matters large and small as if it were universal.

Contrary to claims of majoritarian advocates of the general will, there is nothing trivial or superficial, or thin-skinned about this struggle for cultural recognition. It is as real as any material oppression. There does appear to be some kind of basic human need for dignity that is attached to our investment in a genealogical project, however imaginary that project really is. Groups that organize against the mainstream to protect their heritage are a permanent part of the political landscape.

Whatever has been said here about race can be said about the symbolic politics of any other status struggle as well, for example, gender identity, religious affiliation, sexual orientation, ability status, but not class. That is unless class is understood as a social status and not a feature of economic interdependence. The dignitarian imagination is about the worthiness of a group and the tendency for a hegemonic power to denigrate and marginalize members of it. It is about the politics of evaluation, and although the root narrative will play out a little differently in the three sub-varieties, the core of the idea, even when it is inflected by institutional or legal complications, orbits the concept of group membership not economic or political power, in itself.

We get a better sense of the material reality of symbolic life from the writers of the Birmingham School of cultural studies, figures like Richard Hoggart, Stuart Hall and Dick Hebdige, who helped to reformulate the notion of culture using insights from the Cultural Marxist, Antonio Gramsci, so that it might play a central role in political theory. Hebdige, in particular, has a way of turning our attention toward the defining feature of the Recognition narrative in a way that provides for differentiation with respect to the other two forms of the dignitarian thought. His interest is in style as it relates to the formation of sub-cultures, in music, art, and lifestyle more generally.[12]

Hebdige, writing about the inchoate quasi-politics of the punk rock sub-culture, pointed out how important were the seemingly surface aberrations from the cultural styles of the hegemonic mainstream. His work points us to the politics of everyday life, the characteristic subject matter and field of conflict on which struggles for recognition play out. His work ties in well with the kind of story that someone like Ta-Nehisi Coates tells in contrast to more traditional civil rights leaders, because so much of Coates's story is about African American styles of dress, celebration, intellectual argument, love and intimacy and so on. It is easy to dismiss these markers of difference as trivial, but Hebdige helps us to see that they are anything but.

The Dream of whiteness that Coates vilifies is problematic because it derogates, but also because it is so complete, so totalizing, driving the familiar forms of African American lifestyle and culture to the margins. As long as the Dream survives, the good stuff will be harder to enjoy. To behave as a black person in this kind of world becomes a way to kowtow to the mainstream. Cultural politics—the dignitarian imagination—is the mechanism for countering this tendency. It encourages new forms of respect, new habits of evaluation and revolution in the realm of symbolic culture.

> However, the challenge to hegemony which subcultures represent is not issued directly by them. Rather it is expressed obliquely, in style. The objections are lodged, the contradictions displayed (and, as we shall see, 'magically resolved') at the profoundly superficial level of appearances: that is, at the level of signs. For the sign-community, the community of myth-consumers, is not a uniform body.
>
> *(Hebdige, p. 17)*

Dominated groups express their resistance not only in ideological terms, but also at the "profoundly superficial level" of style. This is why conflicts explode over seemingly silly disputes over reciting the Pledge of Allegiance, end zone celebrations, and kneeling for the national anthem. In these struggles, dominant groups define their positions in terms of securitarian themes of unity, defense, and stability while in their dissenting formulation, critics draw on some conception of cultural style, often implicit, to highlight historical particularity, status discrimination, group difference, and cultural oppression. Their politics works on the level that Max Weber described as the "style of life" against what Antonio Gramsci described as hegemony. It is an inherently cultural politics in which the personal becomes political. Because the dominant culture of the modern context has in most places been white, male, Christian (even protestant), English speaking, able-bodied, and straight, the groups that have sought the protection of the moral politics of dignity are defined against this matrix of oppression. The fact that these margins are often found in complex combinations helps to explain why the concept of intersectionality has become so attractive a concept among dignitarians.

This sense of intersectionality brings up one last point that is really essential to prevent misunderstandings about how the dignitarian root narratives work (in fact all the root narratives, but these in particular). As I have said repeatedly, almost no one tells her political stories from the perspective of the logic of only one root narrative. Most people draw on a wide variety of orienting and justifying perspectives in any given political statement. Any given statement by a rhetor might be characterized as 30 percent securitarian, 20 percent libertarian, 10 percent egalitarian, and 40 percent dignitarian, and the process of profiling can be further sub-divided into the sub-root categories as well. In fact, many individual sentences authored by the same person will also display a blend of root narratives. In this sense, all political thought is highly intersectional or, perhaps, blended like the colors of light absent a prism. The authors I highlight in this book are distinctive in their emphasis on certain root narratives at the expense of the others, although even the purists tend to tap into many of the roots in their thinking. Intersectionality should be a given in these analyses, but we also need to guard against the tendency to treat "intersectionality" only related to or as a species of dignitarian morality, thereby reducing its power by ignoring the moral force of the other three major root narratives.

Because a root narrative is such a powerful rhetorical device, it is so easy to forget the rest of the world when under the spell of one. This witchcraft is what makes ideology so compelling and so dangerous. It is important to remember this as we delve deeper into the dignitarian imagination, because it is the living story of our own times, and therefore has a correspondingly greater potential to draw us to our downfall, like Odysseus unbound from the mast. Marxists went wrong when they made every problem a nail for their egalitarian rhetorical hammer as do American libertarians who see the oppressive government behind every tree. Because we are so recently awake to the abuses of cultural power, we should learn to recognize it wherever it manifests, but guard against the tendency to lose sight of the full spectrum of the color wheel that defines the various forms of abusive power that are alive in the world around us.

In the end, the Recognition narrative is fairly simple and our struggles with it can be summarized with Marcel Mauss's prescient observation at the dawn of the twentieth century, "there are no uncivilized people, only peoples with different civilizations."[13] As simple as this is to say, the ongoing struggle for respect, for *dignitas* is evidence of how challenging it can be to realize.

The Liberation narrative

The dignitarian root narrative manifests in a similar way in all of its three differentiating aspects. It can be hard to discern when the moral authority of an author
relyies more on recognition logic, which demands respect for difference itself,
inclusion logic, which demands equity in economic rewards and opportunity for
achievements for outgroups, and liberation. The logic of the Liberation narrative is
based on the core principle of respect for difference, but its *summum malum* differs
from the other two in a decisive way. Where the perceived evil of slight and insult
drives recognition, and institutional discrimination drives inclusion, the ethic of
liberation is defined more by opposition to state persecution and political oppression than in the other two cases. In recognition stories, the majoritarian ingroup
abuses its control over symbolic resources and cultural institutions to glorify itself.
In inclusion stories, the ingroup abuses control over economic resources and those
institutions that grant access to them like the education system to improve its
relative material conditions. In a liberation story, the ingroup abuses the very
powers of the state to discipline the bodies of the outgroup, to the extreme of
torture, imprisonment and genocide. Liberation stories do not always end with a
call for self-government or independence, but they do always involve some criticism of state power, the criminal justice system, or political oppression that is based
on cultural biases. Liberation is a rebellion against perceived cultural persecution at
the level of the state itself.

Dignitarian stories apply well to any status differential. Any marker of group
difference would work as a matter of illustration of liberation narratives, but some
of the most arresting of examples are drawn from the conversation that developed
in response to anti-Semitism. More than any other group in Western history,
Jewish people have been targets of group-based discrimination, often crossing over
into over persecution. The Jewish experience is therefore a tragically fertile source
for extracting liberation stories.

A good place to begin the excavation is with Theodor Herzl, the spiritual father
of the project of Zionism. In Herzl's writings, the concept of a Jewish state is
developed under conditions of democratically sanctioned persecution. For Herzl,
anti-Semitism was a problem that democracy alone could not solve. Liberation
through national independence was the only option he could accept. This selection
is from his *The Jewish State*. [14]

> The Jewish question still exists. It would be foolish to deny it. It is a remnant
> of the Middle Ages, which civilized nations do not, even yet seem able to
> shake off, try as they will. They certainly showed a generous desire to do so
> when they emancipated us. The Jewish question exists wherever Jews live in
> perceptible numbers. Where it does not exist, it is carried by Jews in the course
> of their migrations. We naturally move to those places where we are not per-
> secuted, and there our presence produces persecution. This is the case in every
> country, and will remain so, even in those highly civilized—for instance,

France—until the Jewish question finds a solution on a political basis. The unfortunate Jews are now carrying the seeds of Anti-Semitism into England; they have already introduced it into America.

Herzl's perspective is interesting as a form of threat narrative. He recognizes that it is the movement of Jews to new locations, often in search of security, that is the proximate cause of anti-Semitism, although it is the natural barrier that he refers to as a "national" one that sits at the root of the problem.

I think the Jewish question is no more a social than a religious one, notwithstanding that it sometimes takes these and other forms. It is a national question, which can only be solved by making it a political world-question to be discussed and settled by the civilized nations of the world in council.

The concept of nation is notoriously complex, but it implies some community of descent, a tie of blood that can be traced back as far as one wishes. It is, obviously, a provocative claim to assert that all Jews are part of a single nation or that they all share a line of descent, but it is less contentious to claim that Jews are often treated as if they were all of a piece and therefore worthy subjects of persecution. This was, again, best stated by Jean Paul Sartre in his investigation of anti-Semitism.

The Jew is one whom other men consider a Jew: that is the simple truth from which we must start. In this sense the democrat is right as against the anti-Semite, for it is the anti-Semite who makes the Jew.[15]

Herzl's familiarity with the enduring perception that the Jew is a physical Other, an internal foreigner, a representative of a nation apart, coming from an alien line of descent with all the invidious status distinctions that form around such a concept, made it clear to him that Jews would never be safe where they formed only a small part of larger and latently hostile nations. His story of persecution locates EVIL clearly in the political structures of a quasi-colonial sovereignty, escape from which he argues lies as the centerpiece of his plan to solve the problem of anti-Semitism.

Let the sovereignty be granted us over a portion of the globe large enough to satisfy the rightful requirements of a nation; the rest we shall manage for ourselves.

Rarely has a story been so clear as this one, and even as familiar as it is, it remains a shocking fact of history to consider that much of the persecution that Herzl most feared when he was writing in the 1890s came to pass, as did the development of a Jewish state with the founding of Israel in 1948. Democracy in Germany and elsewhere in Europe was no cure for National Socialism. National Socialism was, in fact, the product of democratic process, emerging under one of the most progressive constitutions in history: The Weimar Constitution of 1919. The Holocaust may not have been inevitable in 1896, when Herzl imagined his Jewish State, but one can easily imagine why a Jewish person, having grown up in eastern Europe in the nineteenth century and who had covered the Dreyfus Affair would be concerned about the misuse of democratic power and the pressures of public opinion. When the people control the sovereign powers of the state for racist ends, abominations are easy to imagine.

New abuses require the invention of new languages to make sense of them. Figures like Theodor Herzl and later Raphael Lemkin, who would invent the term genocide, emerged in this period because pressures on the collective moral imagination required them. Root Narrative Theory provides us with a language with which to describe the nature of Herzl's insight and Lemkin's innovation.[16] Majoritarian social power, the organizational power of informal networks of socialization and group representation, had turned Germany and much of Europe into a field of nightmares. As Lemkin described it, "it is for this reason that I took the liberty of inventing the word, 'genocide.' The term is from the Greek word *genes* meaning tribe or race and the Latin *cide* meaning killing."[17] It is the act of using state power to kill an entire race of people.

When the language lacks a word with which to describe a pivotal phenomenon, it is clear that we are confronting the problem of radical disagreement, a problem for which we need something like Root Narrative Theory to solve. Lemkin recognized that we needed a new kind of story to describe the kinds of events that he had witnessed, and most of us now have learned how to see the world as he began to in the immediate aftermath of World War II. He described his new word, Genocide, as follows:

> More often it refers to a coordinated plan aimed at destruction of the essential foundations of the life of national groups so that these groups wither and die like plants that have suffered a blight. The end may be accomplished by the forced disintegration of political and social institutions, of the culture of the people, of their language, their national feelings and their religion. It may be accomplished by wiping out all basis of personal security, liberty, health and dignity. When these means fail the machine gun can always be utilized as a last resort. Genocide is directed against a national group as an entity and the attack on individuals is only secondary to the annihilation of the national group to which they belong.[18]

How can we fail to see the notion of group rights and the problem of dignity against this historical backdrop? Individual rights are not enough to explain what kind of moral politics is needed, nor is the concept of democracy. After all, it is consistent with democracy for the 51 percent to kill the 49 percent. Lemkin makes a new story form available to us, offering a lens onto a form of power that resides in informal networks and patterns of socialization and group evaluation that once seemed apolitical but can no longer once an event like the Holocaust has occurred.

It is the nature of root narratives that once innovative thinkers learn to use them, other thinkers find it possible to use the new language to frame new classes of events, using the new images, and linkages to powerful creative effect. In fact, the rhetorical power of the liberation root narrative, fueled by the unparalleled ferocity of the perversion of the forces of modernity in the Holocaust, is such that most political leaders become desperate to avoid having the genocide label attached to their activities for fear that to concede it would leave them vulnerable to any number of future claims for restitution. It is bad enough if states are accused of human rights violations (typically a kind of libertarian critique of the abuse of government power), but if the same events can be framed as genocide, the full weight of the dignitarian worldview might fall on the perpetrators. This helps to explain why it is so difficult to have honest conversations about what happened in Turkey in 1918 with respect to Armenians. Although Adolph Hitler may have learned from this example when he imagined his "final solution" to the Jewish problem, no Turkish leader wants to have his national history associated with this cardinal moral stigma of group persecution.

With the rise of the dignitarian thought around the world, it is increasingly common for authors to float the genocide concept. This is common in relation to United States history as well. After World War II, American segregationists, like Georgia's Richard Russell, found it more difficult to defend their cherished racial caste system, now that racial ideas had become associated with mass killing in Hitler's Germany. This proved to be a rhetorically important part of the rise of civil rights discourse in the United States.[19] More recently, in a book about the mass killing of Native Americans in California in the nineteenth century, Benjamin Madley used this narrative form to tell the story of misuse of the monopoly of legitimate violence by California settlers, producing Californian history in less flattering terms than is typical in American history books.[20]

> Genocide is violence, and the study of direct killing is the heart of this book. Disease, starvation, and exposure played major roles in California's Indian population decline between 1846 and 1873, but this project focuses on documenting and analyzing deaths due to direct acts of violence such as shootings, stabbings, hangings, beheadings, and lethal beatings. Ancillary to the direct killings were mass deaths in incarceration—particularly on federal Indian reservations—as well as other genocidal acts described by the UN Genocide Convention. This book does not investigate questions of cultural genocide, the systematic, deliberate destruction of a culture.
>
> *(p. 11)*

Based on the facts themselves, in some sense it is striking that it took so long for the genocide label to begin to take hold in American storytelling, which may have had something to do with the salience of the legacy of African American slavery in the development of dignitarian stories in the United States (slavery was unspeakably cruel but was not an attempt to eradicate a people). It might also have resulted from the somewhat desperate unifying populism of the imagery of the melting pot (Nation narrative) and the rugged individual (Property narrative). Whatever the reasons for its absence in the past, in the current narrative ecology, liberation stories about Native Americas are much easier to tell and much better received than they once were. It is also telling that Americans are sufficiently horrified by the history of ethnic violence that a world-famous Holocaust Museum was dedicated on the National Mall in Washington D.C. in 1993. All of this demonstrates increasing American commitment to the Liberation narrative.

One of the most influential of the dignitarian philosophers, Will Kymlicka, uses part of his groundbreaking analysis of how individual rights and group rights can coexist in liberal society to portray in the spirit of liberation in his must-read book, *Multicultural Citizenship.* [21]

> As I discuss later, virtually all American political theorists treat the United States as a poly-ethnic nation-state, rather than a truly multination state. Perhaps this is because national minorities in the United States are relatively small and isolated (e.g. Puerto Ricans, American Indians, native Hawaiians, Alaskan Eskimos). These groups are virtually invisible in American political theory. If they are found at all, it is usually as an afterthought. This has had a profound effect on liberal thought around the world, since American theorists have become the dominant interpreters of liberal principles since World War II.
>
> *(p. 56)*

Not only did Kymlicka's analysis provide liberal thinkers with a way to think about the material need for group rights based on traditions of language, culture, and land tenure, it also served as an example on which to resuscitate liberation thinking within and about the United States itself, and helped to bring attention to the centrality of dignitarian root narratives around the world. When this Liberation lens is directed at the United States, there are plenty of examples to highlight.

The most famous early example of a movement dedicated to the Liberation narrative in American history was the *Universal Negro Improvement Association* of Marcus Garvey in the early twentieth century, in which he tried to provide a rationale for a pan-African nationalist movement to give black people the kind of liberation through self-determination that other ethnic groups were demanding in the aftermath of World War I.

> This war has that been won by the allied nations was fought for a great principle. It was that of giving to all people the right to govern themselves. Now that there is peace and the affairs of the world are to be settled, we find that every race except the negro will have a voice in the principle of self-determination. And why is it so? Because all of them are organized...The time for the peaceful penetration of the black man's right by the white man is past, and the time for a determined resistance has come.[22]

Garvey is not as celebrated as many other, subsequent African American liberationists, perhaps because of the fraught and uneven history of his movement in contrast to the great "revolution of 1963" that brought such impressive legislative change in the Johnson administration. Garvey's example is too morally complex to render him suitable for romantic stories of racial liberation, but other figures fit much better.

History has made more of later leaders like Malcolm X, whose memory is often used in productive contrast to Martin Luther King. The durability and rhetorical power of this contrast between the two icons of the Civil Rights Era suggests that each man stands not much for his own life and contributions but for distinctive ideas. In this case, ideas represented by the contrasting aspects of the dignitarian root narrative: King for the Inclusion narrative and Malcolm X for the Liberation narrative. The classic Martin/Malcolm divide is really about root narrative emphasis. Here is Malcolm X in liberation mode:

> Every time I mentioned "separation," some of them would cry that we Muslims were standing for the same thing that white racists and demagogues stood for. I would explain the difference. No! We reject segregation even more militantly than you say you do! We want separation, which is not the same! The Honorable Elijah Muhammad teaches us that segregation is when your life and liberty are controlled, regulated, by someone else. To segregate means to control. Segregation is that which is forced upon inferiors by superiors. But separation is that which is done voluntarily, by two equals—for the good of both! The Honorable Elijah Muhammad teaches us that as long as our people here in America are dependent upon the white man, we will always be begging him for jobs, food, clothing, and housing. And he will always control our lives, regulate our lives, and have the power to segregate us.[23]

This tension between segregation and separation is a natural part of the development of the dignitarian imagination, visible whenever ethnic domination intersects with economic exploitation. Just as critical, however is how the Liberation narrative butts up against the Reciprocity narrative, often in an ideological mélange that confuses those who are frightened by the whole complex. This is an apt description of how the various Latin American revolutionaries have been understood over the past hundred years. Here, themes of ethnic liberation have been mingled with a Marxist revolutionary patina to generate hybrid movements of radical dissent from neoliberal orthodoxy and the policy of shareholder supremacy throughout the hemisphere.

Although the Latin revolutionaries were commonly quite orthodox in their Marxism, their rhetoric was often balanced between the demonization of capital and of the gringo: between the language of reciprocity and liberation. Their rhetoric was a thorough blend of these perspectives. It is not hard to find examples of this kind, and they become more common whenever tensions with the United States rise.

Consider the radical movement in Nicaragua, which was initiated in opposition
to interventions in Nicaragua by American forces perceived to be oppressive and
the rebel leader Augusto Cesar Sandino, after whom the Marxist rebels of the late
twentieth century were named, the Sandinistas, of FSLN for *Frente Sandinista de
Liberación Nacional*. The following example is from an open letter Sandino wrote to
Latin American leaders in 1928, a year in which he was being actively hunted
throughout Nicaragua by American Marines. In the letter, Sandino blends a variety
of idioms—there is an anti-aristocratic/anti-monarchist feel to his rhetoric as
well—but this dedicated Marxist had a distinctly cultural flare to his identification
of the *summum malum*: "Yankee imperialism."

> Today it is with the peoples of Spanish America that I speak. When a gov-
> ernment does not reflect the aspirations of its citizens, the latter, who gave it
> power, have the right to be represented by virile men with concepts of effec-
> tive democracy, and not by useless satraps whose lack of moral valor and
> patriotism are a disgrace to a nation's pride. We are ninety million Spanish
> Americans, and we should think only about our unity, recognizing that
> Yankee imperialism is the most brutal enemy that now threaten us and the
> only one that intends to put an end to our racial honor and our peoples'
> freedom through conquest. Tyrants do not represent nations, and freedom is
> not won with flowers.[24]

This blend of anti-capitalism and anti-Anglicism in Latin American Marxism is a
stable feature of the idiom, but in recent history, as economic theory drifted
toward the libertarian mode, and as critical theory shifted its focus from class to
race, it became more difficult to defend technical economic arguments that supported that egalitarian worldview; accordingly, it has become more common to
emphasize the cultural abuses over economic, much as culture has supplanted class
rhetoric around the world over the course of the latter half of the twentieth century. As this cultural drift in axiology developed in Latin contexts, the indigenous
movements became more successful in promoting a new ideological cocktail with
strictly dignitarian ingredients.

An apposite example is the legacy of the Nobel laureate Rigoberta Menchú who
captivated the world with her story about political oppression in Guatemala in its
economic and cultural dimensions. Her Mayan heritage and the ways that this
made people like her a target of persecution was a critical part of the development
of the justice movements in that part of the world in the 1980s and beyond.
Menchú's story was all the more interesting in that many parts of the auto-
biographical material turned out not to be a true account of her own life, applying
instead to people like her. In this sense, Menchú's story said more about the pre-
ferred root narratives of the audience for her work in that epoch than it did about
her own personal experience. These were the kinds of stories her audience was
prepared to hear. In some sense, it didn't matter if they were really hers. We can
get a sense of that audience and its dignitarian concerns from the introduction of

her *I Rigoberta Menchú: An Indian Woman in Guatemala*, written by her ghost writer Elisabeth Burgos-Debray.[25]

> Rigoberta learned the language of her oppressors in order to use it against them. For her, appropriating the Spanish language is an act which can change the course of history because it is the result of a decision. Spanish was a language which forced upon her, but it has become a weapon in her struggle. She decided to speak in order to tell of the oppression her people have been suffering for almost five hundred years, so that the sacrifices made by her community and her family will not have been made in vain.

There is distinctive dignitarian flavor in Burgos-Debray's reference to "the language of her oppressors," and the use of the imagery of weaponry in her struggle has more of a Liberation narrative than a Recognition narrative feel to it. The rest of the book maintains this flavor as we can see from some of the arresting material in the chapter titles: "The torture and death of her little brother"; "Kidnapping and death of Rigoberta's Mother"; "Hunted by the Army." These are all clear signals of stories of political persecution and the call for liberation, and cultural oppression far outweighs the class analysis in her tale. Culture here is the source of oppression and font of EVIL, whether its form is symbolic, economic, or political. The central threat in Menchú's account is a Guatemalan army that is animated by its cultural biases. Hers is a liberation story.

Where the celebration of Menchú's work on behalf of the indigenous women of central America marked a change in how Latin conflicts were narrated, these stories demonstrated their practical effects just over twenty years later with the election of the Amaryan Indian, Evo Morales, to the presidency of Bolivia. With Morales, the full force of the dignitarian imagination is deployed, eclipsing the old socialist motivations in a blend that is far more about Christopher Columbus than Goldman Sachs, also revealing how important it is to project your opponent's root narrative into your own narrative categories. In this tale, "rule of law" becomes just another tool of cultural oppression.

> What happened these past days in Bolivia was a great revolt by those who have been oppressed for more than 500 years. The will of the people was imposed this September and October and has begun to overcome the empire's cannons. We have lived for so many years through the confrontation of two cultures: the culture of life represented by the indigenous people, and the culture of death represented by West. When we the indigenous people—together with the workers and even the businessmen of our country—fight for life and justice, the State responds with its "democratic rule of law." What does the "rule of law" mean for indigenous people? For the poor, the marginalized, the excluded, the "rule of law" means the targeted assassinations and collective massacres that we have endured. Not just this September and October, but for many years, in which they have tried to impose policies of

hunger and poverty on the Bolivian people. Above all, the "rule of law" means the accusations that we, the Quechuas, Aymaras and Guaranties of Bolivia keep hearing from our governments: that we are narcos, that we are anarchists. This uprising of the Bolivian people has been not only about gas and hydrocarbons, but an intersection of many issues: discrimination, marginalization, and most importantly, the failure of neoliberalism.[26]

Circumstances in most parts of the world make it necessary to moderate practical demands even if the logic of the case could lead to more radical solutions in other circumstances. Among the most celebrated example of this type of pragmatic liberationism is that of Nelson Mandela's "speech from the dock" of 1964, in which he declared that his cause was "an ideal for which I am prepared to die." Mandela, the great peacemaker, proposed a set of demands true to the cause of black liberation, but in a way that was perfectly consistent with democratic politics in the complex ethnic space of South African politics. Most important for our purposes, Mandela's is a liberation not an inclusion speech. The EVIL here results from ethnic abuse of state not private power.

> Above all, My Lord, we want equal political rights, because without them our disabilities will be permanent. I know this sounds revolutionary to the whites in this country, because the majority of voters will be Africans. This makes the white man fear democracy. But this fear cannot be allowed to stand in the way of the only solution which will guarantee racial harmony and freedom for all. It is not true that the enfranchisement of all will result in racial domination. Political division, based on colour, is entirely artificial and, when it disappears, so will the domination of one colour group by another. The ANC has spent half a century fighting against racialism. When it triumphs as it certainly must, it will not change that policy. This then is what the ANC is fighting. Our struggle is a truly national one.[27]

What matters most here is not the conciliatory tone that Mandela takes, even as he is facing the most dire peril of his life, but the target of his indignation. Whenever the dignitarian root is projected against the contrast of the national sovereignty of a discriminatory government and its police and army forces, the Liberation narrative tends to emerge. It can be difficult to differentiate when a particular empirical passage favors one of mode of dignitarian thinking over another, but it is always a good bet that if status oppression is linked in the passage to threats to life and limb of the persecuted, the person is telling a liberation story.

Nevertheless, the task of demarcating the various aspects of the larger complex is extremely important because the assumptions and logical implications for practice of recognition, inclusion, and liberation can be so different. It is not only the attitude of a figure like Malcolm X that comes along with his liberationism, the concrete policy of separation is a natural extension of his point of view. Over long stretches of time, despite the plastic relations between policy and narrative, moral logic tends to drive the policy agenda of those who employ it. National separation follows a liberation logic, racial integration follows an inclusion logic. If the analysis produced in the spirit of the root narrative is not well matched to the current state of the world and the nature of its current and leading injustices, the root narrative itself will simply fall out of use and its problems will become more difficult to solve. This is the performative dimension of root narratives. They have to work to live, and to work, they have to fit the objective circumstances.

This brings me to my final example, which links the ethic of liberation to the current case of race relations in the United States. This is the electric work of Michelle Alexander and her best-selling book, *The New Jim Crow: Mass Incarceration in the Age of Colorblindness.* [28] This book is among the best examples of successful political storytelling in recent memory and provides a helpful illustration of what is at stake in coming to terms with the phenomenon that I am trying to capture with Root Narrative Theory. Hers is the story of awakening that reveals both the power of narrative and the need for something like Root Narrative Theory to explain what it is about the emergence of new story structures—new forms of storytelling—that is so explosive.

> Like many civil rights lawyers, I was inspired to attend law school by the civil rights victories of the 1950s and 1960s. Even in the face of growing social and political opposition to remedial policies such as affirmative action, I clung to the notion that the evils of Jim Crow are behind us…Never did I seriously consider the possibility that a new racial caste system was operating in this country. The new system had been developed and implemented swiftly, and it was largely invisible, even to people, like me, who spent most of their waking hours fighting for justice.
>
> *(p. 3)*

This is a remarkable story of coming to consciousness. But why would a person like her need to come to consciousness? Because, at that time, there was no appropriate and available language through which to narrate current events and abuses of social power. Alexander came to awareness of the absence of a root narrative that fit the circumstances of mass incarceration to the right target of moral indignation. She had to teach people to care about the problem of mass incarceration, and this required that she shift the root narrative from inclusion to liberation. She argued that mass incarceration was not about inclusion as her civil rights law training had taught her to believe, but rather about liberation, an idea that in its novelty felt more radical.

Keep in mind that Alexander identifies herself as a serious player in the quest for racial justice and demonstrates her commitment to overcoming the kinds of structural barriers to economic advancement that are typically developed in inclusion stories. She knew very well why prior activists, like Dr. Martin Luther King and Rosa Parks, had pushed for the cause of desegregation as she began her own quest for racial justice, and yet still she needed to come to consciousness. She had to invent a new way of seeing the problems before her. Alexander's awakening is not about her increasing familiarity with concrete problems. She was already well aware that an inordinate number of black men were being sent to prison and she knew how tough life was for victims of police violence. It was not so much the facts that she awoke to, but the story, a narrative process that forced her to abandon her legal training with its focus on discrimination and inclusion so that she might see the facts in a different light—see them as political persecution, just like in the days of Jim Crow. Michelle Alexander awoke to the uses of the Liberation narrative in American history and brought us along with her.

The term Jim Crow was so effective because it redirected the interpretation of EVIL, pivoting from economic discrimination to political persecution with a literary device that was both compelling and vivid, an ideological move as definitive as Malcolm X ever made.

There is no necessary connection between policy and story. There is no need to imagine an African American state like that which Hertzl imagined for the Jews to tell her liberation story. Instead, all that is needed is a vision of state sanctioned persecution. Root narratives are defined by the source of their indignation and by the experience of abusive power, by Hobbes's *summum malum*. To be expert storytellers, we need to be alive to the EVIL in the text (the emotional, vivid, intense, and literary devices the author uses to make her point). The image of the New Jim Crow accomplishes the narrative turn Alexander wants to make in a single metaphor.

> Such a movement is impossible, though, if those most committed to abolishing racial hierarchy continue to talk and behave as if a state-sponsored racial caste system no longer exists. If we continue to tell ourselves the popular myths about racial progress or, worse yet, if we say to ourselves that the problem of mass incarceration is just too big, too daunting for us to do anything about and that we should instead direct our energies to battles that might be more easily won, history will judge us harshly. A human rights nightmare is occurring on our watch. A new social consensus must be forged about race and the role of race in defining the basic structure of our society, if we hope ever to abolish the New Jim Crow.
>
> *(p. 15)*

Alexander would agree with the conservative thinker, Richard Weaver, that ideas have consequences.[29] She provides us with a complexly textured story about how, in the vernacular, to "stay woke."[30] She wants us to recognize that the kind of story we tell matters, that our choice of root narrative matters. True, there is something unavoidably arbitrary about how facts fit with story, we can tell whatever story we please about the events we experience, but the stories we tell have enduring implications for the change we are likely to see.

The Inclusion narrative

If a large portion of the previous sections were dedicated to the politics of race and ethnicity in their relation to the dignitarian imagination, a large portion of this one will be dedicated to the politics of gender. This is not because it would be difficult to find illustrative material for the entire section on the Inclusion narrative that relied entirely on racial and ethnic examples (in fact the central pillar of the Civil Rights Movement was an inclusion message), but just as some of the most pressing challenges in the race debate were best illustrated with the logic of recognition, so too is the current conversation about gender most incisively and convincingly narrated in the rhetorical space of inclusion. This is because the Inclusion narrative is the terrain where concerns about the abuse of status privilege meet concerns about access and control of material resources, and this is a front burner concern of the modern feminist movement.

All stories are hard to tell when the audience for them is not prepared to be persuaded by the moral logic of the story structure. When people are not familiar or habituated to a root narrative, they see problems as vaguely troubling but apolitical. Early innovators of an unpopular root narrative come across as savants dealing in a kind of ethereal realm. This was true of early gender theorists inspired by the Inclusion narrative like Betty Friedan, whose book *The Feminine Mystique*, published in 1963, began to change the way people thought about gendered work roles.

> The problem lay buried, unspoken for many years in the minds of American women. It was a strange stirring, a sense of dissatisfaction, a yearning that women suffered in the middle of the twentieth century in the United States. Each suburban housewife struggled with it alone. As she made the beds, shopped for groceries, matched slipcover material, ate peanut butter sandwiches with her children, chauffeured Cub Scouts and Brownies, lay beside her husband at night, she was afraid to ask even of herself the silent question—"Is this all?"[31]

If working in the home was not enough for modern women, the workplace was the alternative, but when women began to join the workforce on a mass scale, inequities in pay kept the gender hierarchy in place. This was clear in phenomena like the gender pay gap. Because the primitive logic of the Inclusion narrative speaks so well to this kind of institutionalized discrimination, most critiques of the gender wage gap or pay equity are told as inclusion stories. It is a natural home for these arguments, and good examples are not hard to find. Here is one from the National Partnership on Women and Families and the opening lines from a report on the problem published in April, 2018.

> Nationally, the median annual pay for a woman who holds a full-time, year-round job is $41,554 while the median annual pay for a man who holds a full-time, year-round job is $51,640. This means that, overall, women in the

United States are paid 80 cents for every dollar paid to men, amounting to an annual gender wage gap of $10,086.[32]

This is a powerful argument with a clear moral to the story. If men and women are really considered to be equals in the workplace, how can it be that such a gap could endure over so many decades of ever more assertive labor force engagement by women who have been educated to match or exceed their male peers?

For our purposes, it is most important to recognize that this is an inclusion story. Why? Because the implied EVIL force that keeps women from earning the same pay that men do is a male-dominated and institutionalized structure of market relationships that are themselves determined by the otherwise free choices of economic actors. The report targets the absence of policies to better protect women in the workforce, but the implicit antagonists are the decision makers who hire workers, set pay, and grant promotions. Not male chauvinism or sexual violence, but the system of free contracts in which masculine norms dominate is the antagonism. In such a biased environment, the free choices of individuals is not sufficient to ensure that men and women will be compensated fairly. This is rather implicit in the document, but in this story, women need to be protected from a system that allows individuals to set the terms of contracts on the free market. To close the wage gap, women need protections from liberal economics, from freedom itself.

Remember that economics, as a field, is overwhelmingly dominated by libertarian root narratives. It's in the DNA of the discipline. No sooner were gender equity problems noted than orthodox apologists were available to provide technical explanations demonstrating that the system of free contract under given conditions of supply and demand produced optimal results for both men and women, just as they explained why labor unions, public goods, and minimum wage laws were ultimately destructive. Undaunted, to cope with enduring problems like the pay gap, many economists and sociologists guided by the muse of the dignitarian imagination, began to pick apart the various libertarian rationalizations, building ideological momentum with each successful foray.

One of the early voices in this debate was the economist, Paula England, who, among other things, took one libertarian rationalization known as "occupational sex segregation," a phenomenon in which women and men are imagined to gravitate toward different kinds of jobs and careers, explaining a part of why they are compensated differently. The following excerpt is drawn from her 1982 article titled, "The Failure of Human Capital Theory to Explain Occupational Sex Segregation," in which she attempts to debunk the libertarian rationalizations of an economist named Solomon Polachek.

A striking characteristic of workplaces is the segregation of women and into different occupations. In several recent papers [Solomon] Polachek argues human capital theory can provide an explanation for occupational segregation. In this paper I show that the propositions derived from Polachek's theory conflict with empirical evidence and conclude that human capital theory cannot explain the bulk of occupational sex segregation.[33]

If the rationalization was not valid, then something else must be in play, something like the gender caste structure as it plays out in the tastes of its freely contracting gatekeepers, and if you want to combat a caste structure, you have to do it at the institutional not the individual level. England is just an example of how important technical expertise can be for dislodging existing story structures. If you can only rely on moral suasion without empirical warrants to challenge existing experts, your story is vulnerable to counter-narration.

There are so many good examples of feminist critiques of economic, education and family structures that it is hard to choose among the best illustrations. One that homes in on the logic of inclusion in a slightly different way is the argument made by Joan Williams in *Unbending Gender: Why Family and Work Conflict and What to Do About It.* [34] As a leading scholar of work and family balance, Williams helps us to see that although sexism is a problem much like racism, because of unavoidable links between biology and reproduction, motherhood is a problem all its own. For Williams, unbending gender becomes an extremely delicate ideological operation insofar as it mixes ancient and enduring essentialist ideas about raising children with sexist beliefs about work qualifications.

> Domesticity remains the entrenched, almost unquestioned, American norm and practice. As a gender system, it has two defining characteristics. The first is its organization of market work around the ideal of a worker who works full time and overtime and takes little or no time off for childbearing or child rearing. Though this ideal-worker norm does not define all jobs today, it defines the good ones: full-time blue-collar jobs in the working-class context, and high-level executive and professional jobs for the middle class and above. When work is structured in this way, caregivers often cannot perform as ideal workers. Their inability to do so gives rise to domesticity's second defining characteristic: its system of providing for caregiving by marginalizing the caregivers, thereby cutting them off from most of the social roles that offer responsibility and authority.
>
> *(p. 1)*

As in all root narrative analyses, we find the greatest clarity when we can identify the melodramatic aspects of a passage, its heroes and villains: in other words, EVIL. In this case, there are no clear antagonists, but there is a clear source of antagonism and that is domesticity, a gender system that combines expectations of market work and domestic labor in a way that militates against the liberal hope that men and women can compete for life's rewards on an equal footing. Domesticity is no mustachioed villain, but it is the source of injustice in this story as clearly as if it were. It organizes market work around a masculinized conception of what ideal work is.[35] It defines what good work and a good worker are and defines ideal work to correspond to what men do. Domesticity marginalizes the caregiver who makes the reproduction of society possible, and in all of this it assigns women and men to differential roles in society. Domesticity must go down.

In this story of gender inequity, we learn that we had better pay attention to our larger conceptions of how functional institutions work together to produce exclusionary injustice. Simply overcoming sexism, understood as how women and men are valued in isolated situations (say a job interview or performance evaluation), will not be enough to overcome gender inequities. And we should also remember that the difference between the logics of recognition and inclusion is not between a structural and an individualistic perspective. This is what marks them both off from libertarian views. What makes inclusion different from recognition is that the Recognition narrative focuses on a structure of differential status *evaluations* where the Inclusion narrative focuses on a structure of differential status *expectations*. In the former, the key issue is respect. In the latter, it is access.

The Inclusion narrative has been the source of some of the most inspired sociological analyses, a launchpad for countless careers. Arlie Hochschild is a leading example. A sociologist who spent most of her career in Berkeley California, she begins the afterward to one of her most famous books, *The Second Shift*, [36] with an anecdote that proves the case.

> Sometime after this book first appeared, I had to laugh. Once when I was in a hotel hallway at a sociology conference, an elevator door opened. A man unknown to me peered out of the elevator, saw my name tag, fixed me in the eye and blurted out, "I cook!!! But my wife doesn't *appreciate* it. She thinks I cook to control what we eat. You see, I like fish but she doesn't..." Suddenly the elevator door closed, and that is all I will ever know about this man, his wife and their relative preference for fish.
>
> *(p. 271)*

Hochshild's story is funny and revealing. She points out how her work brought out the defensiveness of her male colleagues, provoking irrational and inappropriate responses like this one in professional settings. It is just a story, but the moral force of the story derives from the Inclusion narrative. It is not just a story about sexism, but how gender expectations about housework intermingle with expectations about professional life, and female social scientists who specialize in the Inclusion narrative can expect awkward experiences that are often less funny than this one.

Inclusion stories take on as many forms as the examples of any other forms of root narrative, but a common one in the United States context is related to welfare policy and government support. A libertarian perspective would try to limit any government expenditure on private needs, as our discussion on Wilhelm von Humboldt revealed, but those who recognize the perversities of gender expectations in the domestic sphere often point out how welfare policy has to be understood in relation to inequitable gender expectations. A good example is from the book *Pitied but not Entitled: Single Mothers and the History of Welfare* by the historian Linda Gordon.[37]

The perverse tendency of our welfare system to deepen inequality has been particularly pronounced in the case of AFDC [Aid for Families with Dependent Children]. The stigmas of "welfare" and of single motherhood intersect: hostility to the poor and hostility to deviant family forms reinforce each other. The resentment undercuts political support for the program, and benefits fall farther and farther behind inflation. The resulting immiseration makes poor single mothers even more needy and less politically attractive.

(p. 6)

We see in this excerpt how you can only beat a root narrative with another root narrative. Here, critics of inclusion project stability arguments onto approved family forms. Single motherhood is presented as a threat of instability, which is in turn linked to social welfare programs. In other words, social welfare policy is a threat to security. Gordon's book is a careful history that shows how this process of narrative competition played out and what its implications for social policy were. The basis of her technical innovation was her ability to navigate the structures described by Root Narrative Theory.

This line of inclusive thinking has developed in a variety of settings and in relation to various kinds of government programs while maintaining a commitment to the logic of inclusion. A good example of how critiques like Gordon's have developed over time can be found in Judith Warner's *Perfect Madness: Motherhood in the Age of Anxiety*. [38]

If we were to desacralize the motherhood issue and drop all the narcissistic and ideological goals that now infuse it, what would families need? Simply put: institutions that can help us take care of our children so that we don't have to do everything on our own.

(p. 268)

There is much in Warner's story that dovetails with the egalitarian ethic of reciprocity (or even with stability), but the core contrast here is between liberal merit-based policies in which people are forced to attend to their own personal responsibilities and an inclusive perspective that recognizes the differential expectations around gender that in Warner's words produce a "feeling so many mothers have today of always doing something wrong. (p. 3)"

I hope that these examples have demonstrated that a powerful set of political movements can be developed using the logic of the Inclusion narrative. It is one of the driving aspects of the dignitarian imagination, and given the demographic disparities on income, wealth and opportunity that abound around the world despite economic liberalization, it has much more work to do. In fact, the obvious demand for the perspective has the potential to crowd out other, important root narrative forms as an unintended consequence. The most likely candidates to be overshadowed are those that, like inclusion, are defined against liberal capitalism.

Notice that there are three root narratives that share the antagonist function, *elites use bargaining power to*, that might place them in opposition to liberal capitalism: unity (from the securitarian set), reciprocity (from the egalitarian set) and inclusion. This correspondence among the three root narratives allows for an interesting phenomenon, which I call, for lack of a better term, borrowed energy. That is to say, if a person is well steeped in a narrative tradition dominated by a class critique, some form of socialist thinking (Reciprocity narrative), members can be easily turned to the use of one of the other two root narrative forms that also define themselves against the same antagonism. This happens through the logic captured in the old proverb, "the enemy of my enemy is my friend." For example, it is not hard for a communitarian to use her own critiques of liberal capitalism to convert a socialist to her side of an argument. Similarly, it is not hard for an inclusion-focused feminist to convince a socialist to come to his side for the same reason. In this way, one of the other sympathetic root narratives can be substituted in the public mind for another.

In some cases, there is no substitution, but only a kind narrative alliance in which the priority once invested in socialism as a worldview is melded with feminism as a worldview, revealing only a modest shift in the root narrative profile of priorities. In other cases, especially when ideological challenges take place over long periods of time and are augmented by generational replacement, the shift can be more dramatic, and the original socialist tradition can be wholly supplanted with a feminist perspective. In this way, inclusive feminism "borrows" the energy from the stale socialist critique, casting off the old root narrative like a snake would its skin. From the perspective of the "curious logicality" of ideologies, this allows the inclusive feminist to claim that he is just as critical of liberal capitalism as were his uncles before him, just that his new feminist approach focuses more on the sexism and racism of the institutions than on the non-ascriptive aspects of exploitation. Over time, the critique of capitalism can be wholly supplanted by a critique of status roles. By degrees, one root narrative tradition can morph into another.

No one has been as trenchant in pointing out this tendency for status politics to drift toward neoliberalism than the philosopher Nancy Fraser, who has already played a key role in the story presented in this book. Given the clear separation she has imposed between the politics of redistribution (the egalitarian imagination) and the politics of recognition (the dignitarian imagination), it is little surprise that she would emerge as a critic of neoliberal feminism.

> In a cruel twist of fate, I fear that the movement for women's liberation has become entangled in a dangerous liaison with neoliberal efforts to build a free-market society. That would explain how it came to pass that feminist ideas that once formed part of a radical worldview are increasingly expressed in individualist terms. Where feminists once criticised a society that promoted careerism, they now advise women to "lean in". A movement that once prioritised social solidarity now celebrates female entrepreneurs. A perspective that once valorised "care" and interdependence now encourages individual advancement and meritocracy.[39]

Feminist inclusion in such a case has borrowed from and supplanted the old narrative. Both the socialist and the feminist perspectives are critical of the operation of liberal institutions but for very different reasons and in ways that will tend to generate very different policy prescriptions. One way to put this is to say that a concern for equity has replaced a concern for equality. As it is used here, equity refers to between-group inequalities, say between men, as a group, and women, as a group. Equality refers more to the problems of within-group inequality, men as compared to men and women as compared to women, and everyone compared to everyone else.

This rapprochement between establishment liberalism and cultural radicalism is the very sort of thing that the cultural critic, David Brooks, has quite a bit of fun with in his book *Bobos in Paradise*, [40] which he describes the rise of a new ideological blend he called the bourgeois bohemians, or "bobos" for short.

> When you are amidst the educated upscalers, you can never be sure if you're living in a world of hippies or stockbrokers. In reality you have entered the hybrid world in which everybody is a little of both. Marx told us that classes inevitably conflict, but sometimes they just blur...In the resolution between the culture and the counterculture, it is impossible to tell who co-opted whom, because in reality the bohemians and the bourgeois co-opted each other.
>
> *(pp. 42–43)*

In Brooks's "comic sociology," it is easy to exaggerate the extent of the ideological transformation he describes, but Root Narrative Theory provides us with a way to understand the logic of this blurring of once rival points of view. It does not just happen, but follows lines of interpretation that make sense given the relations among the logical structures of Root Narrative Theory. One can be anti-capitalist (to a degree) by criticizing the gender and racial biases of modern corporations, while still embracing the overall promise of global capitalism. In fact, this is probably the dominant mode of thinking on the American left today.

If a person were to think like this, if he were to support anti-sexist arguments (really anti-supremacism of any kind) and yet reveal a deep commitment to the promise of corporate America, what kind of argument would he tend to make? Well, it might look a lot like the earliest popular example of the metaphor of the glass ceiling. Although the image of the glass ceiling was used in prior publications, we were all introduced to the image of a glass ceiling—describing a phenomenon in which a woman executive was allowed to rise far enough that she could see the top of the corporate ladder, but never to get there herself—in a column titled, "The Glass Ceiling," published in the *Wall Street Journal* on March 24, 1986.

> The result is that in spite of the extraordinary progress women have made in terms of numbers, a caste system of men at the top and women lower down still prevails in corporate America. Only 2% of 1,362 top executives surveyed

by Korn/Ferry International last year were women. Just one woman—Katharine Graham of Washington Post Co.—heads a Fortune 500 company, and she acknowledges that she got the job because her family owns a controlling share of the corporation. Even women who seem very close to the top concede that they don't have a shot at sitting in the chief executive's chair.[41]

The antagonism is here defined as the "caste system of men at the top." EVIL is easy to see in this story. The problem is not to bring the top and bottom closer together, but to make sure that privileged women have as fair a shot at the top as privileged men have. There is nothing socialistic about this article, and there is nothing about even the most radical inclusion story that needs to be socialistic either. Neoliberal feminism remains an authentic form of feminism, because equality and dignity are orthogonal ethical systems, even when they share a common antagonist.

This imagery of the glass ceiling has proven to be profound and influential, revealing just how important clever political narration can be in forming new solidarities and promoting new social movements. Not only is the concept of a glass ceiling familiar to almost anyone who now hears the term, it was a centerpiece of the failed political candidacy of Hillary Clinton in her bid for the presidency in 2016. The logic of inclusion formed the most poignant moments of her concession speech.

> This loss hurts, but please never stop believing that fighting for what's right is worth it. It is—it is worth it. And so we need—we need you to keep up these fights now and for the rest of your lives. And to all the women, and especially the young women, who put their faith in this campaign and in me, I want you to know that nothing has made me prouder than to be your champion. Now, I—I know—I know we have still not shattered that highest and hardest glass ceiling, but someday someone will and hopefully sooner than we might think right now. And to all the little girls who are watching this, never doubt that you are valuable and powerful and deserving of every chance and opportunity in the world to pursue and achieve your own dreams.[42]

This is a highly critical statement that is subversive of American capitalism in some ways, but not of the basic logic of the property system. It is better described as a version of the Inclusion narrative that has come to peace with those aspects of the libertarian imagination that are compatible with inclusion. Little wonder that the men of the white working class in places like Wisconsin, Michigan, and Pennsylvania found little of interest to them in statements like these, preferring, instead, the reciprocity arguments of Bernie Sanders or the nationalist arguments of Donald Trump.

Nevertheless, the Inclusion narrative is among the most vibrant and decisive of narrative forms available in politics today. It is the basis of commitment of millions of people eager to be treated fairly as they pursue livelihoods in what often feels like increasingly precarious conditions. It is a root narrative filled with promise. To get a sense of that promise, remember that Martin Luther King was deeply animated by the spirit of the ethic of inclusion. In fact, what marked Dr. King as different from other civil rights leaders of the time was his commitment to inclusion, an ethic more readily conducive to reconciliation than the other two forms of dignitarian thinking. You can see this in the contrasting example of Malcolm X, who made his name a champion of what I will describe as liberation. Similarly, recognition stories tend to imply a stark distinction between cultural groups, often condemning them to vie for supremacy. In contrast, inclusion is about overcoming separation in cultures on the principle of equity between them. It has a naturally healing resonance, much like the securitarian ethic of unity. We can see this in Dr. King's "Letter from a Birmingham Jail."[43]

> All segregation statutes are unjust because segregation distorts the soul and damages the personality. It gives the segregator a false sense of superiority and the segregated a false sense of inferiority. To use the words of Martin Buber, the great Jewish philosopher, segregation substitutes an "I - it" relationship for the "I - thou" relationship and ends up relegating persons to the status of things. So segregation is not only politically, economically, and sociologically unsound, but it is morally wrong and sinful. Paul Tillich has said that sin is separation. Isn't segregation an existential expression of man's tragic separation, an expression of his awful estrangement, his terrible sinfulness? So I can urge men to obey the 1954 decision of the Supreme Court because it is morally right, and I can urge them to disobey segregation ordinances because they are morally wrong.

This language of overcoming "tragic separation" in the cause of establishing Buberian "I–thou" relationships is as artful an illustration of the Inclusion narrative as they come. Indeed, it is probably because Dr. King saw how well this moral logic could be turned to prosocial and redemptive ends that he remains so indelible in our memory.

Notes

1 Franklin, "Respect."
2 Baltzell, *The Protestant Establishment.*
3 Anon. "John F. Kennedy and Religion."
4 Caro, *The Power Broker.*
5 Tocqueville, *Democracy in America.*
6 Mill, *On Liberty.*
7 Memmi, *The Colonizer and the Colonized.*
8 Myrdal, *An American Dilemma.*
9 Coates, *Between the World and Me.*
10 West, "Ta-Nehisi Coates Is the Neoliberal Face of the Black Freedom."
11 Sharma, "Ta-Nehisi Coates on Cornel West's One-Sided War."
12 Hebdige, *Subculture.*
13 Merton, *Social Science Quotations.*

14 Herzl, *The Jewish State.*
15 Sartre and Walzer, *Anti-Semite and Jew.*
16 Irvin-Erickson, *Raphael Lemkin and the Concept of Genocide.*
17 Lemkin, "Genocide—A Modern Crime."
18 Lemkin, "Genocide—A Modern Crime."
19 Simmons, *The Eclipse of Equality.*
20 Madley, *An American Genocide.*
21 Kymlicka, *Multicultural Citizenship.*
22 Anon. "Article in The West Indian about Marcus Garvey."
23 X et al., *The Autobiography of Malcolm X.*
24 Sandino, "Letter to the Rulers of Latin America."
25 Menchú, *I, Rigoberta Menchú.*
26 Morales, "I Believe Only in The Power of The People."
27 Mandela, "I am Prepared to Die."
28 Alexander, *The New Jim Crow.*
29 Weaver, *Ideas Have Consequences.*
30 Lopez Bunyasi and Watts Smith, *Stay Woke.*
31 Friedan, *The Feminine Mystique.*
32 National Partnership for Women & Families, "Americas Women and the Wage Gap."
33 England, "The Failure of Human Capital Theory to Explain Occupational Sex
    Segregation."
34 Williams, *Unbending Gender.*
35 Robles, *Troubled Trade-Offs.*
36 Hochschild, *The Second Shift.*
37 Gordon, *Pitied but Not Entitled.*
38 Warner, *Perfect Madness.*
39 Fraser, "How Feminism Became Capitalism's Handmaiden."
40 Brooks, *Bobos In Paradise.*
41 Hymowitz and Schellhardt, "The Glass Ceiling."
42 Golshan, "Hillary Clinton's Concession Speech Full Transcript."
43 Locke, *A Letter Concerning Toleration and Other Writings.*

Bibliography

Alexander, Michelle. *The New Jim Crow: Mass Incarceration in the Age of Colorblindness.* New
    York: The New Press, 2012.
Anon. "Article in The West Indian about Marcus Garvey." February 28, 1919. Marcus
    Garvey Tribute website. Accessed July 19, 2018. http://marcusgarvey.com/?p=1763.
Anon. "John F. Kennedy and Religion." John F. Kennedy Presidential Library and
    Museum. Accessed July 19, 2018. https://www.jfklibrary.org/JFK/JFK-in-History/
    JFK-and-Religion.aspx.
Baltzell, E. Digby. *The Protestant Establishment: Aristocracy and Caste in America.* New Haven:
    Yale University Press, 1964.
Brooks, David. *Bobos in Paradise: The New Upper Class and How They Got There.* New York:
    Simon & Schuster, 2001.
Caro, Robert A. *The Power Broker: Robert Moses and the Fall of New York.* New York: Vintage,
    1975.
Coates, Ta-Nehisi. *Between the World and Me.* Melbourne: The Text Publishing, 2015.
England, Paula. "The Failure of Human Capital Theory to Explain Occupational Sex Segre-
    gation." *Journal of Human Resources* 17 no. 3, 1982, 358–370.
Franklin, Aretha. "Respect." *I Never Loved a Man the Way I Love You*, Atlantic, 1967.

Fraser, Nancy. "How Feminism Became Capitalism's Handmaiden – and How to Reclaim It." *The Guardian*, October 14, 2013. Accessed July 19, 2018. https://www.theguardian.com/commentisfree/2013/oct/14/feminism-capitalist-handmaiden-neoliberal.

Friedan, Betty. *The Feminine Mystique*. New York: W.W. Norton & Company, 2010.

Golshan, Tara. "Hillary Clinton's Concession Speech Full Transcript: 2016 Presidential Election." *Vox*, November 9, 2016. https://www.vox.com/2016/11/9/13570328/hillary-clinton-concession-speech-full-transcript-2016-presidential-election.

Gordon, Linda. *Pitied but Not Entitled: Single Mothers and the History of Welfare 1890–1935*. Reprint edition. Cambridge, MA: Harvard University Press, 1998.

Hebdige, Dick. *Subculture: The Meaning of Style*. London: Routledge, 2012.

Herzl, Theodor. *The Jewish State*. Revised edition. New York: Dover Publications, 1989.

Hochschild, Arlie. *The Second Shift*. New York: Avon Books, 1989.

Hymowitz, Carol, and Timothy D. Schellhardt. "The Glass Ceiling: Why Women Can't Seem to Break the Invisible Barrier That Blocks Them from the Top Jobs." *The Wall Street Journal* 24, no. 1 (1986): 1573–1592.

Irvin-Erickson, Douglas. *Raphael Lemkin and the Concept of Genocide*. Philadelphia, PA: University of Pennsylvania Press, 2016.

Kymlicka, Will. *Multicultural Citizenship: A Liberal Theory of Minority Rights*. New York: Oxford University Press, 1995.

Lemkin, Raphaël. "Genocide—A Modern Crime." *Free World* 4, (1945).

Locke, John. *A Letter Concerning Toleration and Other Writings*. New Edition. Indianapolis: Liberty Fund Inc., 2010.

Lopez Bunyasi, Tehama, and Candis Watts Smith (Eds). *Stay Woke: A People's Guide to Making All Black Lives Matter*. New York. New York University Press, 2019.

Madley, Benjamin. *An American Genocide: The United States and the California Indian Catastrophe, 1846–1873*. Reprint edition. New Haven: Yale University Press, 2017.

Mandela, Nelson. "I am Prepared to Die: Nelson Mandela's Statement from the Dock at the Opening of the Defence Case in the Rivonia Trial." April 20, 1964. Nelson Mandela Foundation. Accessed July 19, 2018. http://db.nelsonmandela.org/speeches/pub_view.asp?pg=item&ItemID=NMS010&txtstr=prepared%20to%20die.

Memmi, Albert. *The Colonizer and the Colonized*. London: Routledge, 2013.

Menchú, Rigoberta. *I, Rigoberta Menchú: An Indian Woman in Guatemala*. Edited by Elisabeth Burgos-Debray. Translated by Ann Wright. 2nd Edition. London: Verso, 2010.

Merton, Robert. *Social Science Quotations: Who Said What, When, and Where*. London: Routledge, 2018.

Mill, John Stuart. *On Liberty*. Edited by Elizabeth Rapaport. Cambridge, MA: Hackett Publishing Company, 1978.

Morales, Evo. "I Believe Only in The Power of The People." *Counter Currents*, December 22, 2006. Accessed July 19, 2018. https://www.countercurrents.org/bolivia-morales221205.htm.

Myrdal, Gunnar. *An American Dilemma: The Negro Problem and Modern Democracy*. New York: Harper Publishing, 1944.

National Partnership for Women & Families. "Americas Women and the Wage Gap." Fact Sheet. September2019. National Partnership for Women & Families. Accessed July 19, 2018. http://www.nationalpartnership.org/research-library/workplace-fairness/fair-pay/americas-women-and-the-wage-gap.pdf.

Robles, Andrea. *Troubled Trade-Offs: Inequality and the Struggle for Work-Life Fit*. UMI Dissertation Publishing, n.d.

Sandino, Augusto C. "Letter to the Rulers of Latin America." August 4,1928. Accessed July 19, 2018. http://www.latinamericanstudies.org/sandino/sandino8-4-28.htm.

Sartre, Jean-Paul, and Michael Walzer. *Anti-Semite and Jew: An Exploration of the Etiology of Hate*. Translated by George J. Becker. New York: Schocken, 1995.

Sharma, Swati. "Ta-Nehisi Coates on Cornel West's One-Sided War." *The Atlantic*, January 17, 2018. https://www.theatlantic.com/entertainment/archive/2018/01/ta-nehisi-coates-cornel-west/550727/.

Simmons, Solon. *The Eclipse of Equality: Arguing America on Meet the Press*. Stanford, CA: Stanford University Press, 2013.

Tocqueville, Alexis de. *Democracy in America*. New York: Harper Perennial, 1966.

Warner, Judith. *Perfect Madness: Motherhood in the Age of Anxiety*. Reprint edition. New York: Riverhead Books, 2006.

Weaver, Richard. *Ideas Have Consequences*. Chicago: University of Chicago Press, 1984.

West, Cornel. "Ta-Nehisi Coates Is the Neoliberal Face of the Black Freedom Struggle." *The Guardian*, December 17, 2017. Accessed July 19, 2018. https://www.theguardian.com/commentisfree/2017/dec/17/ta-nehisi-coates-neoliberal-black-struggle-cornel-west.

Williams, Joan C. *Unbending Gender: Why Family and Work Conflict and What To Do About It*. New York: Oxford University Press, 2001.

X, Malcolm, Alex Haley, and Attallah Shabazz. *The Autobiography of Malcolm X: As Told to Alex Haley*. Reissue edition. New York: Ballantine Books, 1992.

9

CONCLUSION

From Root Narrative Theory to root narrative practice

This book has been filled with complicated and abstract arguments drawn from political and social theory along with examples from various aspects of the history of conflict, but it is really all about practice. My goal is to make it easier for parties in protracted conflicts to better understand one another, on the assumption that before they can repair what was broken, they need to free themselves from their own imaginations—the layers of systematic misunderstanding that makes reconciliation impossible even to conceive. This is a theoretical book, but it is inspired by Kurt Lewin's bromide that there is nothing so practical as a good theory. Each of the reflections collected here on power, suffering, values, morality, trauma, and identity is intended to inspire the development of practical tools that can be used by analysts and practitioners in live conflict settings.

On the surface level, Root Narrative Theory is a tool designed to help the analyst to think about more effective ways to get a message across to any given audience without hitting on the alienating trigger words, allusions, and signifiers that are most likely to derail conscious thought. In this way, it is a theory of rhetoric or communication. In a deeper sense, the diagnostic level—it can be used to help us to enter the social imaginary of those with whom we disagree, and in so doing to become creative again with respect to our most debilitating problems. Think of it as applied meta-philosophy, a model for overcoming radical disagreement. As with any model of the world, what the statistician George Box once wrote holds true for this one as well: "essentially, all models are wrong but some are useful."[1] My goal is to make the root narrative model useful for you.

The basic assumptions of Root Narrative Theory are quite simple. Conflicts, by which I mean the deep divides that can lead to violence and hatred lasting for decades or even centuries, are the result of the abuse of power. Power, the basic material of politics, is the only force that can produce social change, gather like-minded actors for collective action, or generate a broader sense of confidence and self-respect, but it is also a force that can and does produce massive cycles of never-ending suffering and violence. Worse yet, the virtues of power are always in the eye of the beholder. Where one party sees a productive use of social power, the other sees its abject abuse, and whatever the reality of a situation, such a clash of interpretations is irreconcilable, implying that all of forms of social power therefore must be seen as a form of (ab)use. That is, they are either good or bad contingent on the story that parties tell about them.

The stories we tell are both moral and explanatory. They have ethical and technical warrants to them that are used to justify our actions. Some parties may place the accent on the moral side, stressing values, while others may place the accent on the technical side, stressing mechanisms, evidence, policies, and solutions, but all of us are trapped in a narrative universe in which we tell the best stories we can about what is to be done. Neither priest nor economist is immune from the need to situate his or her best arguments in some broader narrative about how the world works, and any account of peace or politics can be subjected to root narrative analysis.

Root Narrative Theory provides a solution to an enduring problem in social science: how are we to measure ideology, beliefs, ultimate values, worldviews and the subjective dimension in politics? The solution it proposes is attractive in that it builds on the best interpretivist insights while relying on the assumptions about the dispositive role of power that is favored both by realists and radicals, conservatives and critical theorists, sociopaths, and sociologists. Along the way, Root Narrative Theory builds in cutting-edge insights about attitudes, values, framing, discourse, propaganda, morality, and emotions, but the goal is always practical, not merely aesthetic or intellectual. How can we put Root Narrative Theory into practice?

The uses of narrative style

Conditions of radical disagreement demand the application of radical curiosity. We can look at stories in a new way. The best part of Root Narrative Theory is that it is a narrative theory, which means that it is designed to represent the dynamics of storytelling and the intricacy of the workings of the human imagination. This introduces a degree of flexibility as compared to rival theories in psychology or political science. Where psychological theories tend to be too hot—they are developed to optimize representations of emotional life—and political science theories tend to be too cold—they err in favor of the rational actor—a narrative approach can work unapologetically with the features of the literary mind that are necessarily both emotional and rational, meeting science at its cutting edge, opening the field to human experience in a richer way, and ultimately making the theory more useful for practical intervention.

Among the things we have learned from recent research on narrative and conflict is the importance of narrative style, or what is often called genre. It is in this area where two separate research streams converge in an exciting way. The first stream is from the study of conflict resolution and narrative. In her article entitled,

"Mediation and Genre," Samantha Hardy introduces a distinction between two ideal-typical types of storytelling, Melodrama and Tragedy.[2] Her distinction builds on Sara Cobb's ideas about the importance of using narrative practice to open moral space in mediation processes so that parties can fashion a new narrative,[3] which she later describes with the metaphor of braiding. In the braiding process, oppositional strands are bound together in a novel way while preserving essential features of the original strands.[4] Hardy reflects on the structure of storytelling in escalated conflicts and finds that they are consistent with the melodramatic pole of her distinction, while tragic forms of storytelling are more likely to produce thoughtful elaboration of story structures that open the moral space of conflict. This insight owes much to Cobb as well who wrote about the potential for tragic irony:

> Once parties have opened the possibility of the legitimacy of their Other, they are in a better position to reinvent history via the elaboration of an ironic narrative that displays the tragic interdependence of each side's role in generating the actions of the other in a "more of the same" negative spiral.[5]

The tragic story employs complexity in contrast to the one-dimensional character of melodrama. It tends to demonstrate curiosity, context, choice, the future, and opportunity, in contrast to confidence, blame, passivity, the past, and suffering. The presence of the tragic genre, for Hardy, opens the door to potential conflict resolution.

The second stream of research on narrative genre and conflict has been developed in the cultural sociology of war, especially in the work of Philip Smith and his 2006 book, *Why War?* Smith advocates for the examination of "culture structures" that he sees as generative of social behavior.[6] He believes that if these culture structures could be decoded, we might be in a better position to explain the onset of war and peace, and perhaps also to do something about it. Although Smith's work is cast in the mold of the sort of traditional social science that preserves its purity by avoiding questions of application, tellingly he arrives at a similar distinction between and among conflict genres that Hardy did, although he presents it in the form of a continuum.

On one side of the continuum is the apocalyptic genre in which stories demonstrate strong moral polarization between characters, ideal motivations, global objects of struggle, and extraordinary powers of action at work. On the other side is what he calls a "low mimesis" genre, a more technical form which is opposite to the apocalyptic genre in each respect. Between the two he places tragedy and romance. In his examination of thousands of conflict stories in popular media he demonstrates the close correlation between war and the apocalyptic genre along with peace and low mimesis. He goes so far to say that the apocalyptic genre is a cause of war, binding actors to action scripts from which they have little or no escape.

The similarity between Hardy's melodrama and Smith's apocalypticism is clear, while Smith's portrait of low mimesis is linked to Hardy's view of tragedy in a more nuanced way. It is clear that both research streams are converging on the same distinction, although the remaining gaps between them demand some innovative theory to span the remaining distance. Hardy's theory is limited in the sense that it falls prey to its own critique—it is a bit melodramatic in the way it draws a clean distinction between the simple, linear, and binary sort of story-telling of melodrama and the complex, circular, and nuanced sort of tragedy. There are obviously other genres than these two in play as Smith recognizes, and the features that differentiate the two are better thought of as matters of degree than dichotomies.

Although tragedy is presented by Hardy, following Cobb, as a path to the "sacred space" of resolution, the classical definition of the genre presented it as intensely literary, highly emotional, and logically fixed in its development in very much the same way that comedy is. Unlike Smith's low mimetic form, which feels more like the rational actor model of interest-based bargaining, the tragic form is less of an endpoint for peace theorists, and more of a halfway house as Smith suggests. Moreover, classical definitions of tragedy suggest that it is less of a goad to action and more of a substitute for it, providing a release of emotion through catharsis on viewing the predictable plot. The distinction between the two poles of the continuum itself requires more elaboration, and I think there is a simple way to bridge the gap in ways that may be immediately useful for conflict resolution practitioners.

Throughout this book, I have said that we know we are in the presence of root narrative content when the story we are examining is full of representations of EVIL, where EVIL stands for emotional, vivid, intense, and literary story elements. Representations that lack these features are simply less cleanly associated with any particular root narrative. We might say that the non-EVIL stories are too complex to be associated with the "curious logicality" that is so typical of the stories of abusive power that define a root narrative.

Root narratives demonstrate a kind of moral clarity, demanding action, while other kinds of stories or accounts demonstrate a kind of moral complexity, demanding reflection and recalibration. Root narrative accounts tend toward the melodramatic and apocalyptic side of Hardy and Smith's distinction, while less identifiable accounts tend toward the other side. For simplicity's sake, let me just label the poles for these genres (or narrative styles) moral clarity and moral complexity, respectively. Moreover, in order to avoid the pitfall of becoming trapped by a clever acronym, let me use a table to introduce a set of differentiating criteria for the two narrative styles that is slightly more complicated.

Now that we have all of these differentiating characteristics in place, we can make some claims about how Root Narrative Theory can be used in live conflict settings. The short answer is that it all depends on what you are trying to do. Here is the trick; if you truly believe that you are in a situation in which power is being abused and the people who wield the power are bad actors, it makes good sense to find a way to intervene in the narrative context to promote and augment stories that illustrate moral clarity. Not only will this tend to increase indignation, but it will also serve to promote action in response to the perceived abuse. The best way

TABLE 9.1 Moral Clarity vs. Moral Complexity

	Narrative Feature	Moral Clarity	Moral Complexity
E	Their Motivation	Domination	Rational Interests
	Their Powers	Exaggerated	Banal
	Their Character	Malevolent	Human
	Our Past	Innocent	Complicit
	Our Future	Romantic	Realistic
	Our Focus	Retribution	Cost/Benefit
V	Causal Factors	Vivid and Simple	Multiple and Complicated
	Causal Direction	Linear	Circular
	Causal Context	Individuated	Structural
I	Discursive Tendencies	Polarizing	Elaborating
	Relations with Adversary	Treasonous	Generative
	Conflict Scope	Cosmic	Mundane
L	Story Language	Poetic	Prosaic
	Representation of Time	Compressed	Complicated

to promote moral clarity in a conflict is to use some mechanism for mapping the root narrative profile of the actors you happen to favor, and to couch your policy agenda in a story that hits all the right notes of that profile. This alignment of your story and their root narrative profile should, other things being equal, trigger your audience in the way you hope. Of course, there are sophisticated ways to do this and awkward ways as well, but the overall effort should be supported by the root narrative alignment. This is the business of normal politics and social movement activity, and it is fairly intuitive. Root Narrative Theory will help you in your politics to be more successful in framing your ideas to your audience's worldview, triggering their moral emotions in ways that follow your purpose.

Intriguing as this political use of Root Narrative Theory may be, the theory is more useful in peace studies and conflict resolution settings insofar as it helps us to find ways to introduce moral complexity into the narrative environment, opening the possibility for the elaboration and braiding that Sara Cobb has long advocated. There is a simple way to introduce moral complexity, which we might just describe as lowering the volume, draining the EVIL from our words and images, and presenting stories to our audiences that decrease the probability of triggering events. But this is the boring way to approach things, and one that is not likely to change much.

The reason why Hardy and Cobb latched onto the power of tragedy to move conflicts toward a turning point is because the tragic style was capable of eliciting powerful emotions in a way that forced realizations about the futility of existing patterns of conflict storytelling and courses of action. The tragic genre is full of emotion and drama; in fact, the words drama and tragedy are near synonyms. The more elaborated form of tragic complexity emerges when parties recognize the vital truth of rival moralities. It emerges when one root narrative profile collides with another. The peacemaker can use Root Narrative Theory as a tool, a way to introduce moral complexity into the narrative ecology of the conflict by elaborating the vital truth each party to the other side.

But moral complexity is not enough. The tragic mode makes it possible for more insightful styles of criticism to develop, to more fully elaborate the forms of abusive power in all their destructive force, but it does little to point to future probabilities. Both the melodramatic (apocalyptic) and tragic genres share a critical pessimism that exposes vital truths of moral politics, but they both lack hope. Ask yourself how much sense it makes to talk about how tragic it is that we now live in a world at peace. At a minimum, conflict resolution practice demands that we introduce a distinction between story types that focus on problems and those that focus on possibilities, between those that develop critical awareness of abusive powers, and those that project a future when those powers have been overcome or redeemed. Think of Robert F. Kennedy's speech to a South African audience when the fight against apartheid remained desperately uncertain.

> Each time a man stands up for an ideal, or acts to improve the lot of others, or strikes out against injustice, he sends forth a tiny ripple of hope, and crossing each other from a million different centers of energy and daring, those ripples build a current which can sweep down the mightiest walls of oppression and resistance.[7]

Hope is a tremendously complicated concept, but for the purposes of this discussion, I will follow the lead of Dan McAdams, a prominent researcher on narrative psychology and the interpretation of life stories, to offer a working concept of hope for narrative practice. One of the critical factors that McAdams finds that marks the boundary between people who are what he calls highly generative—inspired, positive, caring, and productive—from those who are not is the kind of life story they tell. McAdams finds evidence that the engaged and proactive people he studied all had a powerful tendency to tell what he calls redemptive stories about their lives.

> Generative adults tend to see their lives as redemptive stories that emphasize related themes such as early advantage, the suffering of others, moral clarity, the conflict between power and love, and leaving a legacy for growth.[8]

It is not hard to see how what McAdams describes in these successful adults is their capacity for hope over pessimism. It is not that they deny that bad things have happened in their lives; they simply work those bad things into new stories that stress how those bad things happened for a good reason, making them better people today. They interpellate, creating a better version of themselves as they narrate. This is important for students of narrative and conflict resolution, because it provides us with something new to look for in the conflict stories. Just as Hardy, Cobb and Smith showed us that conflict stories can be differentiated in terms of moral clarity or moral complexity, they can also be differentiated in terms of what

Erik Erikson called generativity and stagnation—although I will refer to stagnation as critical (to better fit McAdams's use[9]). Blending these two distinctions in a new two-by-two table, we can generate a typology of four different narrative conflict styles, the melodramatic, the tragic, the romantic, and the redemptive. We can think of these four genres as potential moves in the game of narrative intervention. We always have a choice to fashion our narrative in a way that pushes our story from one category to another by exchanging critical elements or by altering the tone or the level of care we place in our story. These four narrative styles are depicted in Table 9.2.

We have seen that the difference between melodrama and tragedy involves the degree to which the story relies on depictions of EVIL, emotional, vivid, intense, and literary accounts and images, with more thorough dimensional differentiators listed in Table 9.1 above. This is also what differentiates a romantic account from a redemptive one. Both romance and redemption conflict stories recall the suffering of the past and both also point to the future with hope, care, and energy, but the romantic story does so without abandoning the moral clarity of the true believer or compromising on his depiction of EVIL. In complex conflict settings, romance is a kind of false hope built on the epic moral logic of one's own cause and ignoring the other's, revealing the wisdom of the phrase, "hope is not a strategy." Because all conflicts are necessarily complex, with plenty of abuse on all sides, short of total victory, generativity alone is not a solution to conflict without the pivot to moral complexity that Hardy and Cobb insisted on.

Generativity without hope only produces what I once described as generativity-based conflict.[10] Before we judge romantic stories, we should recognize that it is likely that they are among the most powerful in promoting and sustaining social movements, especially in their most vulnerable moments. If part of your plan for peace is social mobilization and non-violent resistance, then romance might be your most useful tool. We should just not delude ourselves by hoping that moral complexity and reconciliation will emerge from a group of people whose primary mode of storytelling is glorifying their own past and celebrating their virtues and triumphs over evil as happens in a political romance.

In contrast, a redemptive story looks to overcome the past, but it does so largely by engaging the moral complexity that is always present in every protracted conflict. One way to engage moral complexity is by using the primitive grammar of the root narratives to invert the central elements of its logic. For example, a redemptive securitarian story would not abandon the sentence, *Foreigners use armed violence to create physical deprivation in the State*, but would invert it to read, *Foreigners have also suffered*

TABLE 9.2 Major Conflict Genres

	Moral Clarity	*Moral Complexity*
Generative	Romance	Redemption
Critical	Melodrama	Tragedy

physical deprivation by our use of armed violence. This inversion of the association of the abuse of power and the experience of injustice retains the moral force of the root narrative, but it recognizes the inherent complexity of the case. This is the strategy that Gunnar Myrdal used with the publication of his great *An American Dilemma*. He pointed out to his largely libertarian, white audience that African Americans too had suffered from political coercion at the hands of the government.

But Myrdal's book did more than that, it also proposed an alternative root narrative category, the dignitarian, to open new possibilities in the future conversation. Not only could one identify the suffering of African Americans in terms of classical freedoms (the philosophy of the ingroup), but also in opposition to the abuse from which they suffered: from hate (the philosophy of the outgroup). In the first case you position the outgroup issues (poverty, harassment, and restricted opportunity) in the dominant root narrative, and in the second you position the ingroup issue (crime, dissent, and resentment) in the outgroup root narrative. Myrdal worked in both modes, by projecting the issues of African Americans into the dominant ideology and by taking the ideology of the oppressed seriously. In these ways, redemption stories deal with the abuses of the past of all parties as a way to engage with the story structures of the present. This is how they pave the path to the future.

Although Philip Smith was right that we can read off a state of conflict from the genre profile of the narrative environment—when melodramatic and apocalyptic stories predominate, there is an advanced state of conflict—peacemaking practitioners always have the freedom to intervene in conflicts in a manner of their choosing. They can work to introduce moral complexity into the narrative environment and they can also work to introduce generativity. If they can do both, they are likely to make a difference. In all their efforts, peacemakers will benefit by learning how to map, characterize, depict, imagine, and assess the moral logics that parties deploy in conflicts. Root Narrative Theory is a tool that will help them do just that.

An open question

As with any theory, if Root Narrative Theory is to prove to be a good one, it will have to prove itself in the arena. How it might do so is an open question. Once we learn how to recognize root narratives, to measure them, and apply them to real world situations, we are in a much better position to add value in conditions of radical disagreement. How we do so is dependent on you, the reader. Does Root Narrative Theory trigger new insights for you about the conflicts you study? Can you use it in a way that improves your analyses and enriches your practice? One thing is sure, narrative matters, but life is not just one darn story after another. There are structures at work in the narration of both peace and politics. Root Narrative Theory provides us access to some of those structures, especially those having to do with power and injustice. The analysis of root narratives adds value for both the analyst of escalated conflicts and the practitioner by showing how the ideological perspectives of rival parties drive them forward into patterns of further escalation that are largely beyond their consciousness or control. It is a theory that is quite general and open to a wide variety of practices, most of which I have not begun to consider and in all likelihood would be unqualified to perform. In this sense, Root Narrative Theory should be taken as an invitation to both researchers and practitioners to use and develop. I believe that the simple story structures that I have identified here open new possibilities for theory and action that I hope inspire you to try to make the world a better place.

Notes

1 Lopez Bunyasi and Watts Smith, *Stay Woke.*
2 Hardy, "Mediation and Genre."
3 Hardy, "Mediation and Genre."
4 Cobb, "Narrative Braiding and the Role of Public Officials in Transforming the Publics Conflicts."
5 Cobb, "A Developmental Approach to Turning Points."
6 Smith, *Why War?*
7 Kennedy, "Day of Affirmation Address."
8 McAdams, *The Redemptive Self.*
9 Erikson, *Childhood and Society.*
10 Simmons, "Generativity-Based Conflict: Maturing Microfoundations for Conflict Theory."

Bibliography

Box, George E.P., and Norman R. Draper. *Empirical Model-Building and Response Surfaces.* New York: John Wiley & Sons, 1987.

Cobb, Sara. "Creating Sacred Space: Toward a Second-Generation Dispute Resolution Practice." *Fordham Urban Law Journal* 28 (2001): 1017.

Cobb, Sara. "A Developmental Approach to Turning Points: Irony as an Ethics for Negotiation Pragmatics." *Harvard Negotiation Law Review* 11 (2006): 147.

Cobb, Sara. "Narrative Braiding and the Role of Public Officials in Transforming the Publics Conflicts." *Narrative and Conflict: Explorations in Theory and Practice* 1, no. 1 (2013): 4–30.

Erikson, Erik H. *Childhood and Society.* New York: W. W. Norton, 1963.

Hardy, Samantha. "Mediation and Genre." *Negotiation Journal* 24, no. 3 (2008): 247–268.

Kennedy, Robert F. "Day of Affirmation Address." June 6, 1966. John F. Kennedy Presidential Library and Museum. Accessed July 20, 2018. https://www.jfklibrary.org/Research/Resea rch-Aids/Ready-Reference/RFK-Speeches/Day-of-Affirmation-Address-as-delivered.aspx.

Lopez Bunyasi, Tehama, and Candis Watts Smith (Eds). *Stay Woke: A People's Guide to Making All Black Lives Matter.* New York. New York University Press, 2019.

McAdams, Dan P. *The Redemptive Self: Stories Americans Live By.* Oxford: Oxford University Press, 2013.

Simmons, Solon J. "Generativity-Based Conflict: Maturing Microfoundations for Conflict Theory." In *Handbook of Conflict Analysis and Resolution* by Dennis J.D. Sandole, Sean Byrne, Ingrid Sandole-Staroste and Jessica Senehi (Eds). London: Routledge, 2008, 116–129.

Smith, Philip. *Why War? The Cultural Logic of Iraq, The Gulf War, and Suez.* Chicago: The University of Chicago Press, 2005.

INDEX